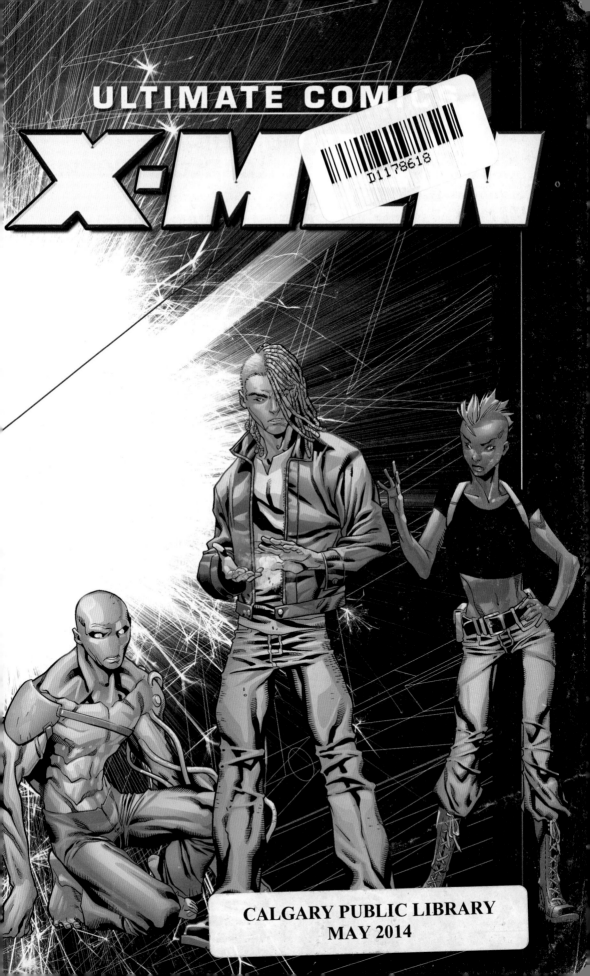

ULTIMATE COMICS
X·MEN

WRITER: **BRIAN WOOD**

WITH **NATHAN EDMONDSON** (#21-22)

PENCILERS: **FILIPE ANDRADE** (#18.1),

PACO MEDINA (#19) & **CARLO BARBERI** (#20-23)

WITH **DAVID BALDEON** (#21)

INKERS: **FILIPE ANDRADE** (#18.1) & **JUAN VLASCO** (#19-22)

WITH **JORDI TARRAGONA** (#21) & **DON HO** (#23)

COLORISTS: **JEAN-FRANCOIS BEAULIEU** (#18.1)

& **JESUS ABURTOV** (#19-23) WITH **JAVIER TARTAGLIA** (#21)

LETTERER: **VC'S JOE SABINO**

COVER ART: **SARA PICHELLI** & **MARTE GRACIA** (#18.1),

DAVE JOHNSON (#19-20 & #22), **MICHAEL RYAN** (#21)

AND **GREG LAND** & **FRANK MARTIN** (#23)

ASSISTANT EDITORS: **EMILY SHAW** & **JON MOISAN**

EDITOR: **MARK PANICCIA**

COLLECTION EDITOR: **CORY LEVINE**

ASSISTANT EDITORS: **ALEX STARBUCK** & **NELSON RIBEIRO**

EDITORS, SPECIAL PROJECTS: **JENNIFER GRÜNWALD** & **MARK D. BEAZLEY**

SENIOR EDITOR, SPECIAL PROJECTS: **JEFF YOUNGQUIST**

SVP OF PRINT & DIGITAL PUBLISHING SALES: **DAVID GABRIEL**

BOOK DESIGNER: **RODOLFO MURAGUCHI**

EDITOR IN CHIEF: **AXEL ALONSO**

CHIEF CREATIVE OFFICER: **JOE QUESADA**

PUBLISHER: **DAN BUCKLEY**

EXECUTIVE PRODUCER: **ALAN FINE**

EN BY BRIAN WOOD VOL. 1. Contains material originally published in magazine form as ULTIMATE COMICS X-MEN #18.1 and #19-23. First printing 2013. ISBN# 978-0-7851-6136-3.)RLDWIDE, INC., a subsidiary of MARVEL ENTERTAINMENT, LLC. OFFICE OF PUBLICATION: 135 West 50th Street, New York, NY 10020. **Printed in the U.S.A.** ALAN President, Marvel Worldwide, Inc. and EVP & CMO Marvel Characters B.V.; DAN BUCKLEY, Publisher & President - Print, Animation & Digital Divisions; JOE QUESADA, Chief Creative Officer; 'ublishing; DAVID BOGART, SVP of Operations & Procurement, Publishing; C.B. CEBULSKI, SVP of Creator & Content Development; DAVID GABRIEL, SVP of Print & Digital Publishing Sales; JIM s & Logistics; DAN CARR, Executive Director of Publishing Technology; SUSAN CRESPI, Editorial Operations Manager; ALEX MORALES, Publishing Operations Manager; STAN LEE, Chairman regarding advertising in Marvel Comics or on Marvel.com, please contact Niza Disla, Director of Marvel Partnerships, at ndisla@marvel.com. For Marvel subscription inquiries, please call **:tured between 4/10/2013 and 5/13/2013 by QUAD/GRAPHICS, VERSAILLES, KY, USA.**

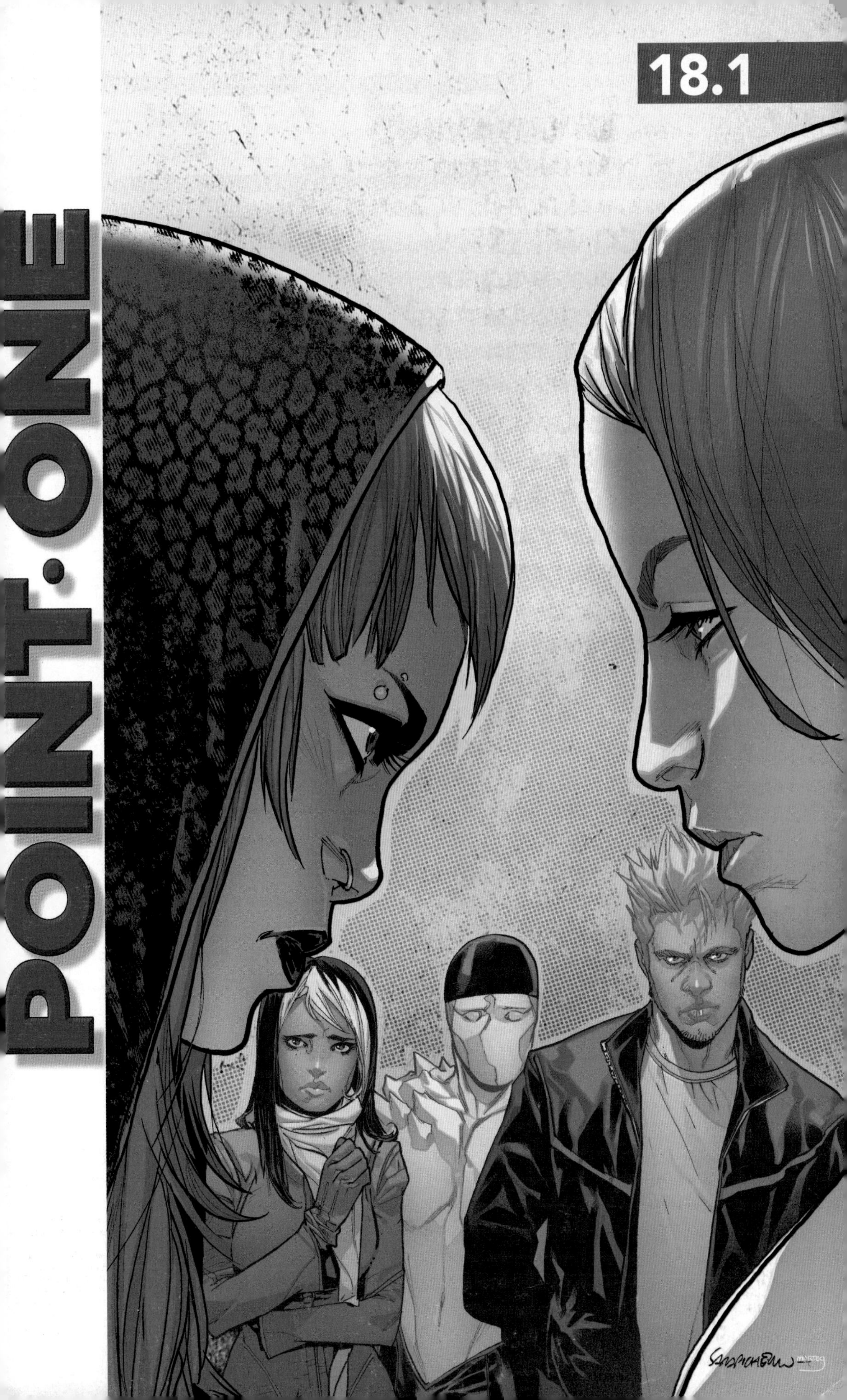
POINT.ONE
18.1

PREVIOUSLY:

With a crippled country undergoing Reconstruction, the mutant population still struggles to find its place in society. President Captain America has offered the community two options: a cure for any mutants willing to lead a "normal" life or a plot of land for those who choose to keep their powers. The cure has been synthesized and camps have been set up to distribute the cure to those that desire it. While many mutants have opted to hold on to their mutations, many more have flocked to these camps under the promise of a brand new life...

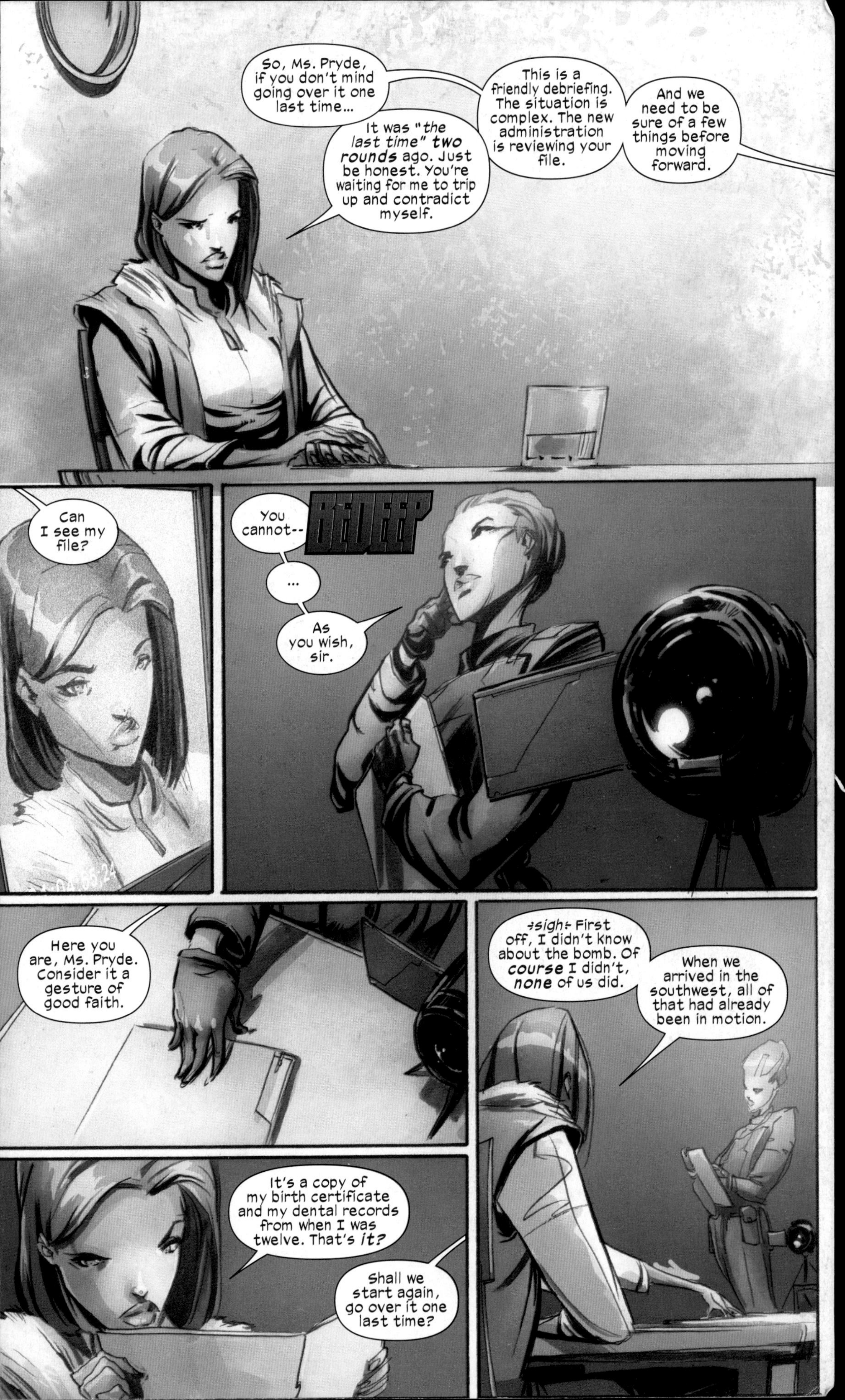
So, Ms. Pryde, if you don't mind going over it one last time...
It was "the last time" two rounds ago. Just be honest. You're waiting for me to trip up and contradict myself.
This is a friendly debriefing. The situation is complex. The new administration is reviewing your file.
And we need to be sure of a few things before moving forward.
Can I see my file?
You cannot--
BEEEEP
...
As you wish, sir.
Here you are, Ms. Pryde. Consider it a gesture of good faith.
=sigh= First off, I didn't know about the bomb. Of course I didn't, none of us did.
When we arrived in the southwest, all of that had already been in motion.
It's a copy of my birth certificate and my dental records from when I was twelve. That's it?
Shall we start again, go over it one last time?

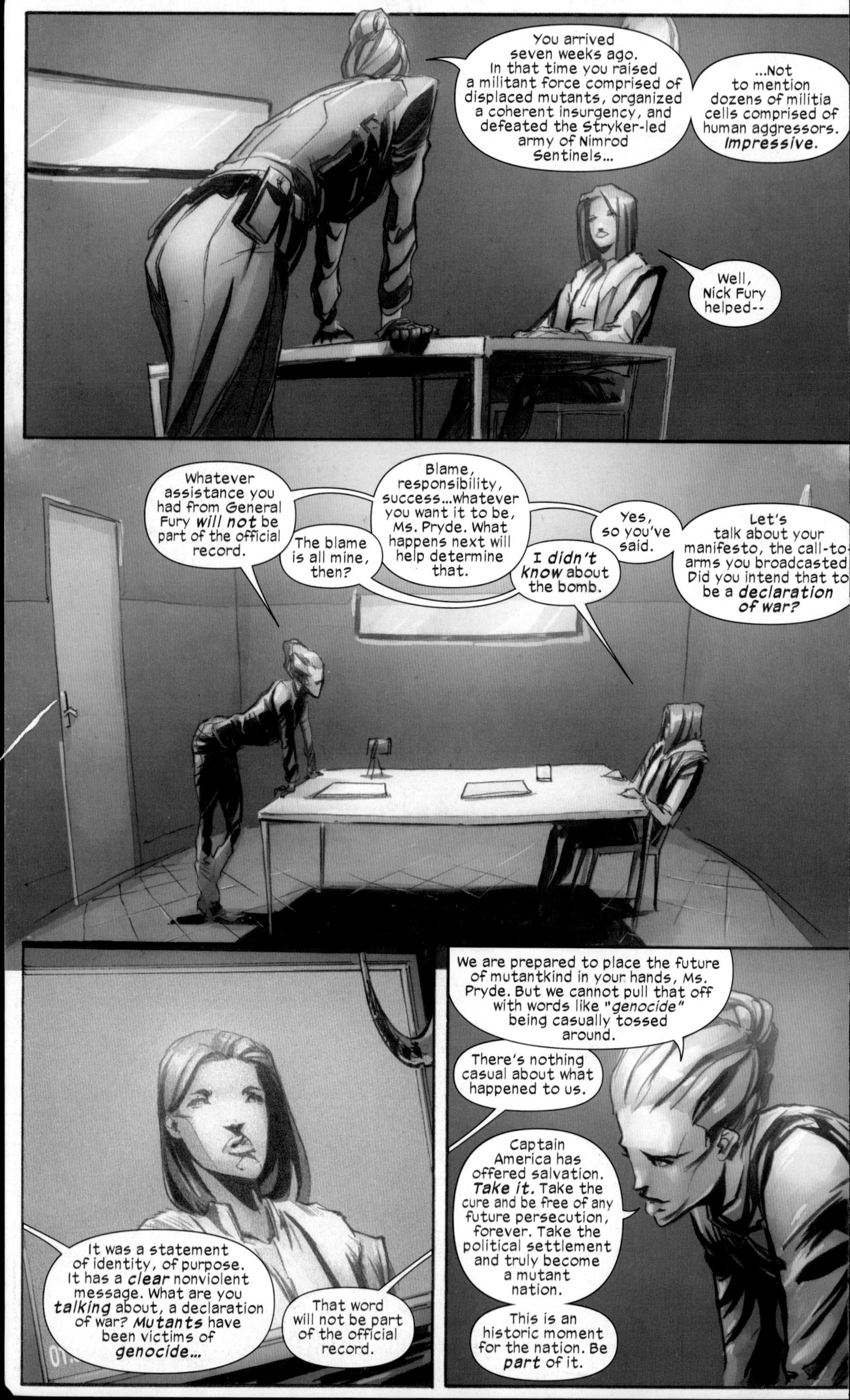
You arrived seven weeks ago. In that time you raised a militant force comprised of displaced mutants, organized a coherent insurgency, and defeated the Stryker-led army of Nimrod Sentinels...
...Not to mention dozens of militia cells comprised of human aggressors. *Impressive.*
Well, Nick Fury helped--
Whatever assistance you had from General Fury *will not* be part of the official record.
The blame is all mine, then?
Blame, responsibility, success...whatever you want it to be, Ms. Pryde. What happens next will help determine that.
I *didn't know* about the bomb.
Yes, so you've said.
Let's talk about your manifesto, the call-to-arms you broadcasted. Did you intend that to be a *declaration of war?*
It was a statement of identity, of purpose. It has a *clear* nonviolent message. What are you *talking* about, a declaration of war? *Mutants* have been victims of *genocide...*
That word will not be part of the official record.
We are prepared to place the future of mutantkind in your hands, Ms. Pryde. But we cannot pull that off with words like "*genocide*" being casually tossed around.
There's nothing casual about what happened to us.
Captain America has offered salvation. *Take it.* Take the cure and be free of any future persecution, forever. Take the political settlement and truly become a mutant nation.
This is an historic moment for the nation. Be *part* of it.

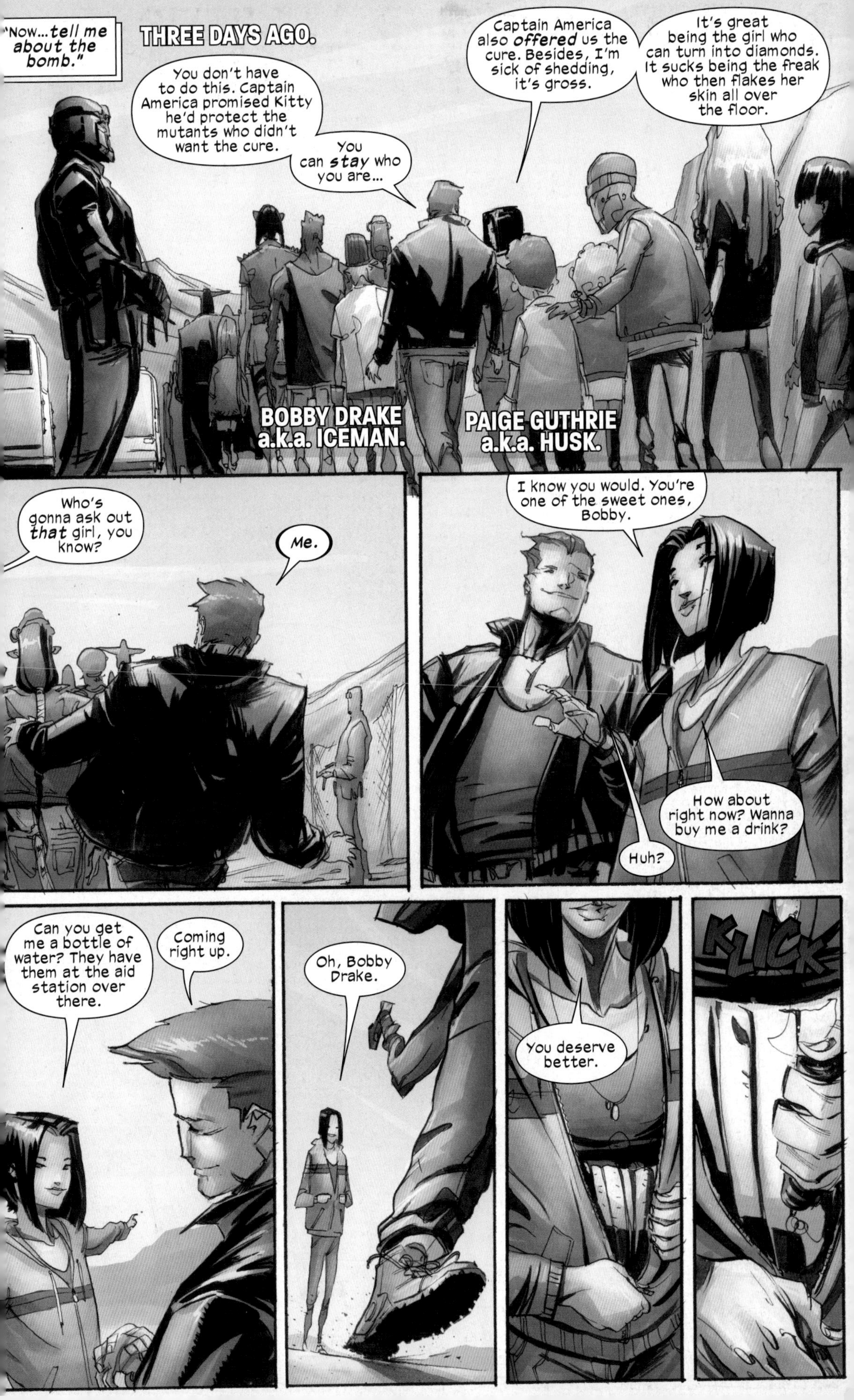
"Now...tell me about the bomb."
THREE DAYS AGO.
You don't have to do this. Captain America promised Kitty he'd protect the mutants who didn't want the cure.
You can stay who you are...
Captain America also offered us the cure. Besides, I'm sick of shedding, it's gross.
It's great being the girl who can turn into diamonds. It sucks being the freak who then flakes her skin all over the floor.
BOBBY DRAKE a.k.a. ICEMAN.
PAIGE GUTHRIE a.k.a. HUSK.
Who's gonna ask out that girl, you know?
Me.
I know you would. You're one of the sweet ones, Bobby.
How about right now? Wanna buy me a drink?
Huh?
Can you get me a bottle of water? They have them at the aid station over there.
Coming right up.
Oh, Bobby Drake.
You deserve better.
KLICK

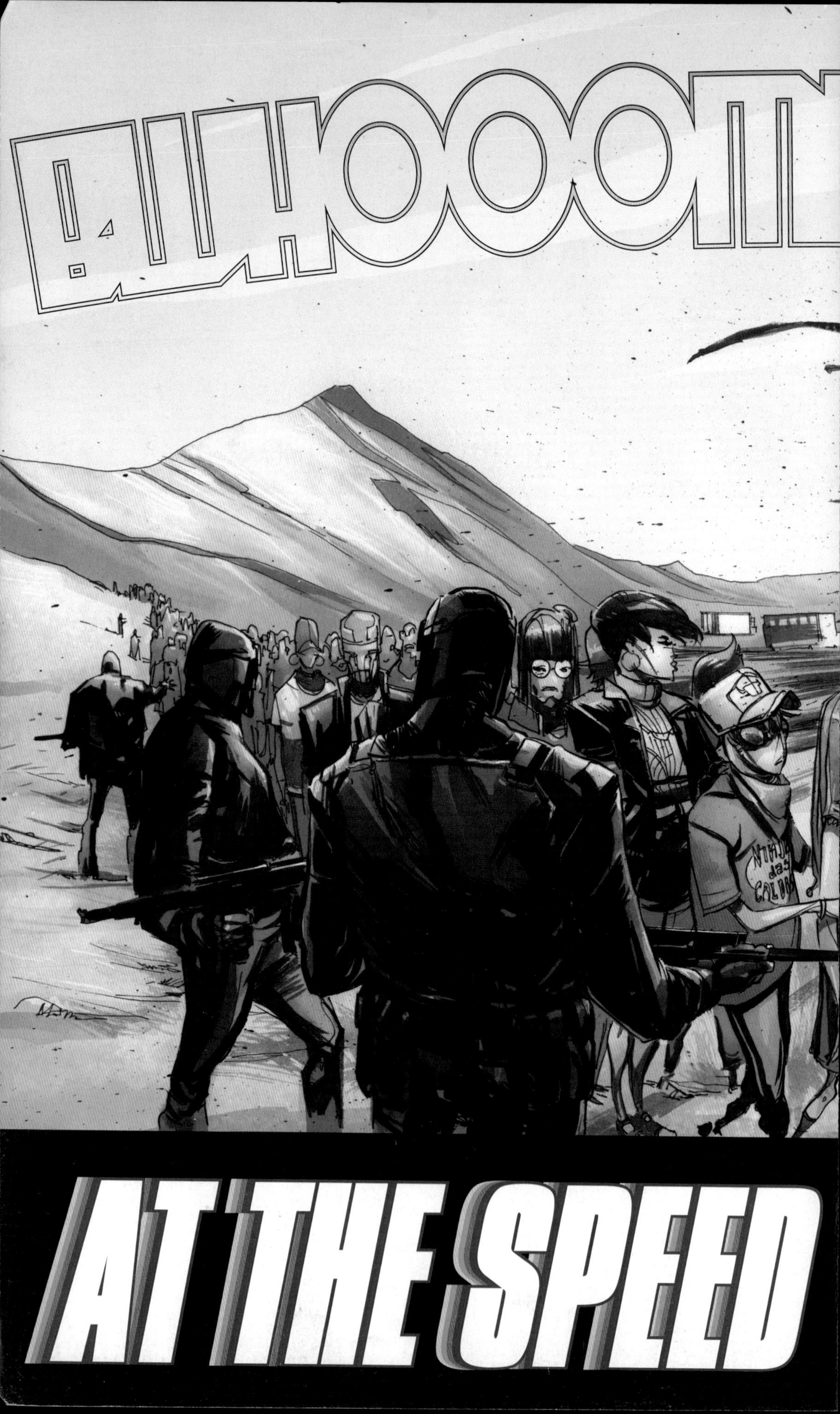
AT THE SPEED

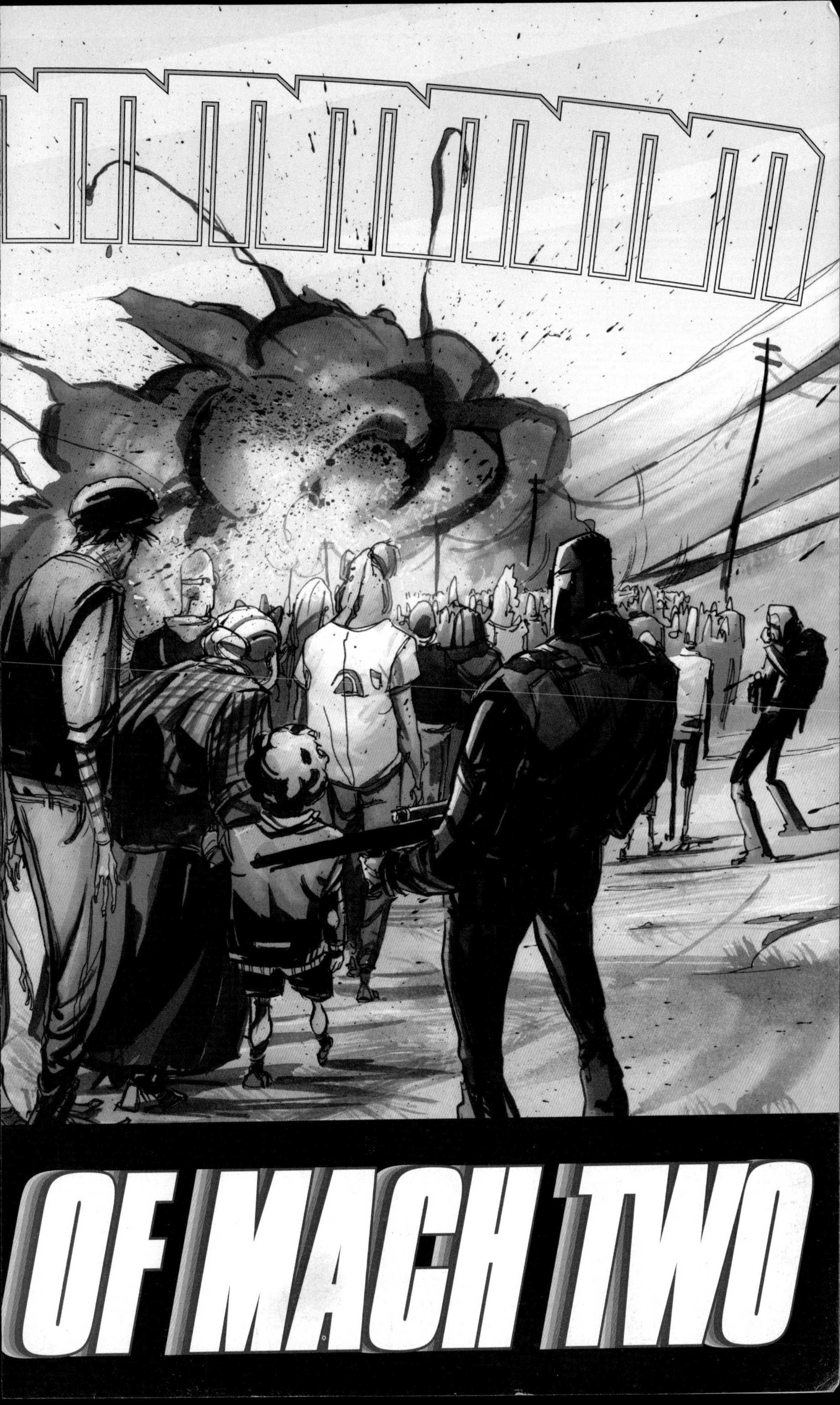
OF MACH TWO

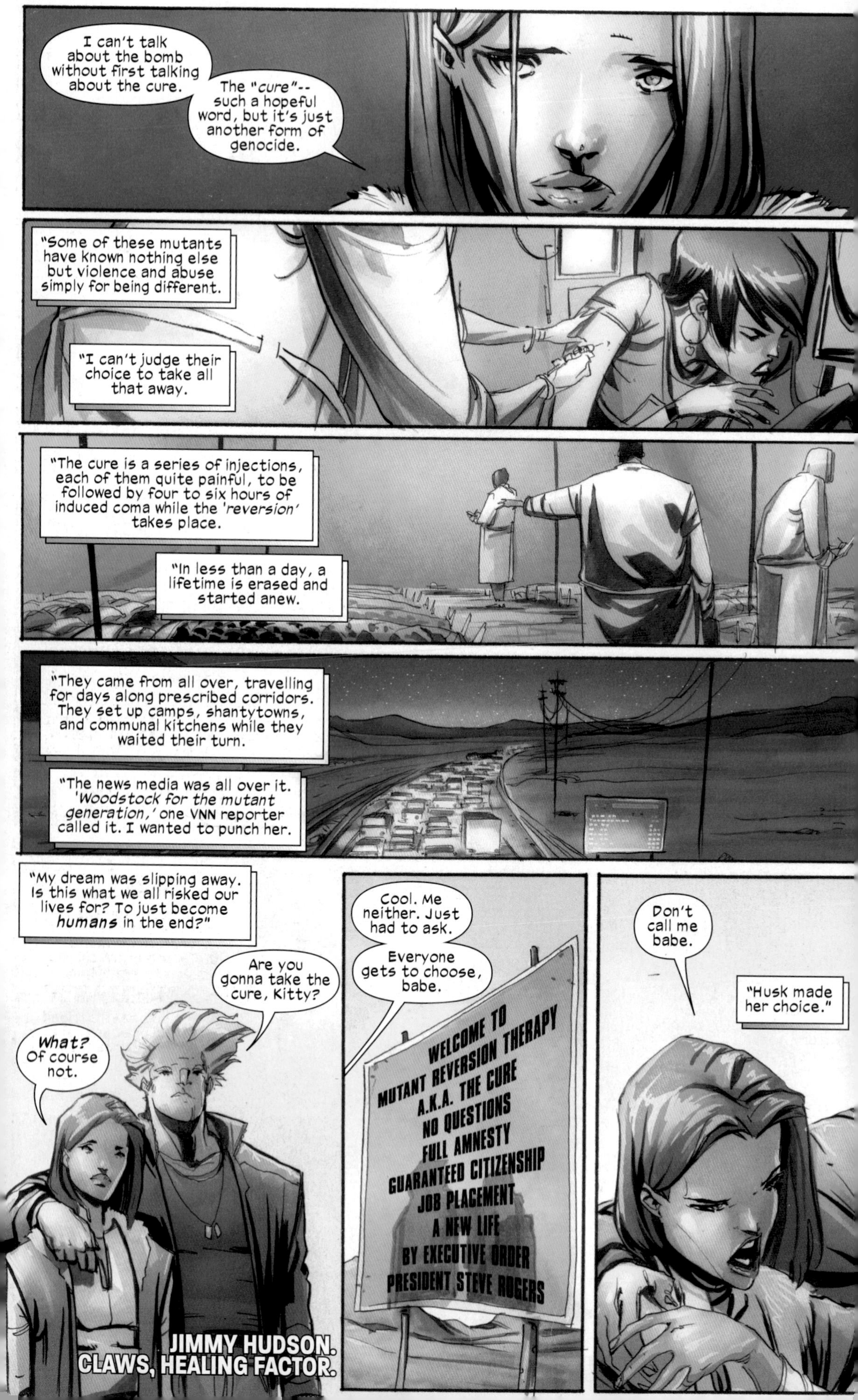

I can't talk about the bomb without first talking about the cure.
The "*cure*"-- such a hopeful word, but it's just another form of genocide.
"Some of these mutants have known nothing else but violence and abuse simply for being different.
"I can't judge their choice to take all that away.
"The cure is a series of injections, each of them quite painful, to be followed by four to six hours of induced coma while the '*reversion*' takes place.
"In less than a day, a lifetime is erased and started anew.
"They came from all over, travelling for days along prescribed corridors. They set up camps, shantytowns, and communal kitchens while they waited their turn.
"The news media was all over it. '*Woodstock for the mutant generation,*' one VNN reporter called it. I wanted to punch her.
"My dream was slipping away. Is this what we all risked our lives for? To just become *humans* in the end?"
Are you gonna take the cure, Kitty?
What? Of course not.
JIMMY HUDSON. CLAWS, HEALING FACTOR.
Cool. Me neither. Just had to ask.
Everyone gets to choose, babe.
WELCOME TO MUTANT REVERSION THERAPY A.K.A. THE CURE NO QUESTIONS FULL AMNESTY GUARANTEED CITIZENSHIP JOB PLACEMENT A NEW LIFE BY EXECUTIVE ORDER PRESIDENT STEVE ROGERS
Don't call me babe.
"Husk made her choice."

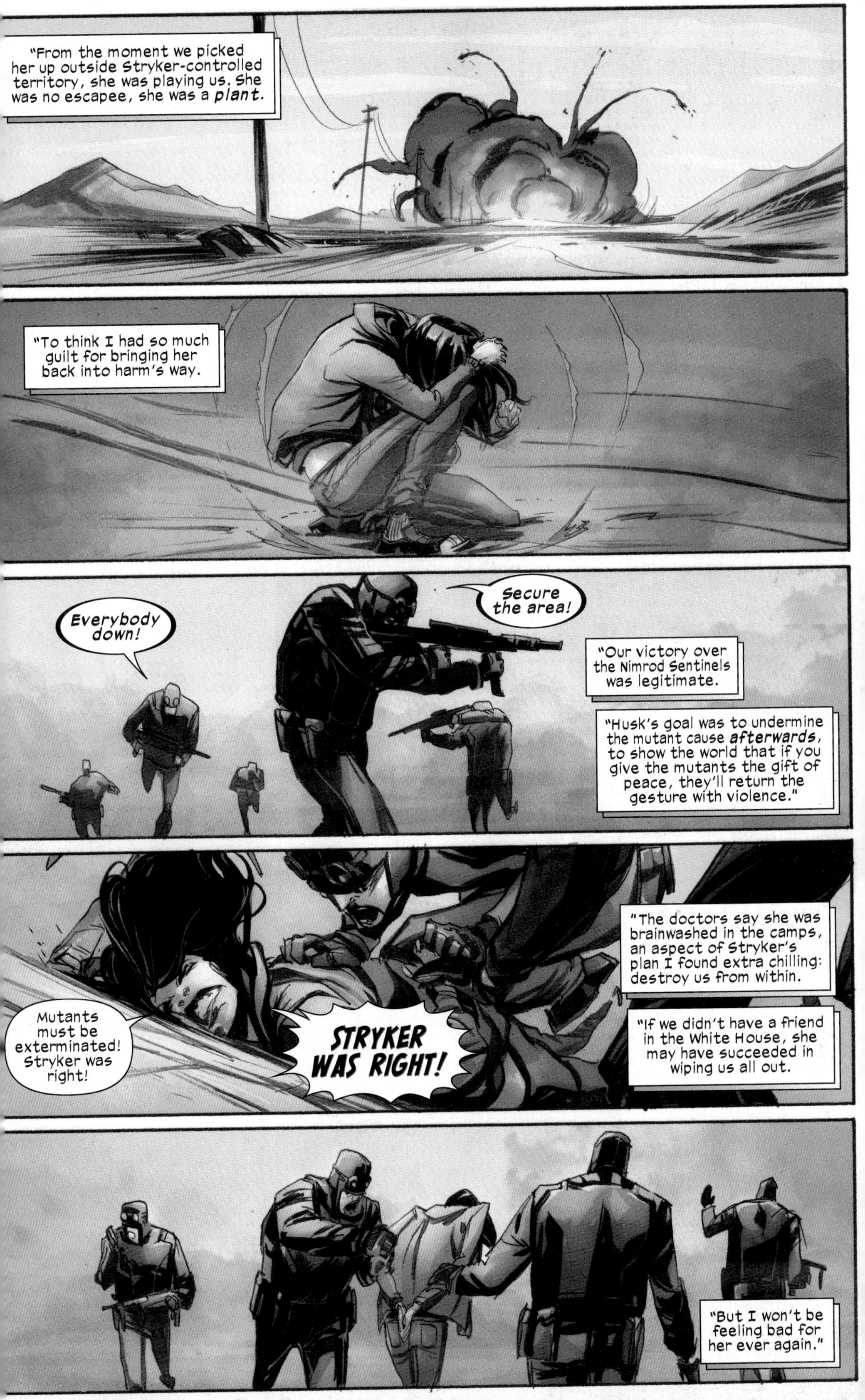
"From the moment we picked her up outside Stryker-controlled territory, she was playing us. She was no escapee, she was a *plant*.
"To think I had so much guilt for bringing her back into harm's way.
Everybody down!
Secure the area!
"Our victory over the Nimrod Sentinels was legitimate.
"Husk's goal was to undermine the mutant cause *afterwards*, to show the world that if you give the mutants the gift of peace, they'll return the gesture with violence."
"The doctors say she was brainwashed in the camps, an aspect of Stryker's plan I found extra chilling: destroy us from within.
"If we didn't have a friend in the White House, she may have succeeded in wiping us all out.
Mutants must be exterminated! Stryker was right!
STRYKER WAS RIGHT!
"But I won't be feeling bad for her ever again."

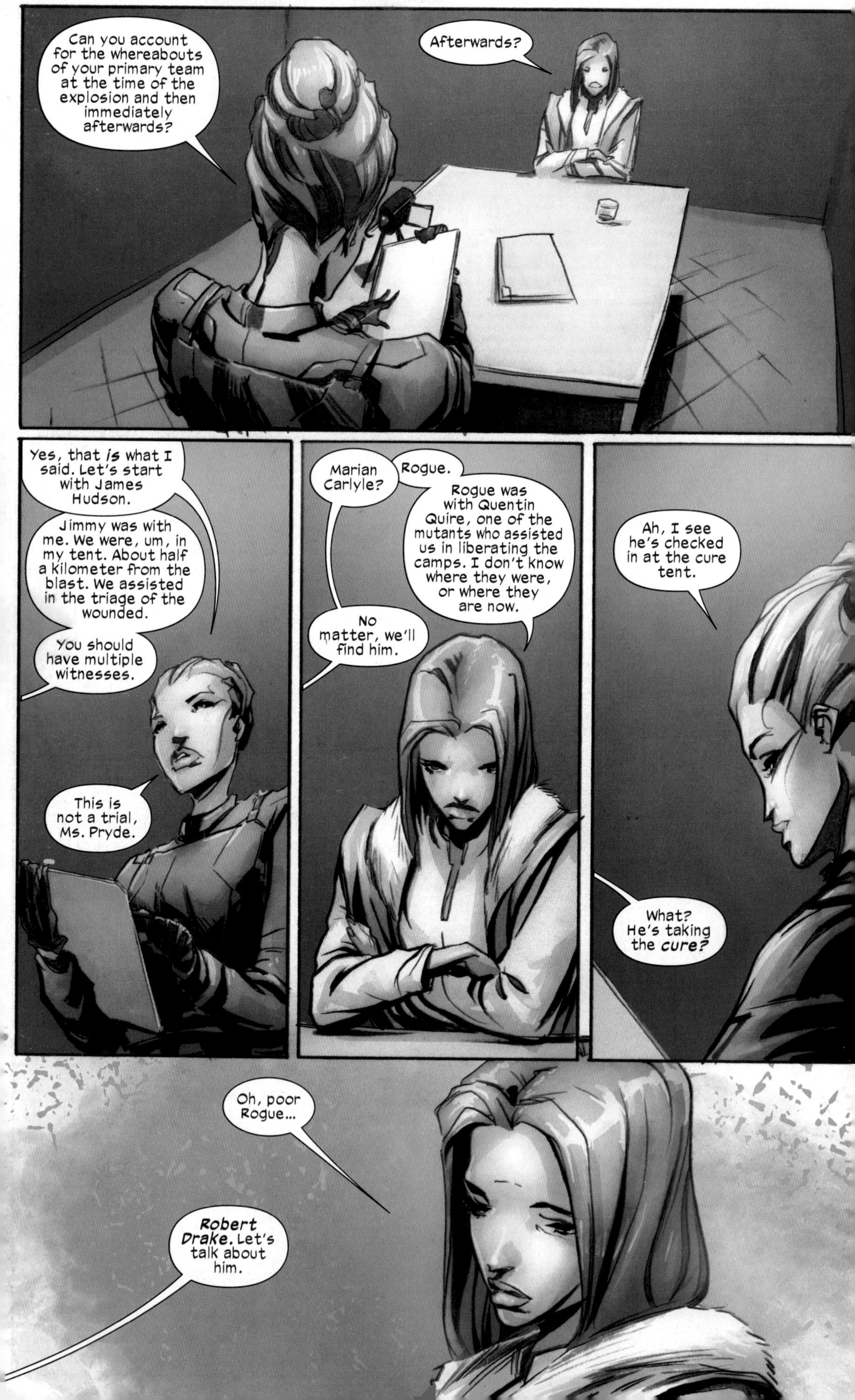

Can you account for the whereabouts of your primary team at the time of the explosion and then immediately afterwards?
Afterwards?
Yes, that *is* what I said. Let's start with James Hudson.
Jimmy was with me. We were, um, in my tent. About half a kilometer from the blast. We assisted in the triage of the wounded.
You should have multiple witnesses.
This is not a trial, Ms. Pryde.
Marian Carlyle?
Rogue.
Rogue was with Quentin Quire, one of the mutants who assisted us in liberating the camps. I don't know where they were, or where they are now.
No matter, we'll find him.
Ah, I see he's checked in at the cure tent.
What? He's taking the *cure?*
Oh, poor Rogue...
Robert Drake. Let's talk about him.

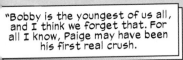

"Bobby is the youngest of us all, and I think we forget that. For all I know, Paige may have been his first real crush.

"Maybe he was even in love with her.

"She didn't return the feelings, but that wouldn't have changed how Bobby felt.

"I couldn't get him to talk to me. He's furious, closed off. Probably suffering from some sort of post-traumatic stress.

"She lied to us all, but Bobby was there when she did what she did. I wish she had died. It might have been easier on all of us. We could have moved past it.

"I don't know how to help him."

"He doesn't want help.

"He just needs space."

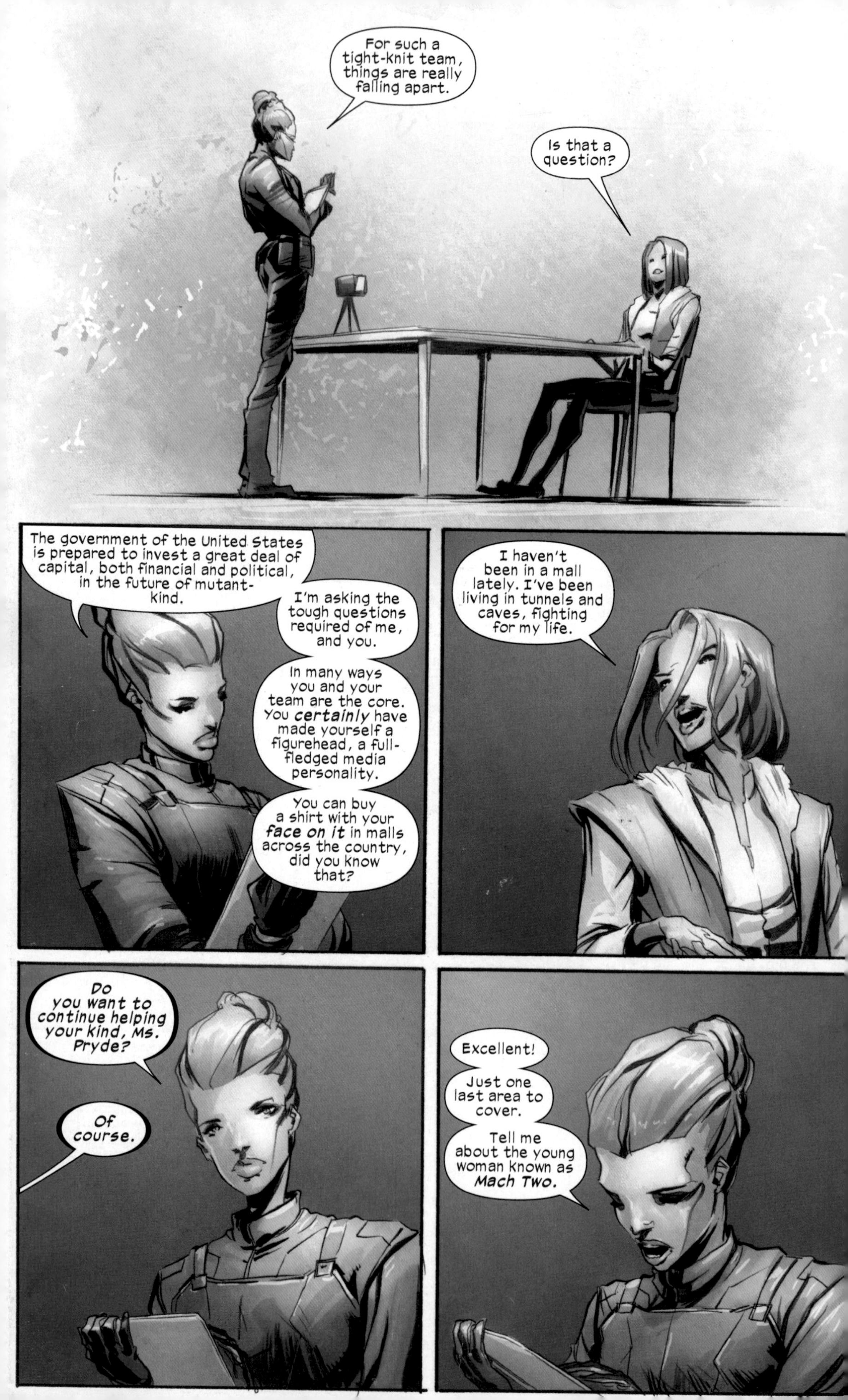
For such a tight-knit team, things are really falling apart.
Is that a question?
The government of the United States is prepared to invest a great deal of capital, both financial and political, in the future of mutant-kind.
I'm asking the tough questions required of me, and you.
In many ways you and your team are the core. You *certainly* have made yourself a figurehead, a full-fledged media personality.
You can buy a shirt with your *face on it* in malls across the country, did you know that?
I haven't been in a mall lately. I've been living in tunnels and caves, fighting for my life.
Do you want to continue helping your kind, Ms. Pryde?
Of course.
Excellent!
Just one last area to cover.
Tell me about the young woman known as *Mach Two*.

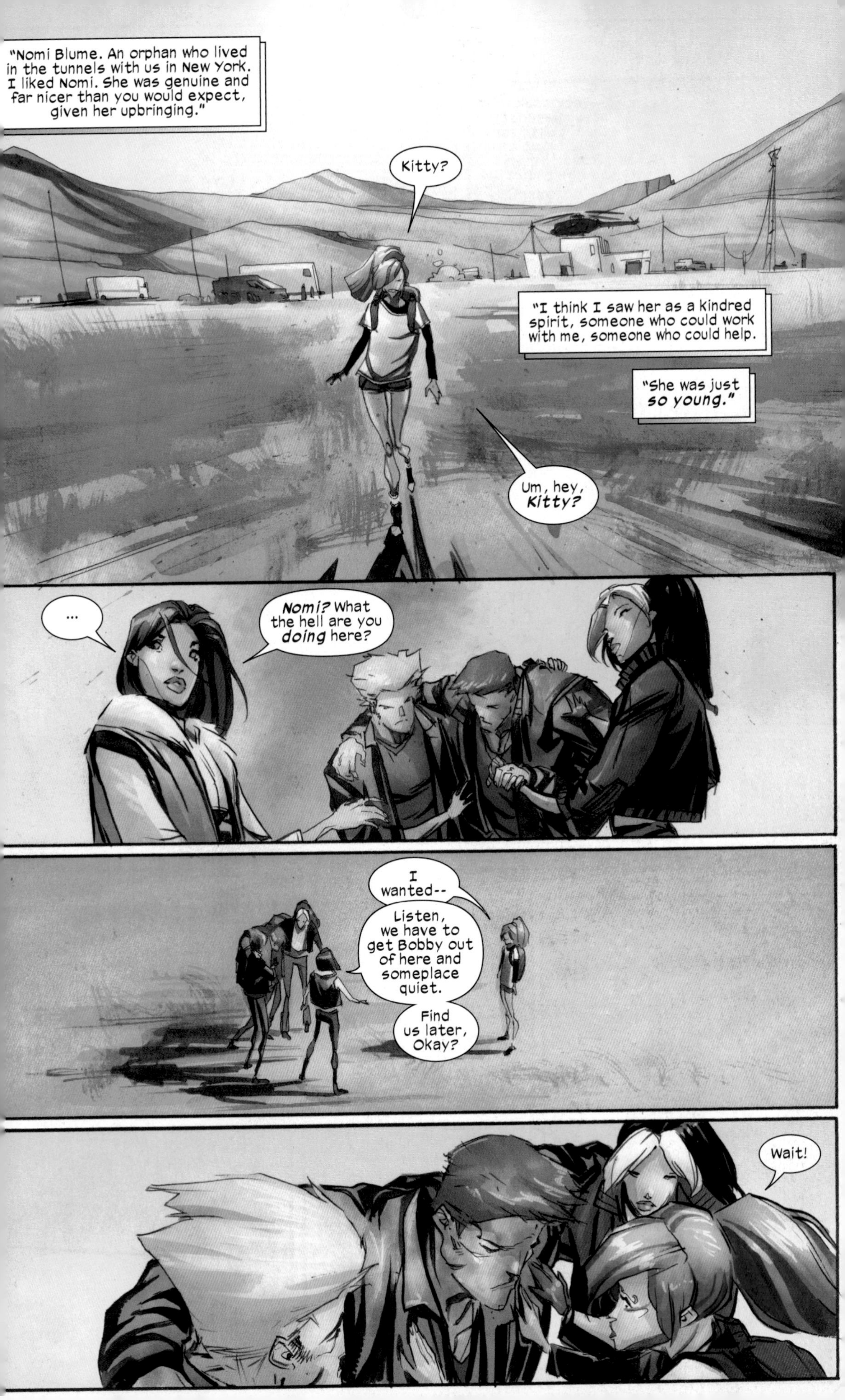
"Nomi Blume. An orphan who lived in the tunnels with us in New York. I liked Nomi. She was genuine and far nicer than you would expect, given her upbringing."
Kitty?
"I think I saw her as a kindred spirit, someone who could work with me, someone who could help.
"She was just so young."
Um, hey, Kitty?
...
Nomi? What the hell are you doing here?
I wanted--
Listen, we have to get Bobby out of here and someplace quiet.
Find us later, Okay?
Wait!

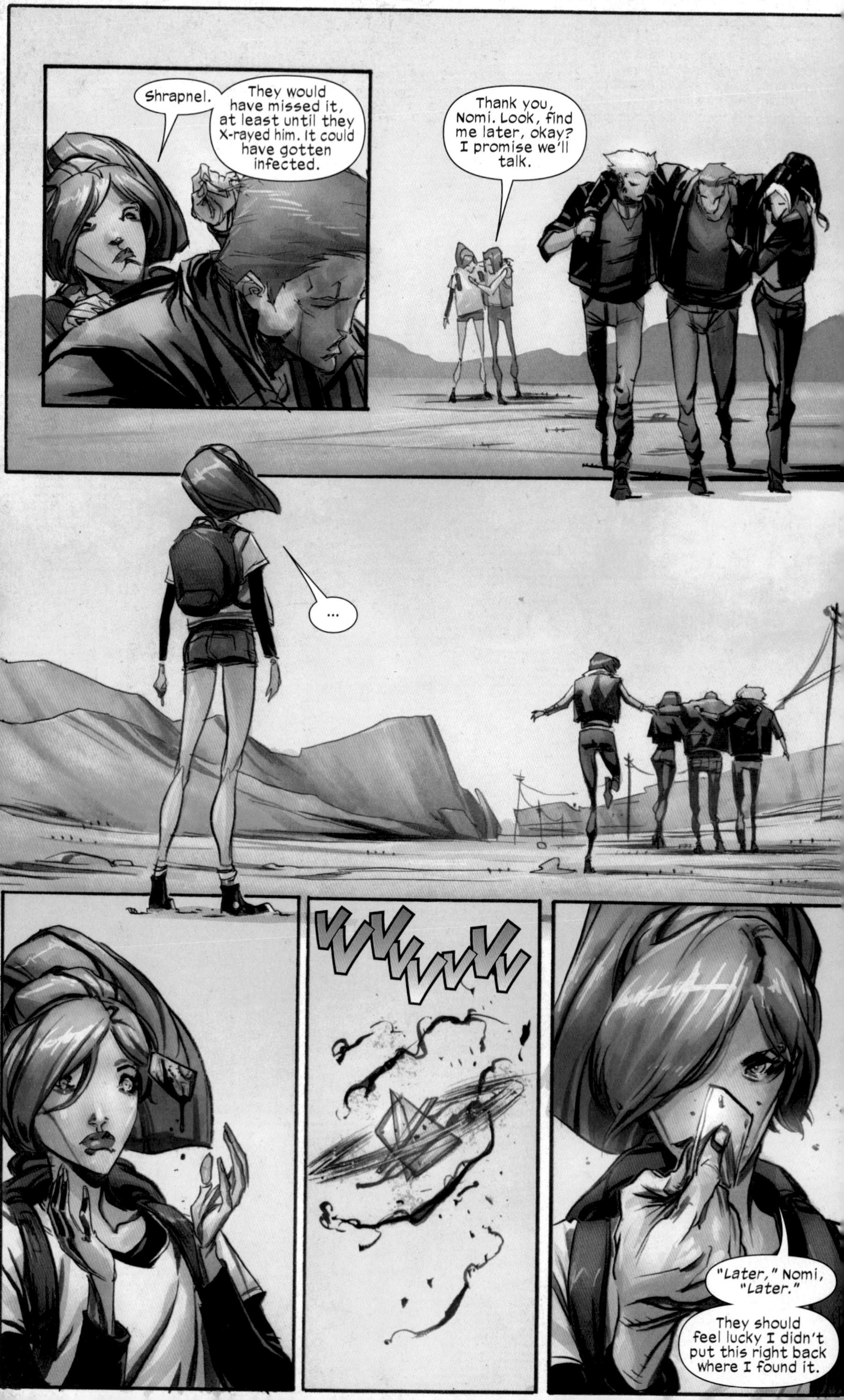
Shrapnel.
They would have missed it, at least until they X-rayed him. It could have gotten infected.
Thank you, Nomi. Look, find me later, okay? I promise we'll talk.
...
VVVVVVVVV
"Later," Nomi, "Later."
They should feel lucky I didn't put this right back where I found it.

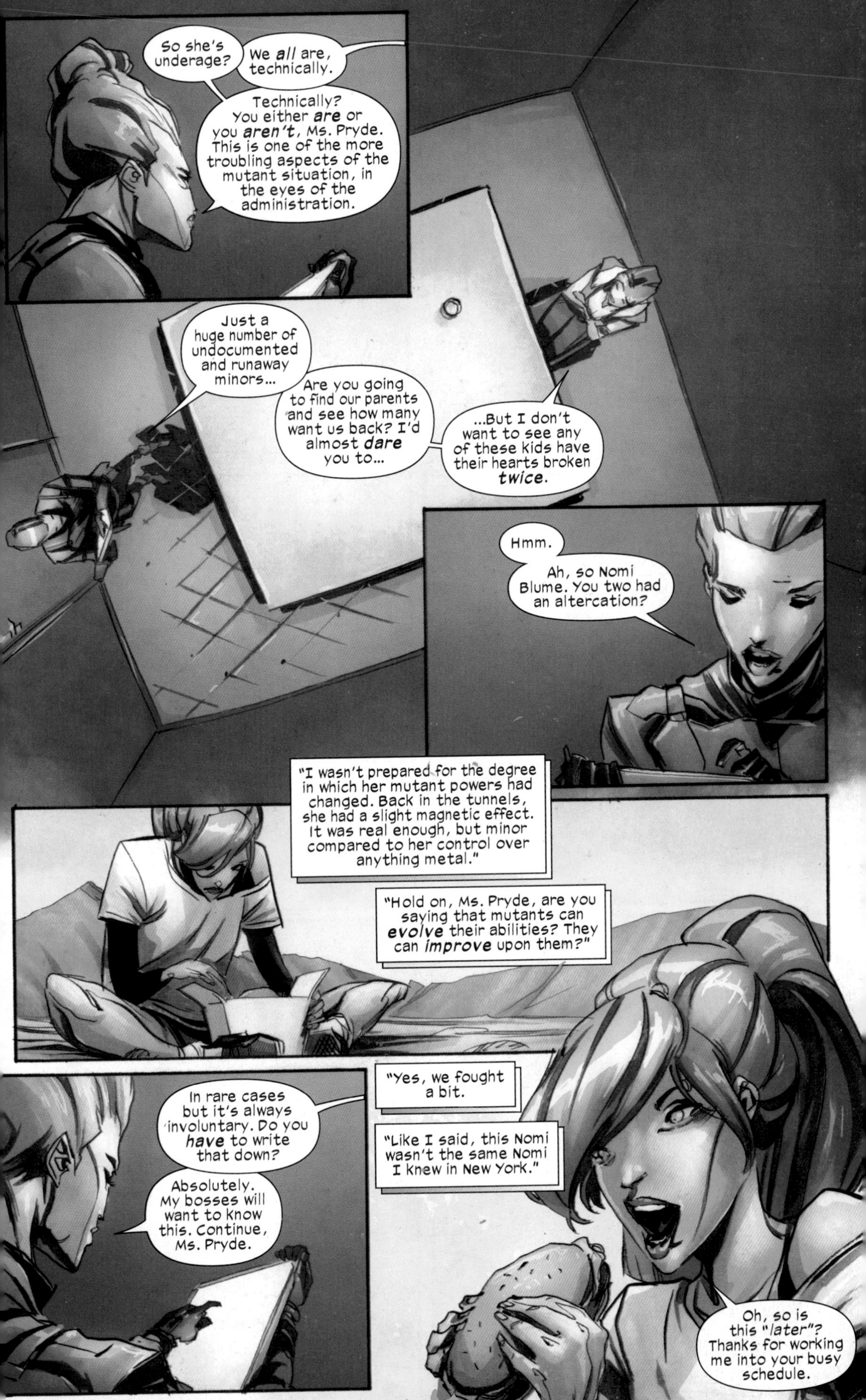
So she's underage?
We all are, technically.
Technically? You either are or you aren't, Ms. Pryde. This is one of the more troubling aspects of the mutant situation, in the eyes of the administration.
Just a huge number of undocumented and runaway minors...
Are you going to find our parents and see how many want us back? I'd almost dare you to...
...But I don't want to see any of these kids have their hearts broken twice.
Hmm.
Ah, so Nomi Blume. You two had an altercation?
"I wasn't prepared for the degree in which her mutant powers had changed. Back in the tunnels, she had a slight magnetic effect. It was real enough, but minor compared to her control over anything metal."
"Hold on, Ms. Pryde, are you saying that mutants can evolve their abilities? They can improve upon them?"
In rare cases but it's always involuntary. Do you have to write that down?
Absolutely. My bosses will want to know this. Continue, Ms. Pryde.
"Yes, we fought a bit.
"Like I said, this Nomi wasn't the same Nomi I knew in New York."
Oh, so is this "later"? Thanks for working me into your busy schedule.

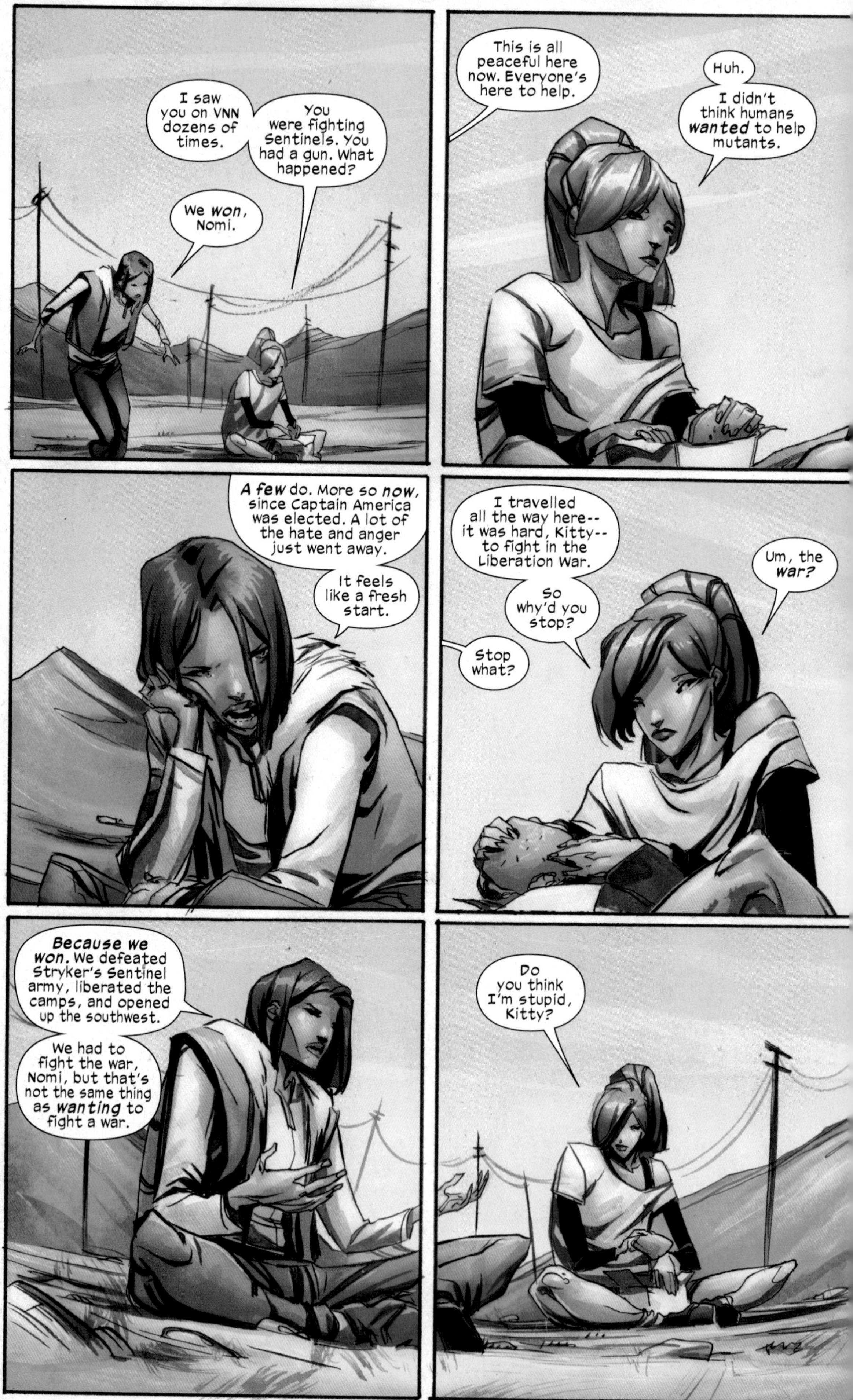
I saw you on VNN dozens of times.
You were fighting Sentinels. You had a gun. What happened?
We won, Nomi.
This is all peaceful here now. Everyone's here to help.
Huh.
I didn't think humans wanted to help mutants.
A few do. More so now, since Captain America was elected. A lot of the hate and anger just went away.
It feels like a fresh start.
I travelled all the way here--it was hard, Kitty--to fight in the Liberation War.
So why'd you stop?
Stop what?
Um, the war?
Because we won. We defeated Stryker's Sentinel army, liberated the camps, and opened up the southwest.
We had to fight the war, Nomi, but that's not the same thing as wanting to fight a war.
Do you think I'm stupid, Kitty?

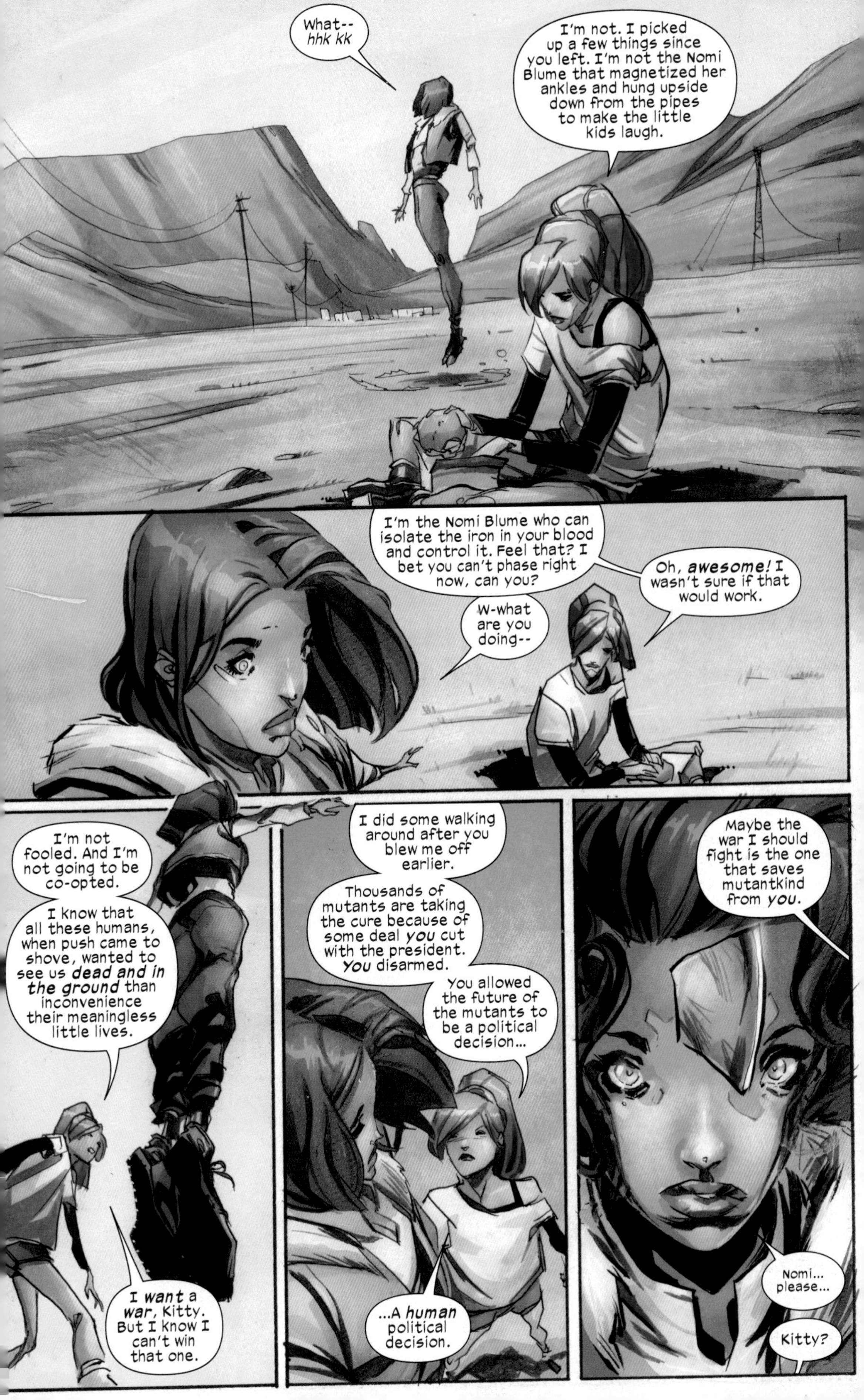
What-- hhk kk
I'm not. I picked up a few things since you left. I'm not the Nomi Blume that magnetized her ankles and hung upside down from the pipes to make the little kids laugh.
I'm the Nomi Blume who can isolate the iron in your blood and control it. Feel that? I bet you can't phase right now, can you?
W-what are you doing--
Oh, *awesome!* I wasn't sure if that would work.
I'm not fooled. And I'm not going to be co-opted.
I know that all these humans, when push came to shove, wanted to see us ***dead and in the ground*** than inconvenience their meaningless little lives.
I *want* a *war*, Kitty. But I know I can't win that one.
I did some walking around after you blew me off earlier.
Thousands of mutants are taking the cure because of some deal *you* cut with the president. *You* disarmed.
You allowed the future of the mutants to be a political decision...
...A *human* political decision.
Maybe the war I should fight is the one that saves mutantkind from *you*.
Nomi... please...
Kitty?

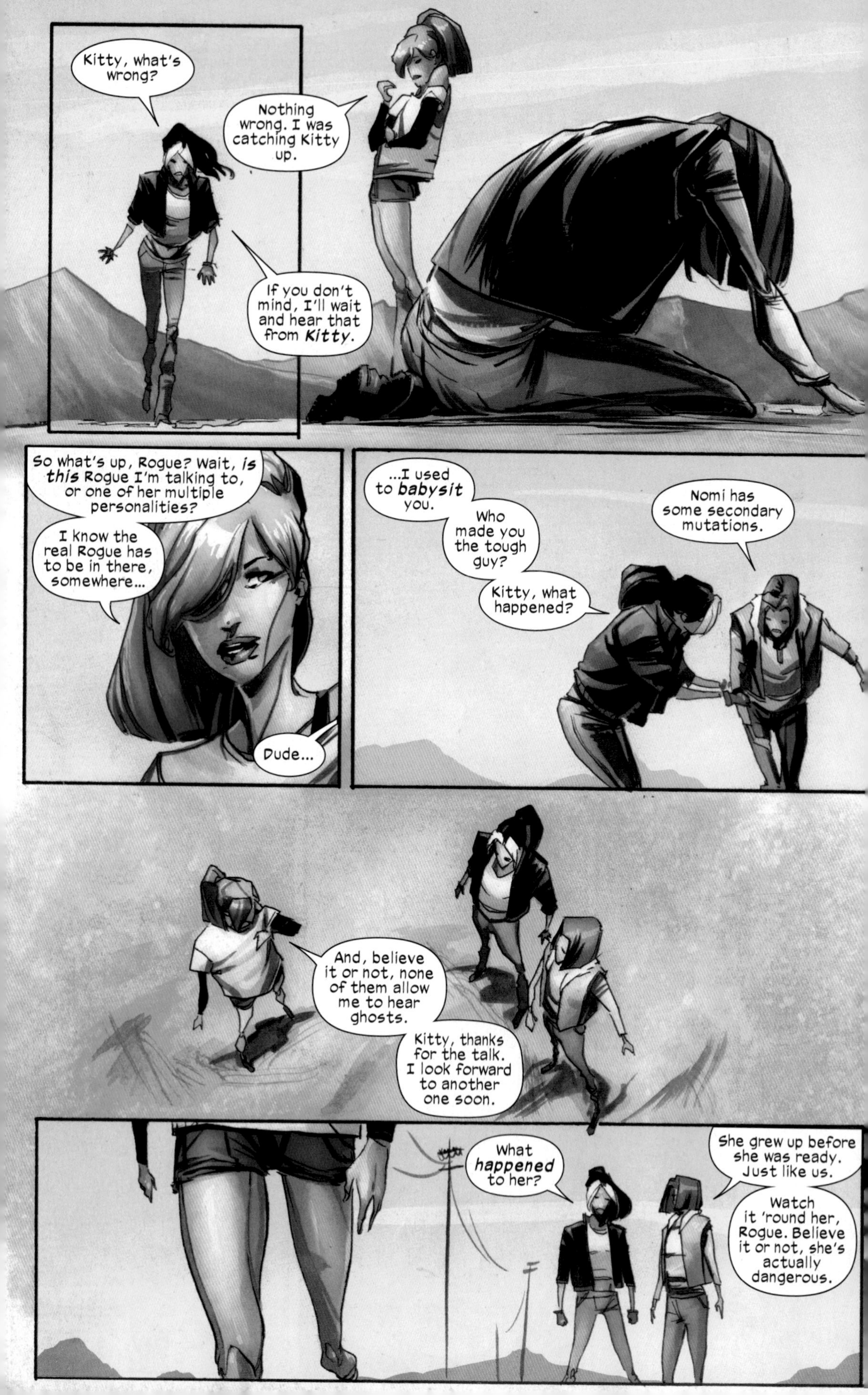

Kitty, what's wrong?
Nothing wrong. I was catching Kitty up.
If you don't mind, I'll wait and hear that from *Kitty*.
So what's up, Rogue? Wait, *is this* Rogue I'm talking to, or one of her multiple personalities?
I know the real Rogue has to be in there, somewhere...
Dude...
...I used to *babysit* you.
Who made you the tough guy?
Kitty, what happened?
Nomi has some secondary mutations.
And, believe it or not, none of them allow me to hear ghosts.
Kitty, thanks for the talk. I look forward to another one soon.
What *happened* to her?
She grew up before she was ready. Just like us.
Watch it 'round her, Rogue. Believe it or not, she's actually dangerous.

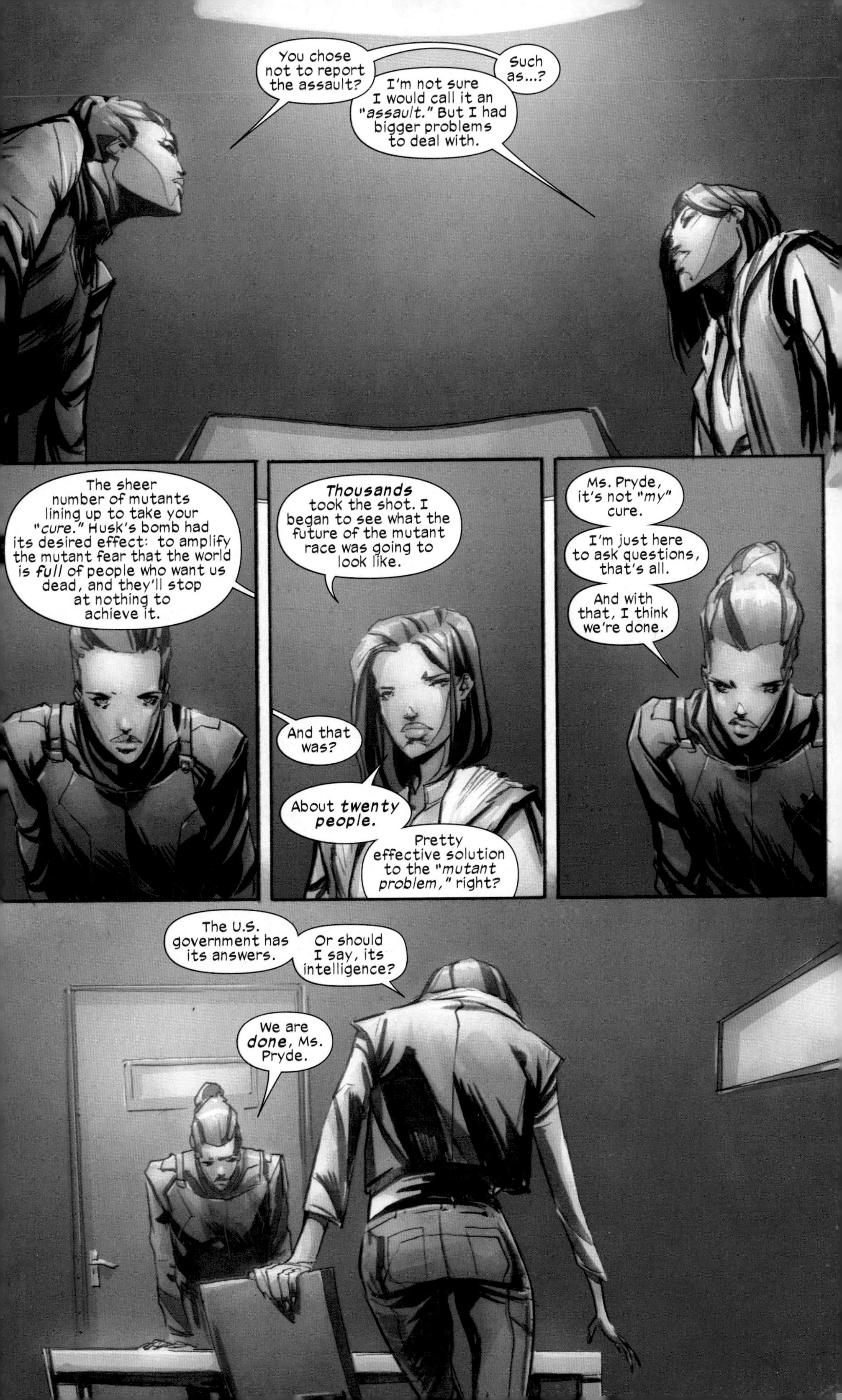

You chose not to report the assault?
Such as...?
I'm not sure I would call it an "assault." But I had bigger problems to deal with.
The sheer number of mutants lining up to take your "cure." Husk's bomb had its desired effect: to amplify the mutant fear that the world is full of people who want us dead, and they'll stop at nothing to achieve it.
Thousands took the shot. I began to see what the future of the mutant race was going to look like.
And that was?
About twenty people.
Pretty effective solution to the "mutant problem," right?
Ms. Pryde, it's not "my" cure.
I'm just here to ask questions, that's all.
And with that, I think we're done.
The U.S. government has its answers.
Or should I say, its intelligence?
We are done, Ms. Pryde.

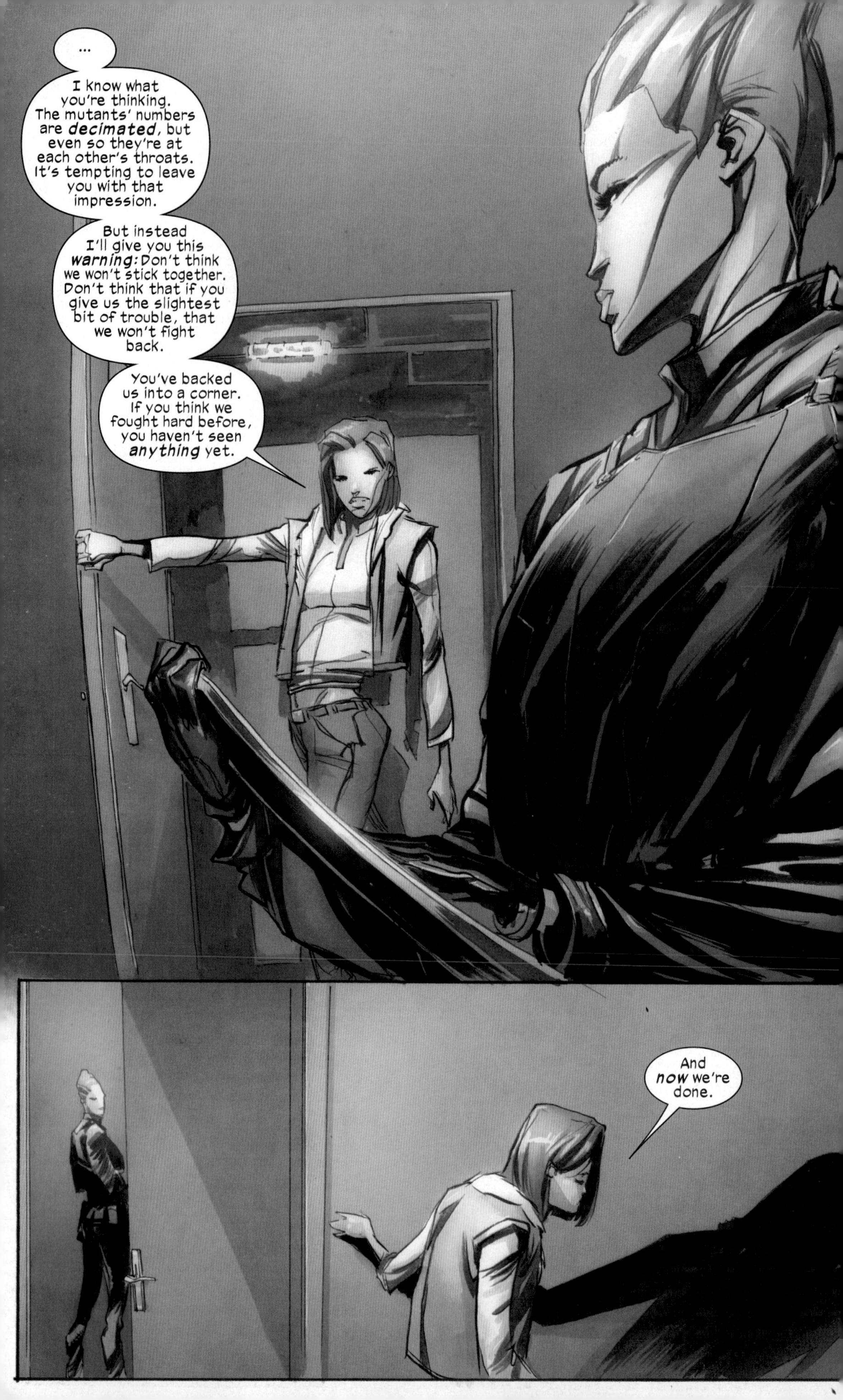
...
I know what you're thinking. The mutants' numbers are *decimated*, but even so they're at each other's throats. It's tempting to leave you with that impression.
But instead I'll give you this *warning:* Don't think we won't stick together. Don't think that if you give us the slightest bit of trouble, that we won't fight back.
You've backed us into a corner. If you think we fought hard before, you haven't seen *anything* yet.
And *now* we're done.

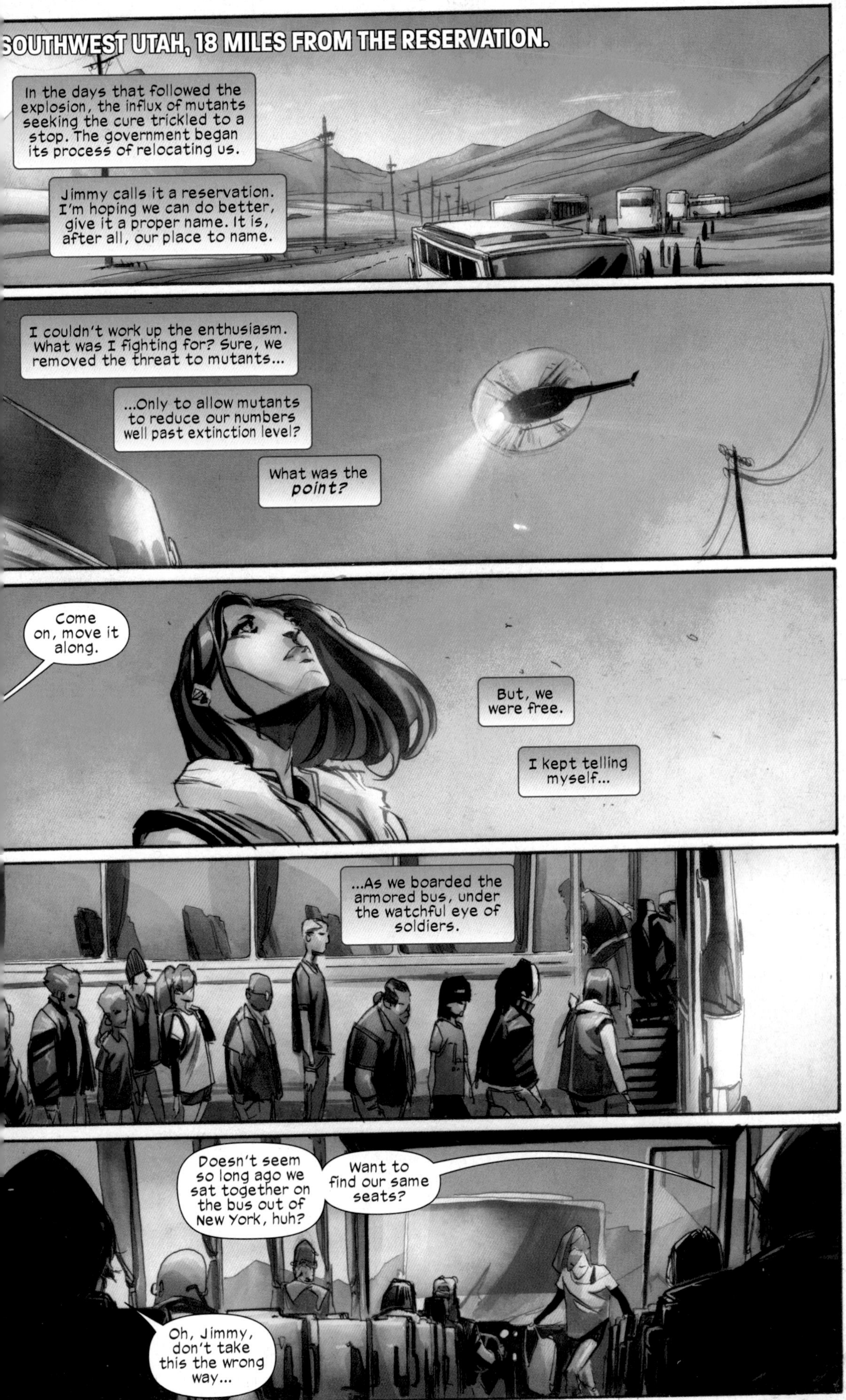
SOUTHWEST UTAH, 18 MILES FROM THE RESERVATION.
In the days that followed the explosion, the influx of mutants seeking the cure trickled to a stop. The government began its process of relocating us.
Jimmy calls it a reservation. I'm hoping we can do better, give it a proper name. It is, after all, our place to name.
I couldn't work up the enthusiasm. What was I fighting for? Sure, we removed the threat to mutants...
...Only to allow mutants to reduce our numbers well past extinction level?
What was the *point?*
Come on, move it along.
But, we were free.
I kept telling myself...
...As we boarded the armored bus, under the watchful eye of soldiers.
Doesn't seem so long ago we sat together on the bus out of New York, huh?
Want to find our same seats?
Oh, Jimmy, don't take this the wrong way...

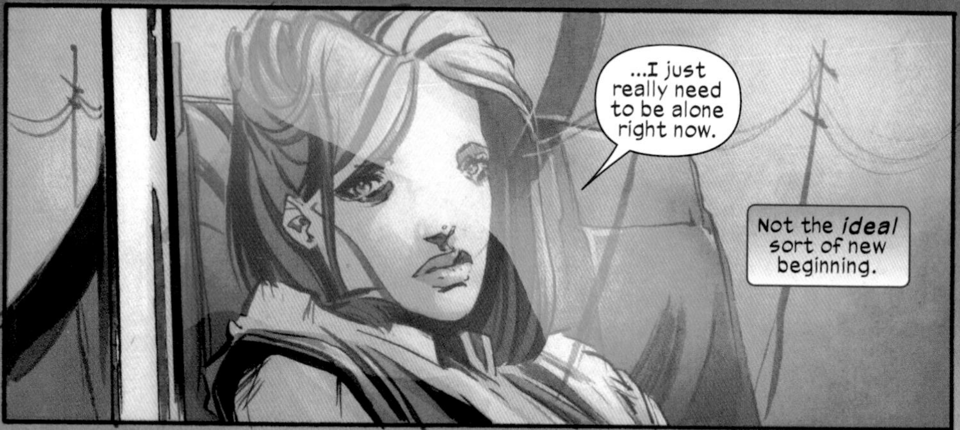
...I just really need to be alone right now.
Not the *ideal* sort of new beginning.

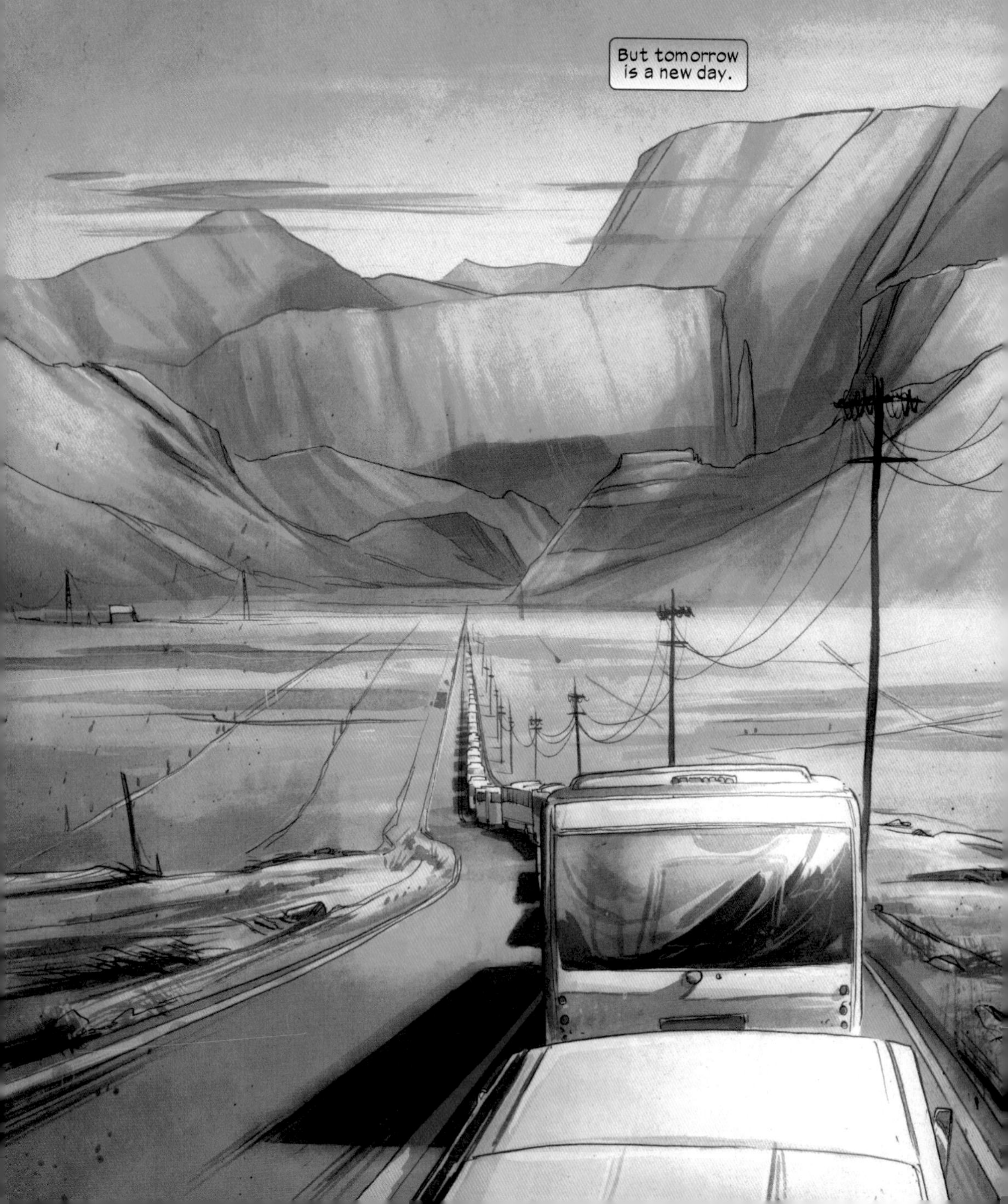
But tomorrow is a new day.

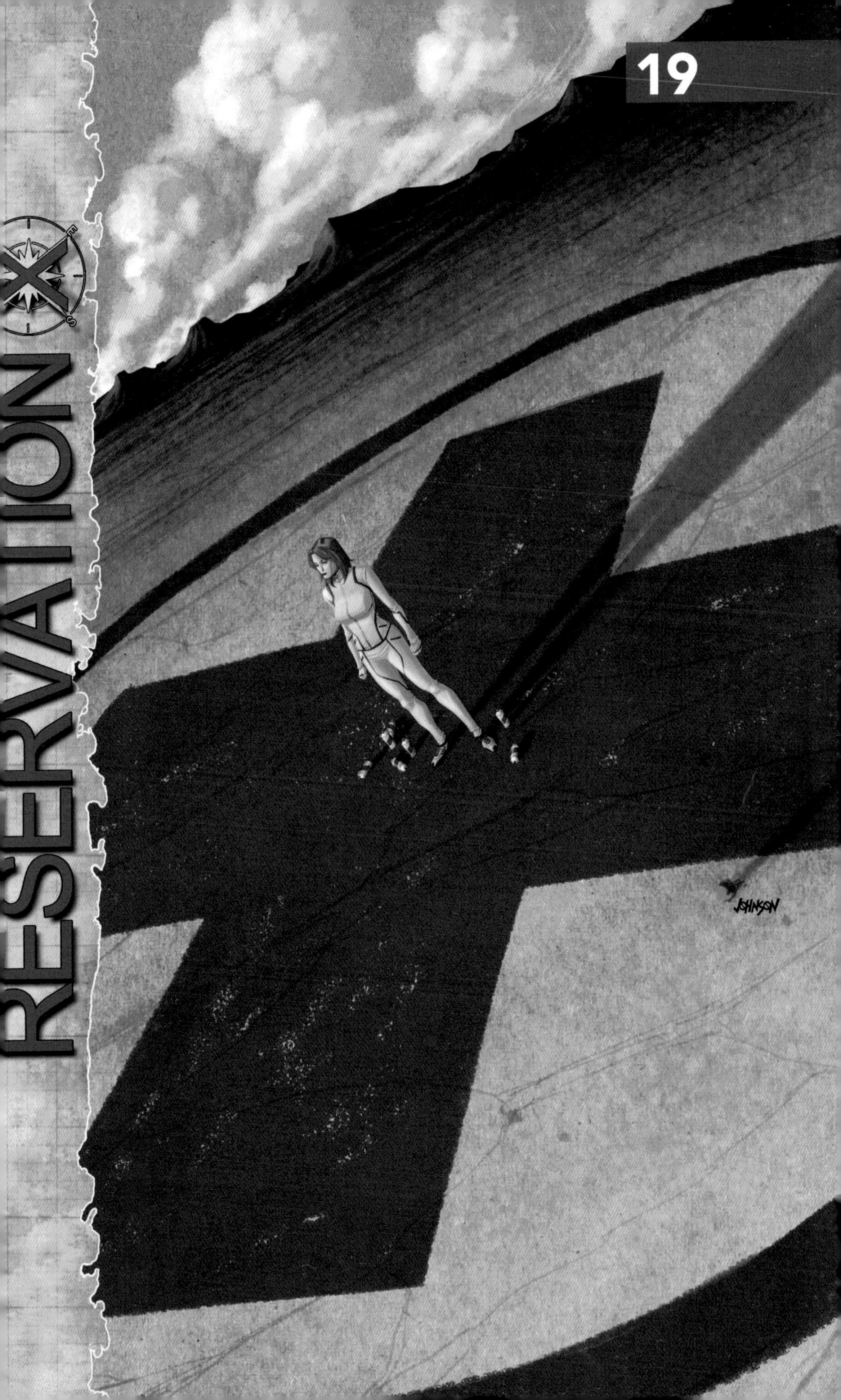
19
RESERVATION
JOHNSON

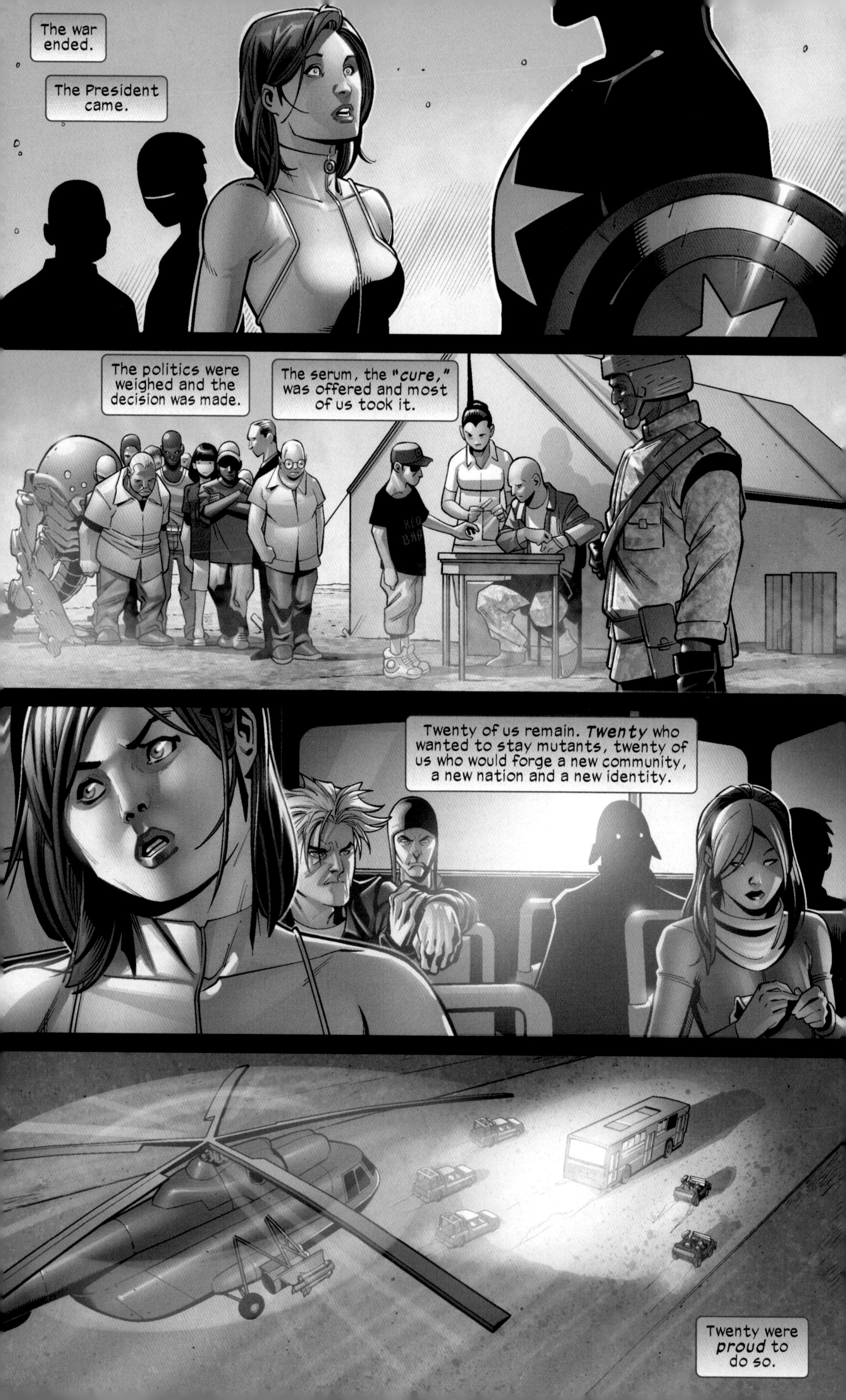

The war ended.
The President came.
The politics were weighed and the decision was made.
The serum, the "*cure*," was offered and most of us took it.
Twenty of us remain. ***Twenty*** who wanted to stay mutants, twenty of us who would forge a new community, a new nation and a new identity.
Twenty were ***proud*** to do so.

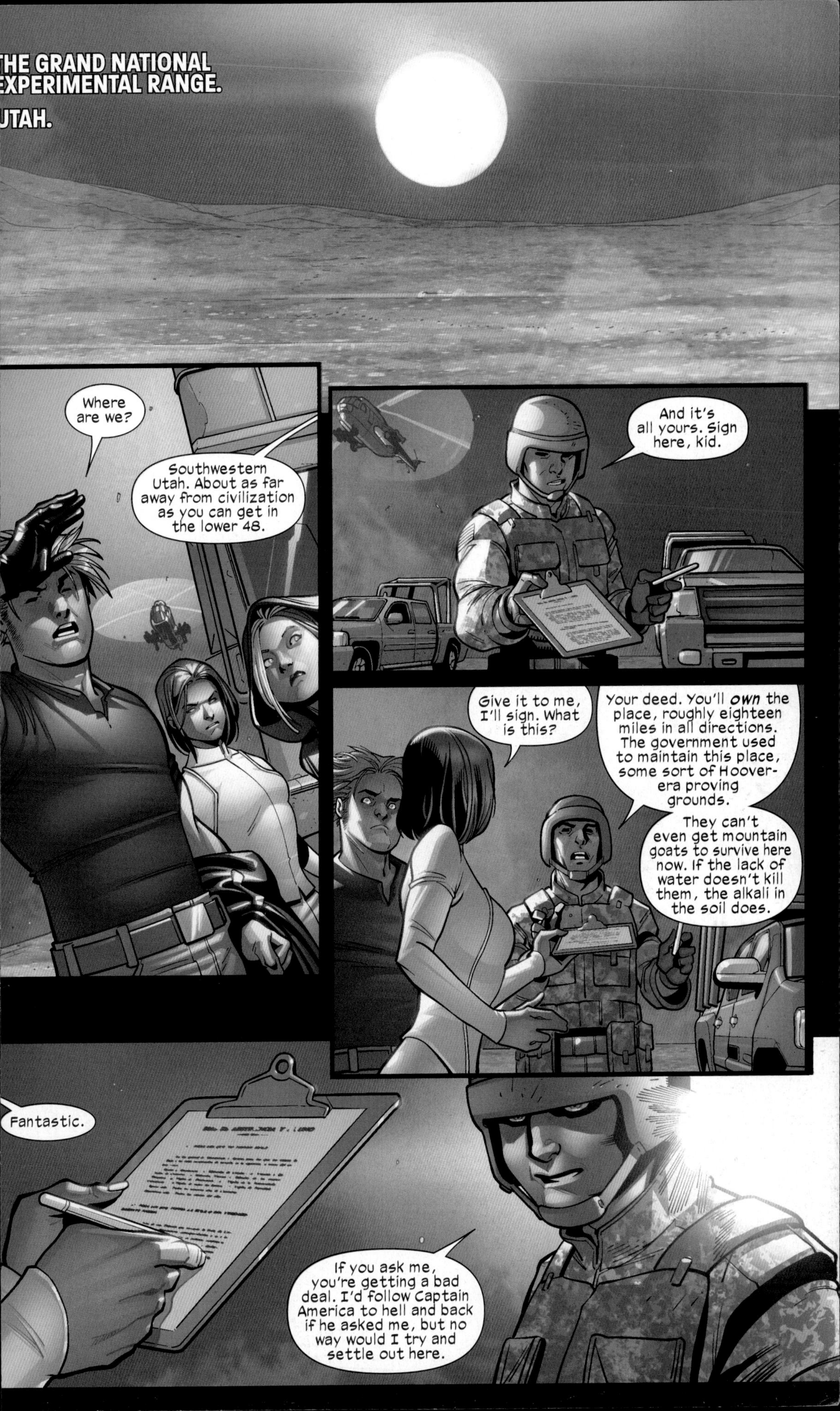
THE GRAND NATIONAL EXPERIMENTAL RANGE.
UTAH.
Where are we?
Southwestern Utah. About as far away from civilization as you can get in the lower 48.
And it's all yours. Sign here, kid.
Give it to me, I'll sign. What is this?
Your deed. You'll *own* the place, roughly eighteen miles in all directions. The government used to maintain this place, some sort of Hoover-era proving grounds.
They can't even get mountain goats to survive here now. If the lack of water doesn't kill them, the alkali in the soil does.
Fantastic.
If you ask me, you're getting a bad deal. I'd follow Captain America to hell and back if he asked me, but no way would I try and settle out here.

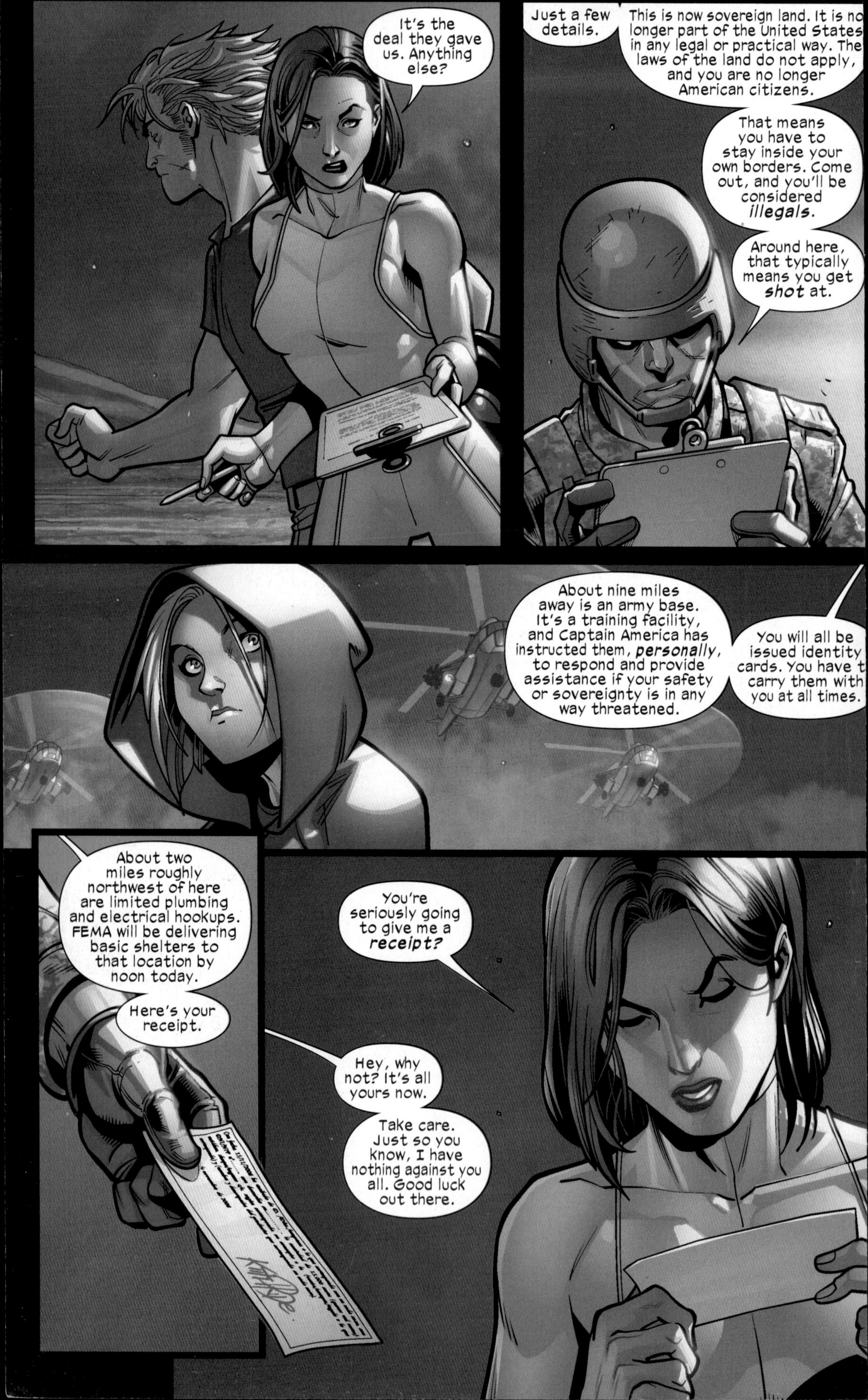
It's the deal they gave us. Anything else?
Just a few details.
This is now sovereign land. It is no longer part of the United States in any legal or practical way. The laws of the land do not apply, and you are no longer American citizens.
That means you have to stay inside your own borders. Come out, and you'll be considered *illegals*.
Around here, that typically means you get *shot* at.
About nine miles away is an army base. It's a training facility, and Captain America has instructed them, *personally*, to respond and provide assistance if your safety or sovereignty is in any way threatened.
You will all be issued identity cards. You have t carry them with you at all times.
About two miles roughly northwest of here are limited plumbing and electrical hookups. FEMA will be delivering basic shelters to that location by noon today.
Here's your receipt.
You're seriously going to give me a *receipt?*
Hey, why not? It's all yours now.
Take care. Just so you know, I have nothing against you all. Good luck out there.

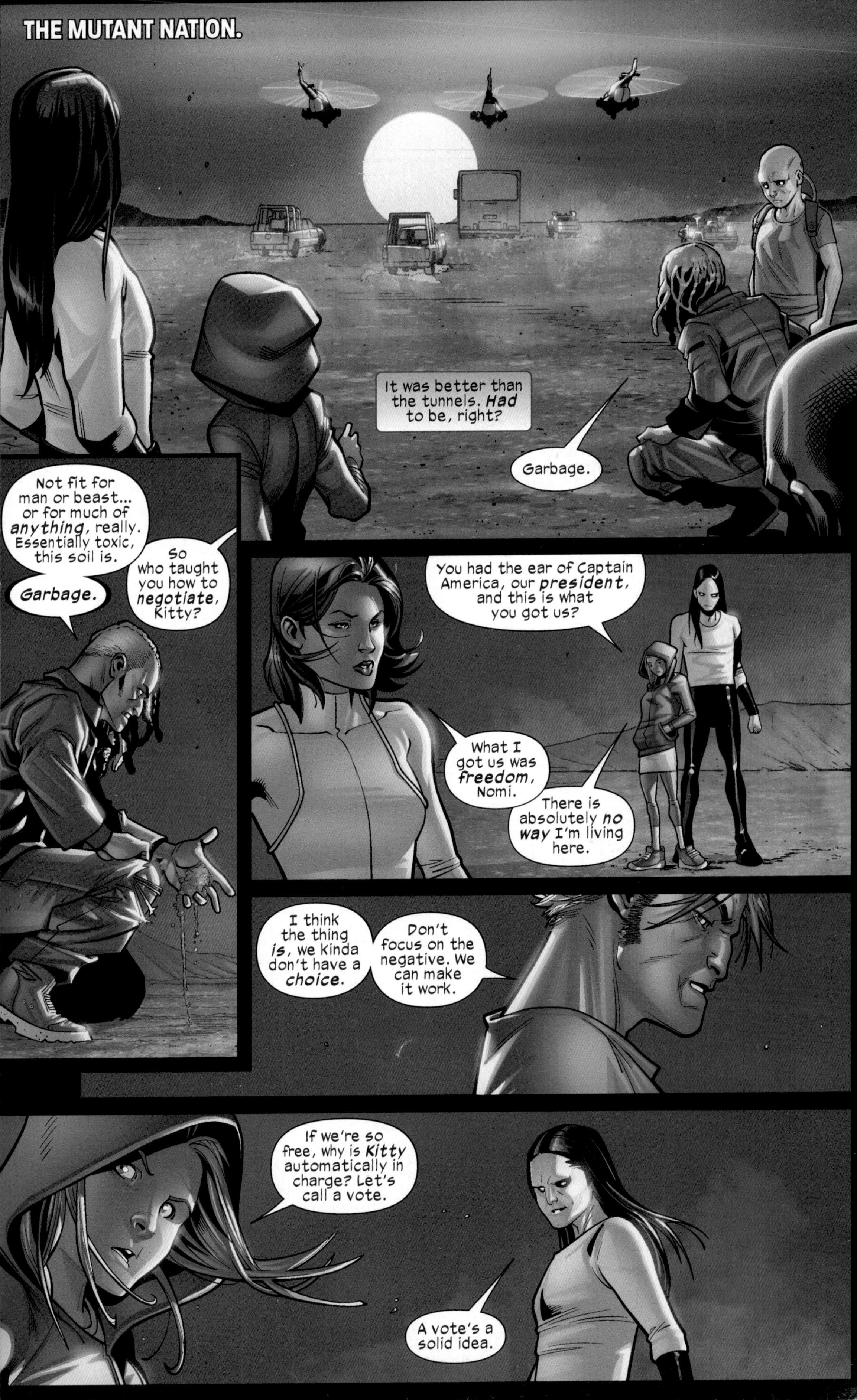
THE MUTANT NATION.
It was better than the tunnels. *Had* to be, right?
Garbage.
Not fit for man or beast... or for much of *anything*, really. Essentially toxic, this soil is.
Garbage.
So who taught you how to *negotiate*, Kitty?
You had the ear of Captain America, our *president*, and this is what you got us?
What I got us was *freedom*, Nomi.
There is absolutely *no way* I'm living here.
I think the thing *is*, we kinda don't have a *choice*.
Don't focus on the negative. We can make it work.
If we're so free, why is *Kitty* automatically in charge? Let's call a vote.
A vote's a solid idea.

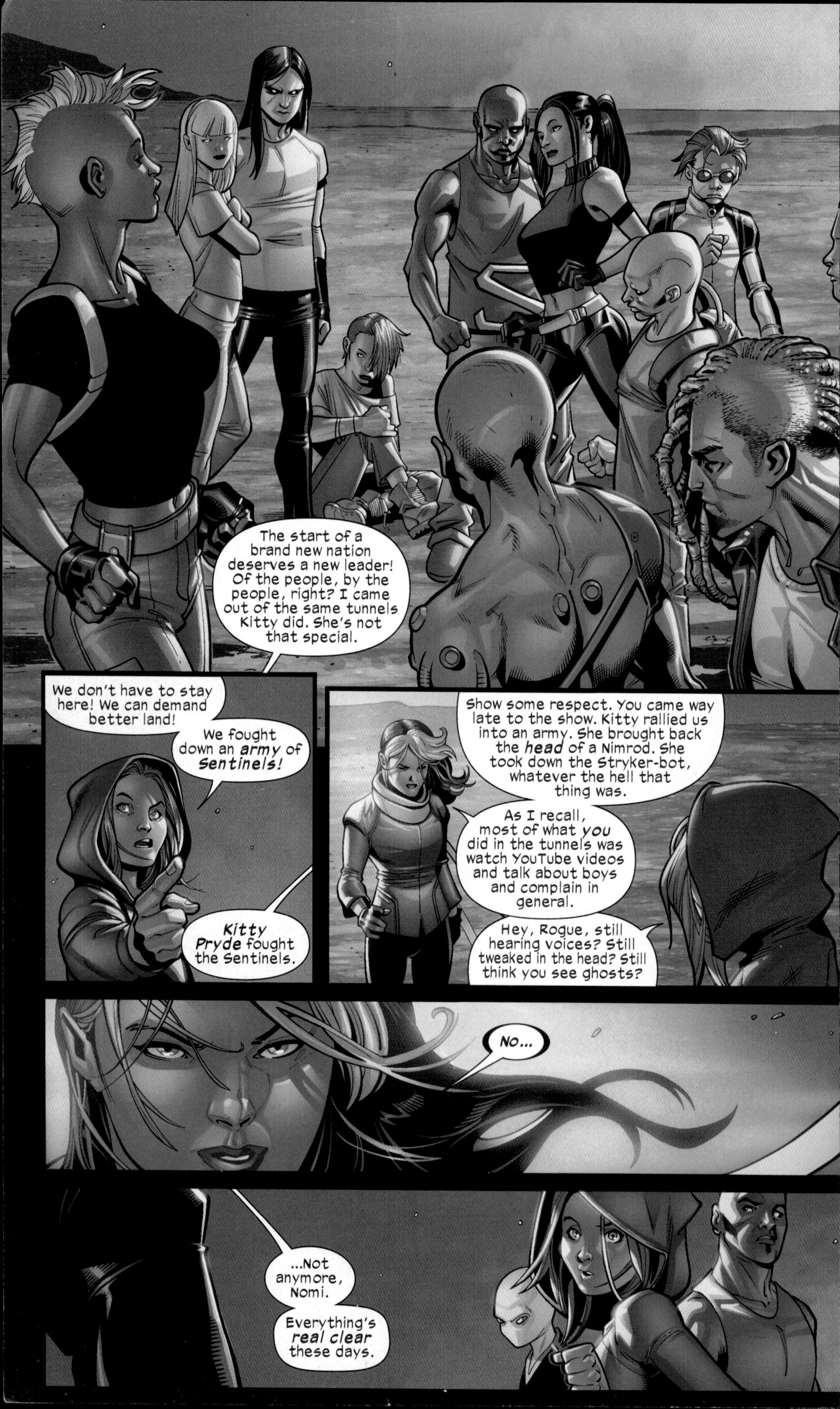
The start of a brand new nation deserves a new leader! Of the people, by the people, right? I came out of the same tunnels Kitty did. She's not that special.
We don't have to stay here! We can demand better land!
We fought down an *army* of *Sentinels!*
Kitty Pryde fought the Sentinels.
Show some respect. You came way late to the show. Kitty rallied us into an army. She brought back the *head* of a Nimrod. She took down the Stryker-bot, whatever the hell that thing was.
As I recall, most of what *you* did in the tunnels was watch YouTube videos and talk about boys and complain in general.
Hey, Rogue, still hearing voices? Still tweaked in the head? Still think you see ghosts?
NO...
...Not anymore, Nomi.
Everything's *real clear* these days.

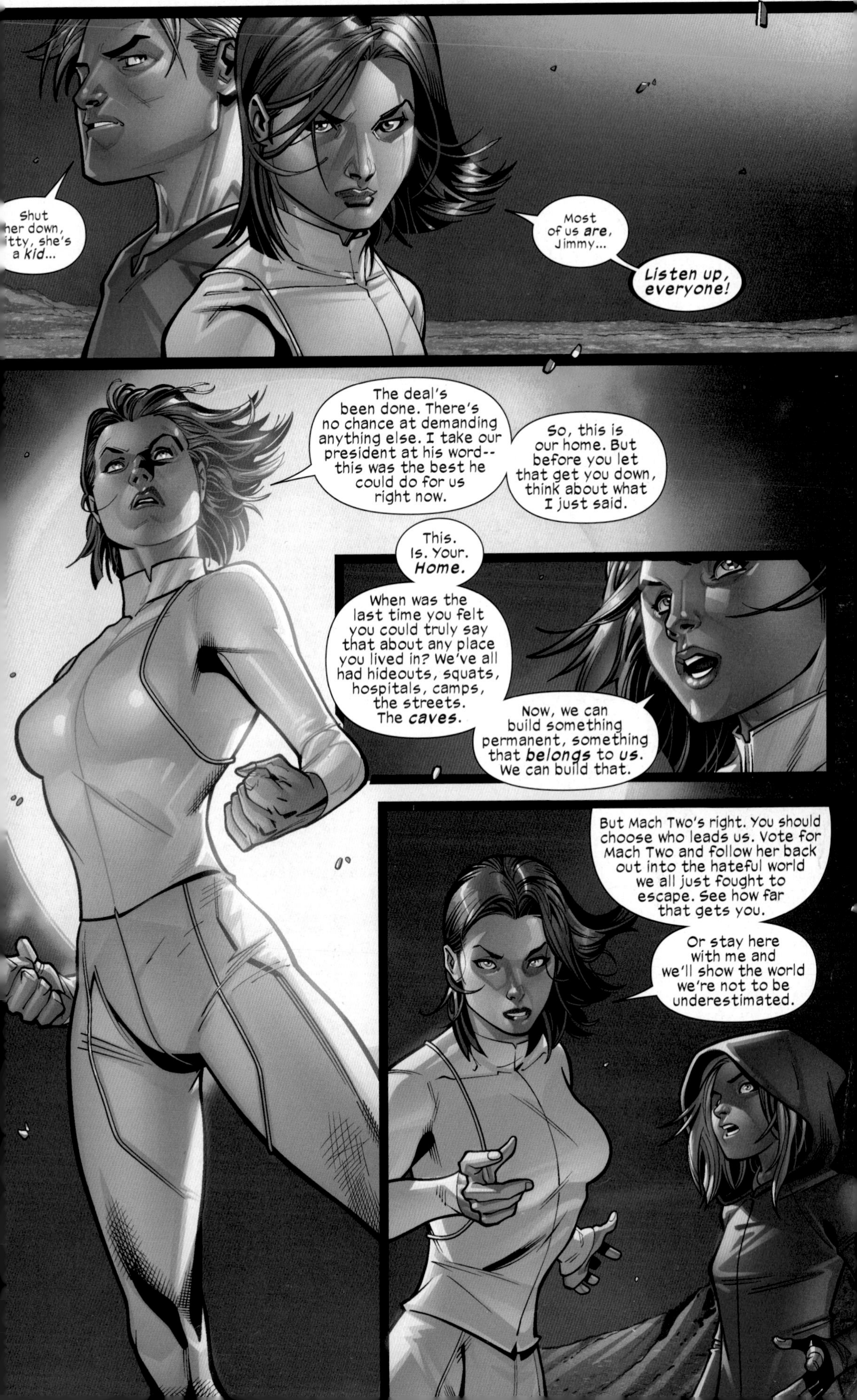

Shut her down, Kitty, she's a kid...
Most of us are, Jimmy...
Listen up, everyone!
The deal's been done. There's no chance at demanding anything else. I take our president at his word-- this was the best he could do for us right now.
So, this is our home. But before you let that get you down, think about what I just said.
This. Is. Your. Home.
When was the last time you felt you could truly say that about any place you lived in? We've all had hideouts, squats, hospitals, camps, the streets. The caves.
Now, we can build something permanent, something that belongs to us. We can build that.
But Mach Two's right. You should choose who leads us. Vote for Mach Two and follow her back out into the hateful world we all just fought to escape. See how far that gets you.
Or stay here with me and we'll show the world we're not to be underestimated.

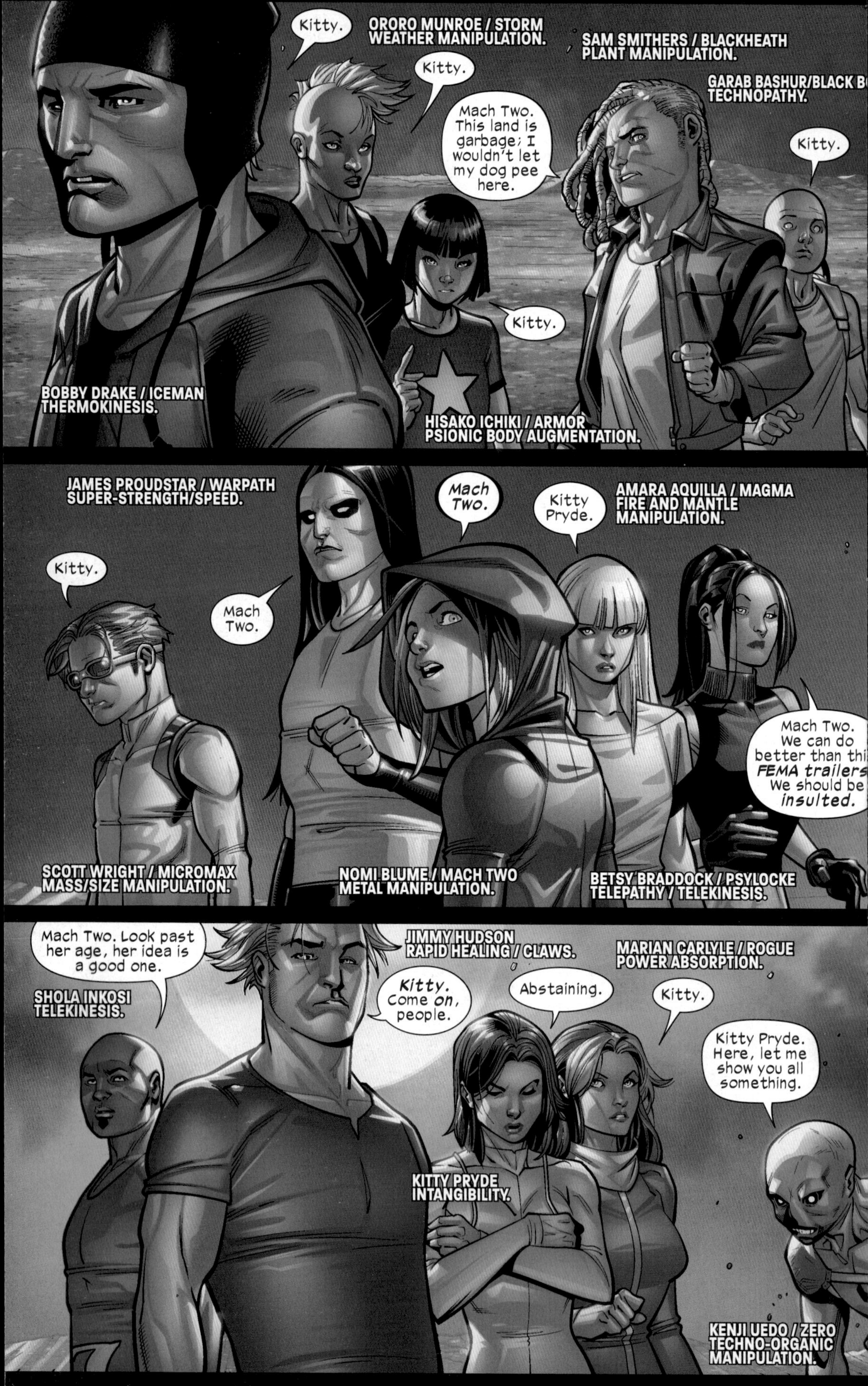

Kitty.
ORORO MUNROE / STORM
WEATHER MANIPULATION.
Kitty.
SAM SMITHERS / BLACKHEATH
PLANT MANIPULATION.
Mach Two. This land is garbage; I wouldn't let my dog pee here.
GARAB BASHUR/BLACK B
TECHNOPATHY.
Kitty.
Kitty.
BOBBY DRAKE / ICEMAN
THERMOKINESIS.
HISAKO ICHIKI / ARMOR
PSIONIC BODY AUGMENTATION.
JAMES PROUDSTAR / WARPATH
SUPER-STRENGTH/SPEED.
Mach Two.
Kitty Pryde.
AMARA AQUILLA / MAGMA
FIRE AND MANTLE MANIPULATION.
Kitty.
Mach Two.
Mach Two. We can do better than thi FEMA trailers We should be insulted.
SCOTT WRIGHT / MICROMAX
MASS/SIZE MANIPULATION.
NOMI BLUME / MACH TWO
METAL MANIPULATION.
BETSY BRADDOCK / PSYLOCKE
TELEPATHY / TELEKINESIS.
Mach Two. Look past her age, her idea is a good one.
SHOLA INKOSI
TELEKINESIS.
JIMMY HUDSON
RAPID HEALING / CLAWS.
Kitty. Come on, people.
Abstaining.
MARIAN CARLYLE / ROGUE
POWER ABSORPTION.
Kitty.
Kitty Pryde. Here, let me show you all something.
KITTY PRYDE
INTANGIBILITY.
KENJI UEDO / ZERO
TECHNO-ORGANIC MANIPULATION.

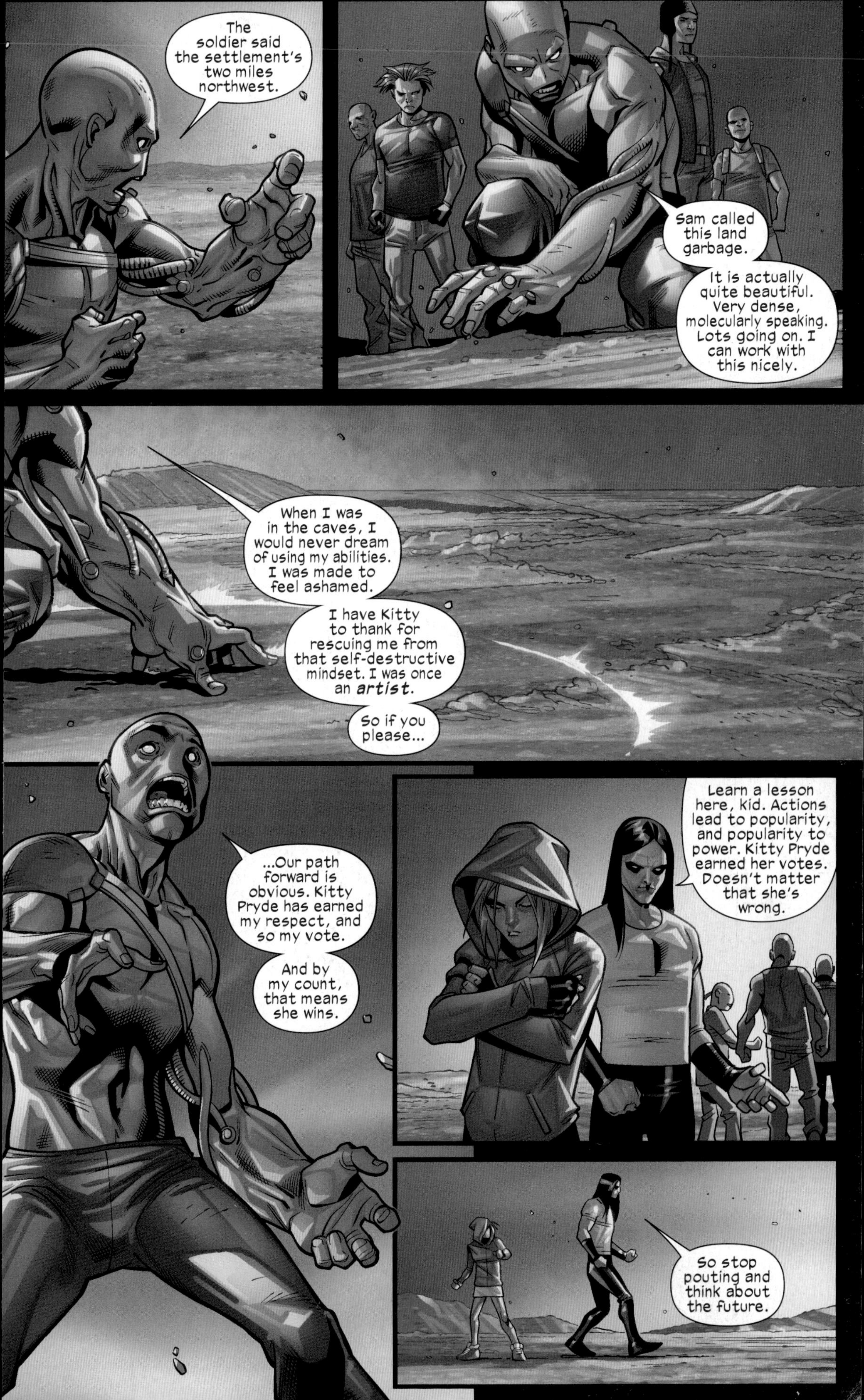

The soldier said the settlement's two miles northwest.
Sam called this land garbage.
It is actually quite beautiful. Very dense, molecularly speaking. Lots going on. I can work with this nicely.
When I was in the caves, I would never dream of using my abilities. I was made to feel ashamed.
I have Kitty to thank for rescuing me from that self-destructive mindset. I was once an *artist*.
So if you please...
...Our path forward is obvious. Kitty Pryde has earned my respect, and so my vote.
And by my count, that means she wins.
Learn a lesson here, kid. Actions lead to popularity, and popularity to power. Kitty Pryde earned her votes. Doesn't matter that she's wrong.
So stop pouting and think about the future.

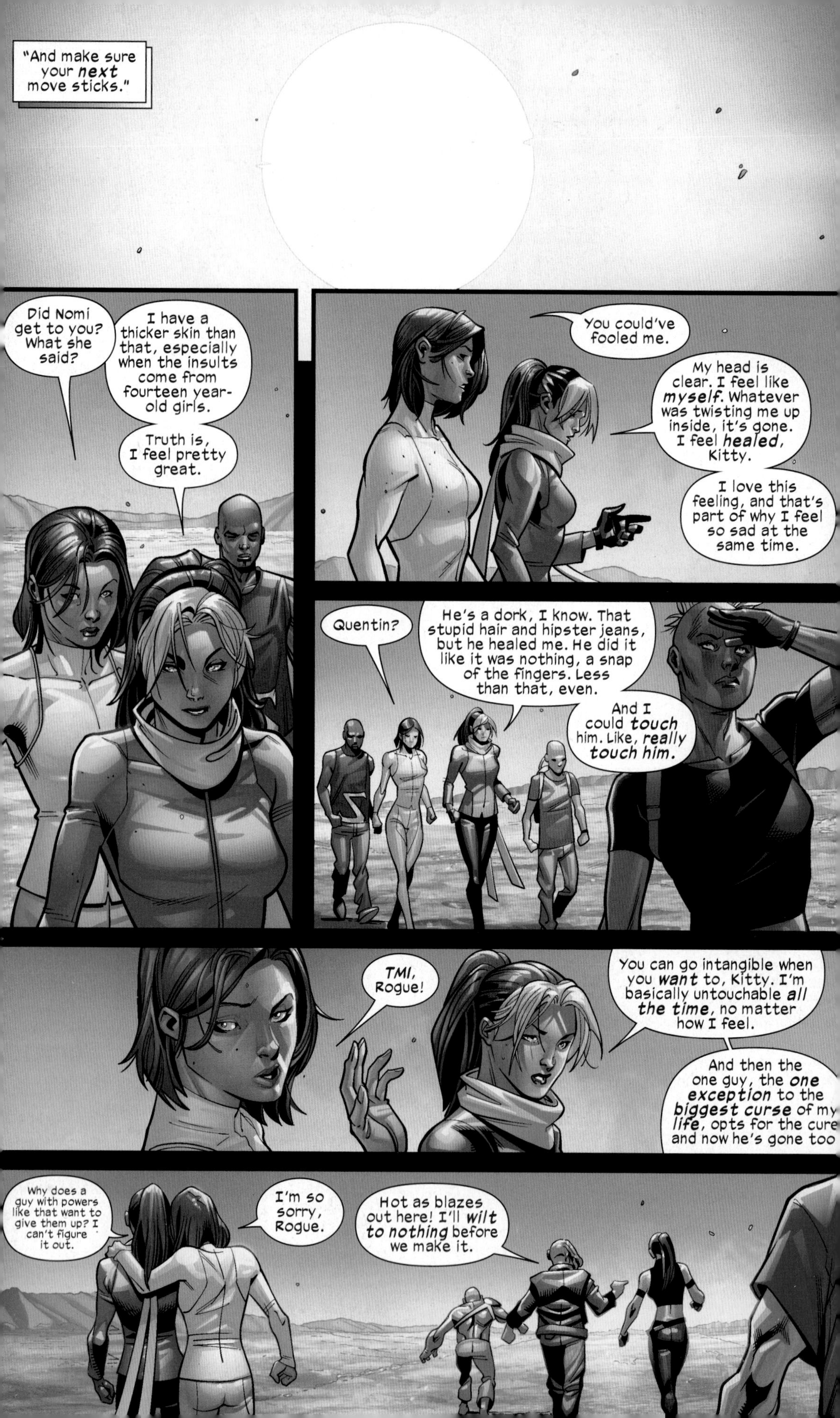
"And make sure your *next* move sticks."
Did Nomi get to you? What she said?
I have a thicker skin than that, especially when the insults come from fourteen year-old girls.
Truth is, I feel pretty great.
You could've fooled me.
My head is clear. I feel like *myself*. Whatever was twisting me up inside, it's gone. I feel *healed*, Kitty.
I love this feeling, and that's part of why I feel so sad at the same time.
Quentin?
He's a dork, I know. That stupid hair and hipster jeans, but he healed me. He did it like it was nothing, a snap of the fingers. Less than that, even.
And I could *touch* him. Like, *really touch him.*
TMI, Rogue!
You can go intangible when you *want* to, Kitty. I'm basically untouchable *all the time*, no matter how I feel.
And then the one guy, the *one exception* to the *biggest curse* of my *life*, opts for the cure and now he's gone too
Why does a guy with powers like that want to give them up? I can't figure it out.
I'm so sorry, Rogue.
Hot as blazes out here! I'll *wilt to nothing* before we make it.

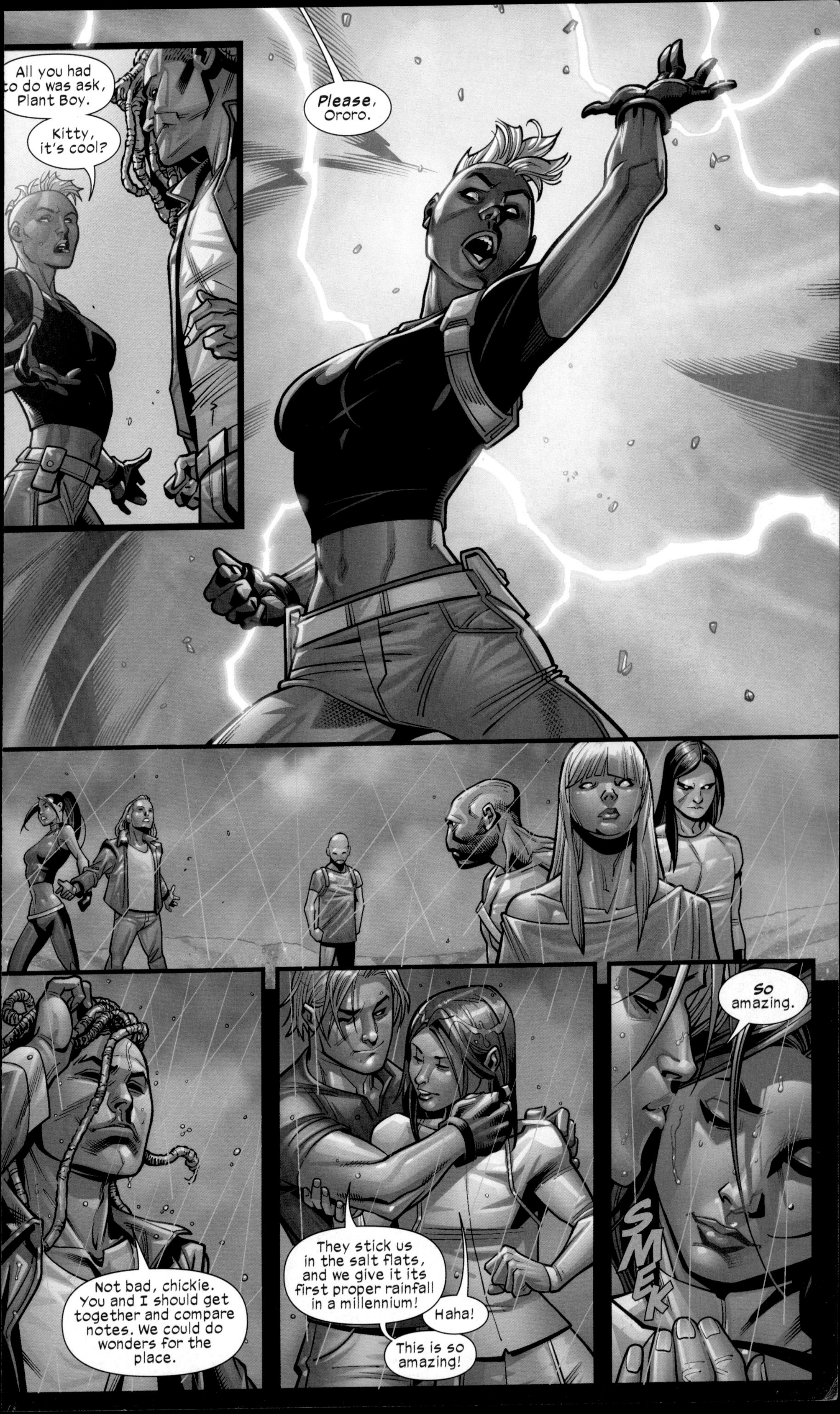

All you had to do was ask, Plant Boy.
Kitty, it's cool?
Please, Ororo.
Not bad, chickie. You and I should get together and compare notes. We could do wonders for the place.
They stick us in the salt flats, and we give it its first proper rainfall in a millennium!
Haha!
This is so amazing!
So amazing.
SMEK

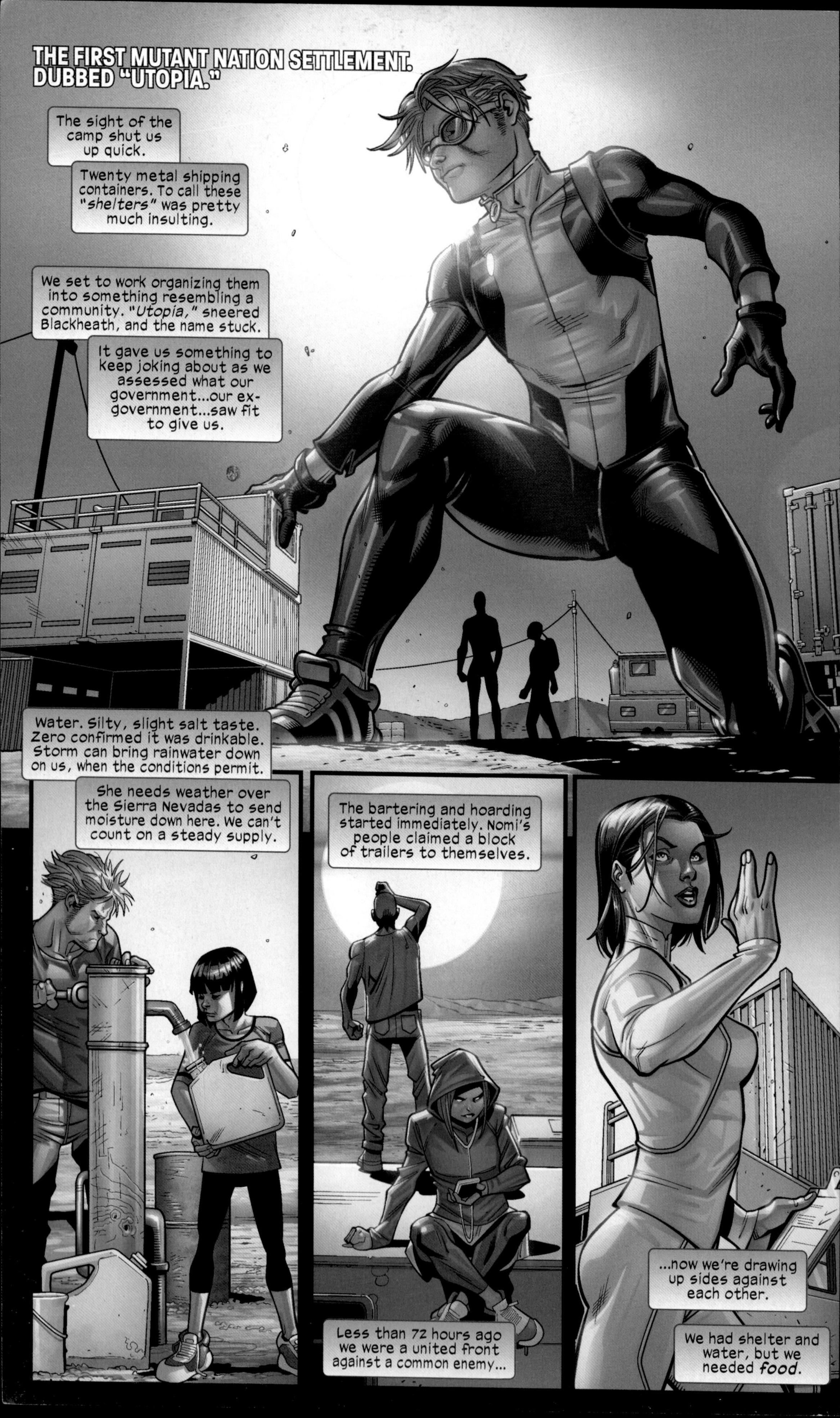
THE FIRST MUTANT NATION SETTLEMENT. DUBBED "UTOPIA."
The sight of the camp shut us up quick.
Twenty metal shipping containers. To call these "shelters" was pretty much insulting.
We set to work organizing them into something resembling a community. "Utopia," sneered Blackheath, and the name stuck.
It gave us something to keep joking about as we assessed what our government...our ex-government...saw fit to give us.
Water. Silty, slight salt taste. Zero confirmed it was drinkable. Storm can bring rainwater down on us, when the conditions permit.
She needs weather over the Sierra Nevadas to send moisture down here. We can't count on a steady supply.
The bartering and hoarding started immediately. Nomi's people claimed a block of trailers to themselves.
Less than 72 hours ago we were a united front against a common enemy...
...now we're drawing up sides against each other.
We had shelter and water, but we needed food.

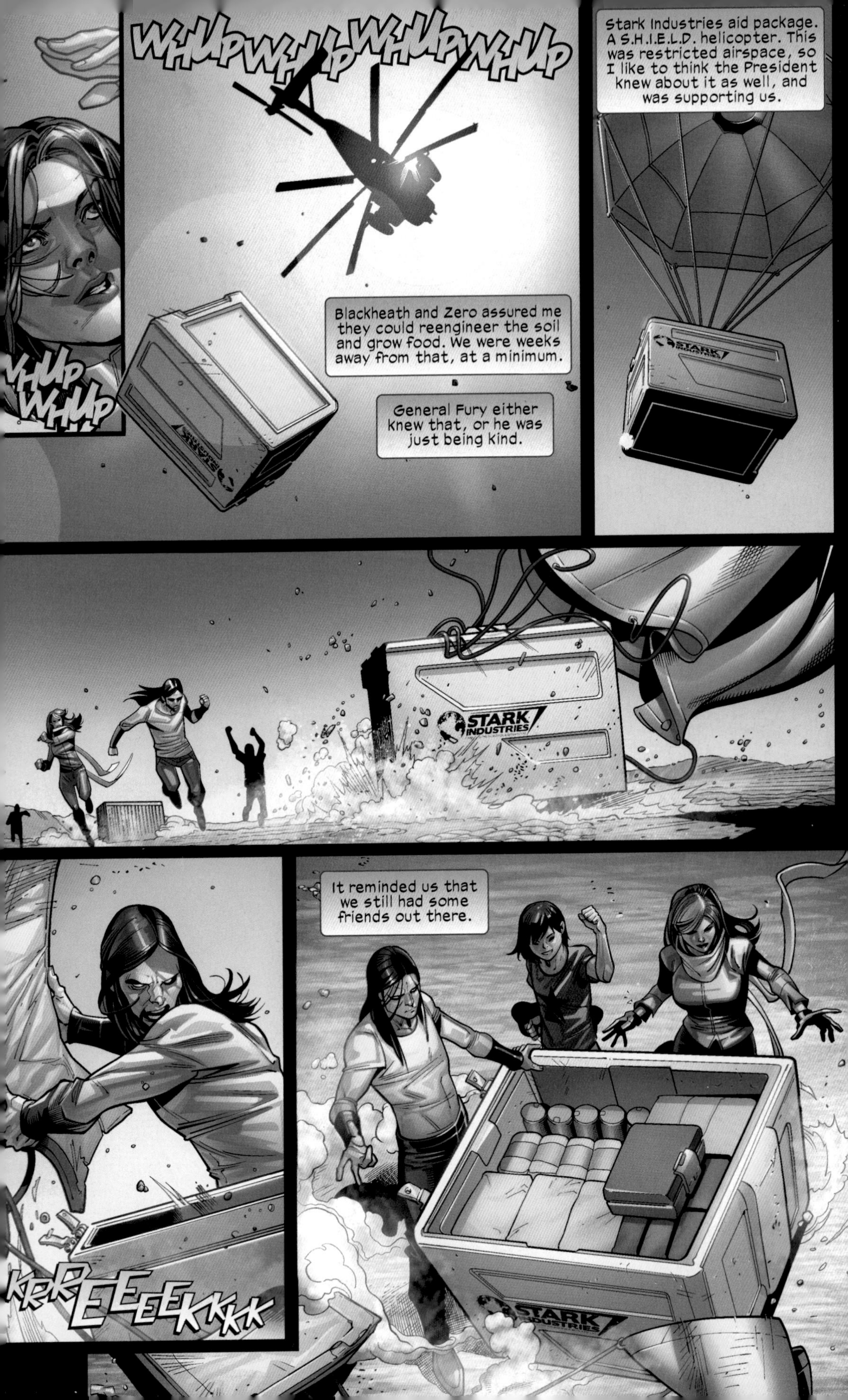
WHUP WHUP
WHUPWHUP WHUPWHUP
Blackheath and Zero assured me they could reengineer the soil and grow food. We were weeks away from that, at a minimum.
General Fury either knew that, or he was just being kind.
Stark Industries aid package. A S.H.I.E.L.D. helicopter. This was restricted airspace, so I like to think the President knew about it as well, and was supporting us.
STARK INDUSTRIES
KRRREEEEEKKKK
It reminded us that we still had some friends out there.
STARK INDUSTRIES

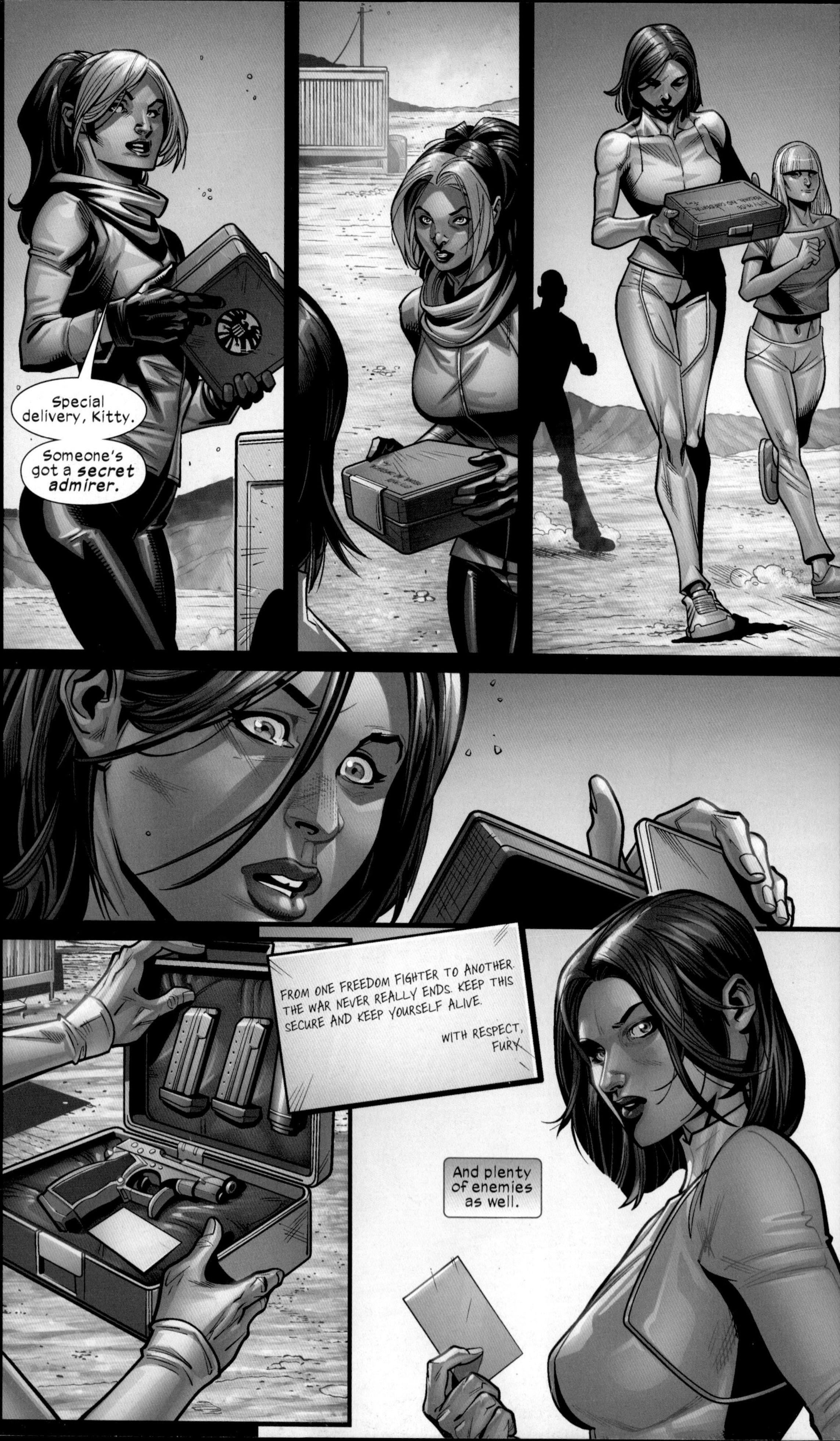

Special delivery, Kitty.
Someone's got a *secret admirer.*
FROM ONE FREEDOM FIGHTER TO ANOTHER. THE WAR NEVER REALLY ENDS. KEEP THIS SECURE AND KEEP YOURSELF ALIVE.
WITH RESPECT, FURY
And plenty of enemies as well.

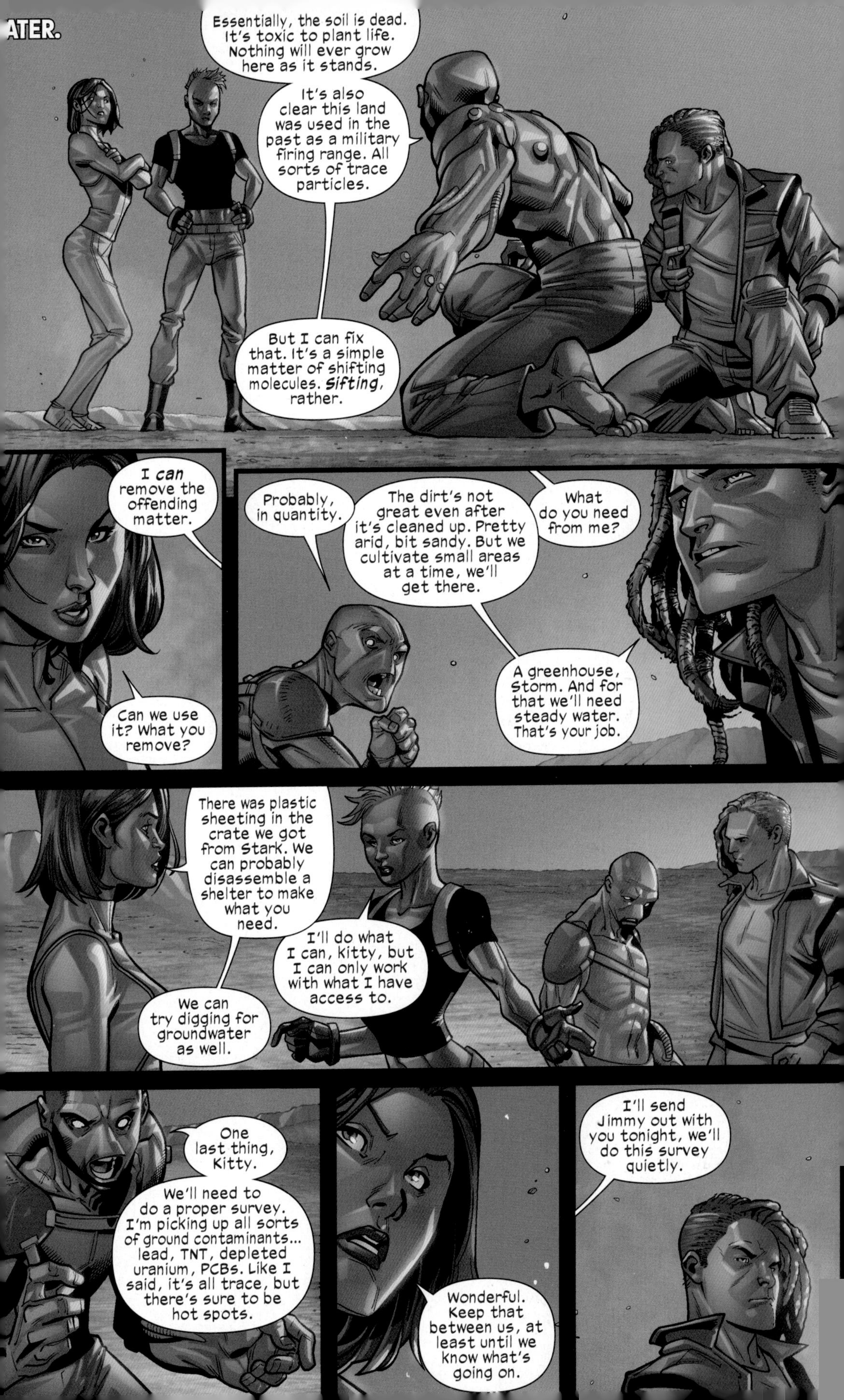
ATER.
Essentially, the soil is dead. It's toxic to plant life. Nothing will ever grow here as it stands.
It's also clear this land was used in the past as a military firing range. All sorts of trace particles.
But I can fix that. It's a simple matter of shifting molecules. *Sifting*, rather.
I *can* remove the offending matter.
Can we use it? What you remove?
Probably, in quantity.
The dirt's not great even after it's cleaned up. Pretty arid, bit sandy. But we cultivate small areas at a time, we'll get there.
What do you need from me?
A greenhouse, Storm. And for that we'll need steady water. That's your job.
There was plastic sheeting in the crate we got from Stark. We can probably disassemble a shelter to make what you need.
We can try digging for groundwater as well.
I'll do what I can, Kitty, but I can only work with what I have access to.
One last thing, Kitty.
We'll need to do a proper survey. I'm picking up all sorts of ground contaminants... lead, TNT, depleted uranium, PCBs. Like I said, it's all trace, but there's sure to be hot spots.
Wonderful. Keep that between us, at least until we know what's going on.
I'll send Jimmy out with you tonight, we'll do this survey quietly.

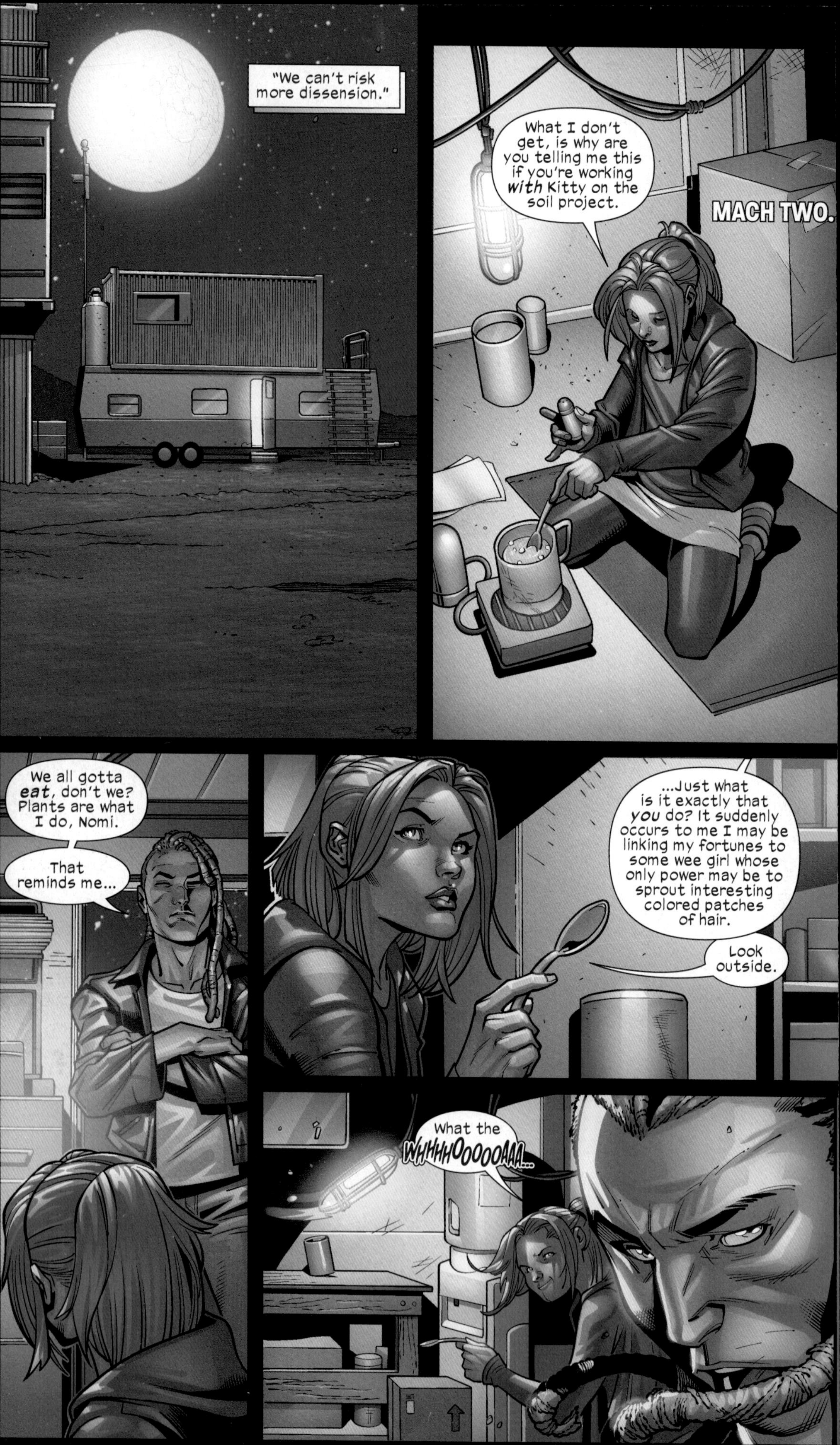
"We can't risk more dissension."
What I don't get, is why are you telling me this if you're working *with* Kitty on the soil project.
MACH TWO.
We all gotta *eat*, don't we? Plants are what I do, Nomi.
That reminds me...
...Just what is it exactly that *you* do? It suddenly occurs to me I may be linking my fortunes to some wee girl whose only power may be to sprout interesting colored patches of hair.
Look outside.
What the
WHHHHOOOOOAAA...

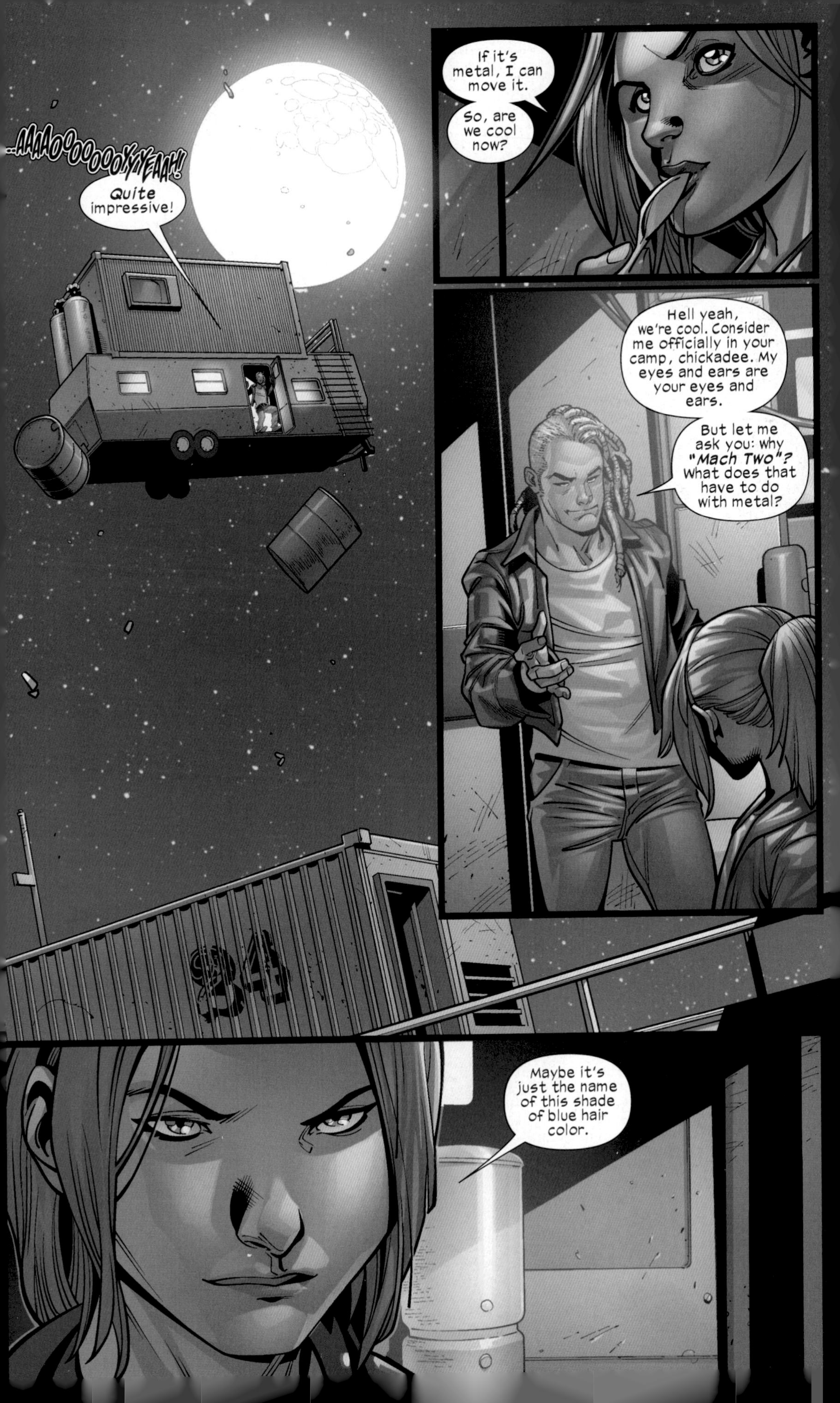

...AAAAOOOOOOOYYYEAAH!!
Quite impressive!
If it's metal, I can move it.
So, are we cool now?
Hell yeah, we're cool. Consider me officially in your camp, chickadee. My eyes and ears are your eyes and ears.
But let me ask you: why "Mach Two"? What does that have to do with metal?
Maybe it's just the name of this shade of blue hair color.

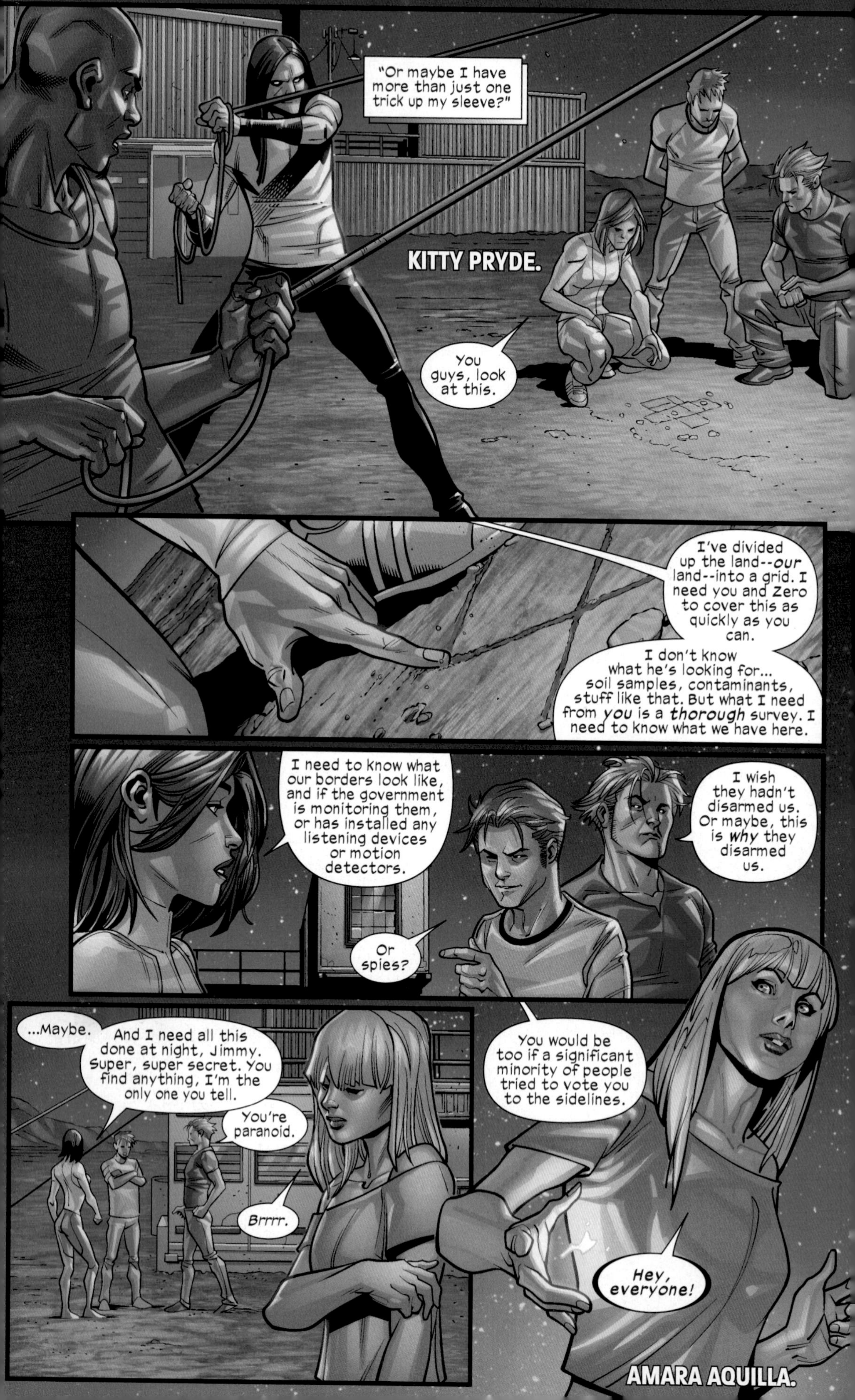
"Or maybe I have more than just one trick up my sleeve?"
KITTY PRYDE.
You guys, look at this.
I've divided up the land--*our* land--into a grid. I need you and Zero to cover this as quickly as you can.
I don't know what he's looking for... soil samples, contaminants, stuff like that. But what I need from *you* is a *thorough* survey. I need to know what we have here.
I need to know what our borders look like, and if the government is monitoring them, or has installed any listening devices or motion detectors.
Or spies?
I wish they hadn't disarmed us. Or maybe, this is *why* they disarmed us.
...Maybe.
And I need all this done at night, Jimmy. Super, super secret. You find anything, I'm the only one you tell.
You're paranoid.
Brrrr.
You would be too if a significant minority of people tried to vote you to the sidelines.
Hey, everyone!
AMARA AQUILLA.

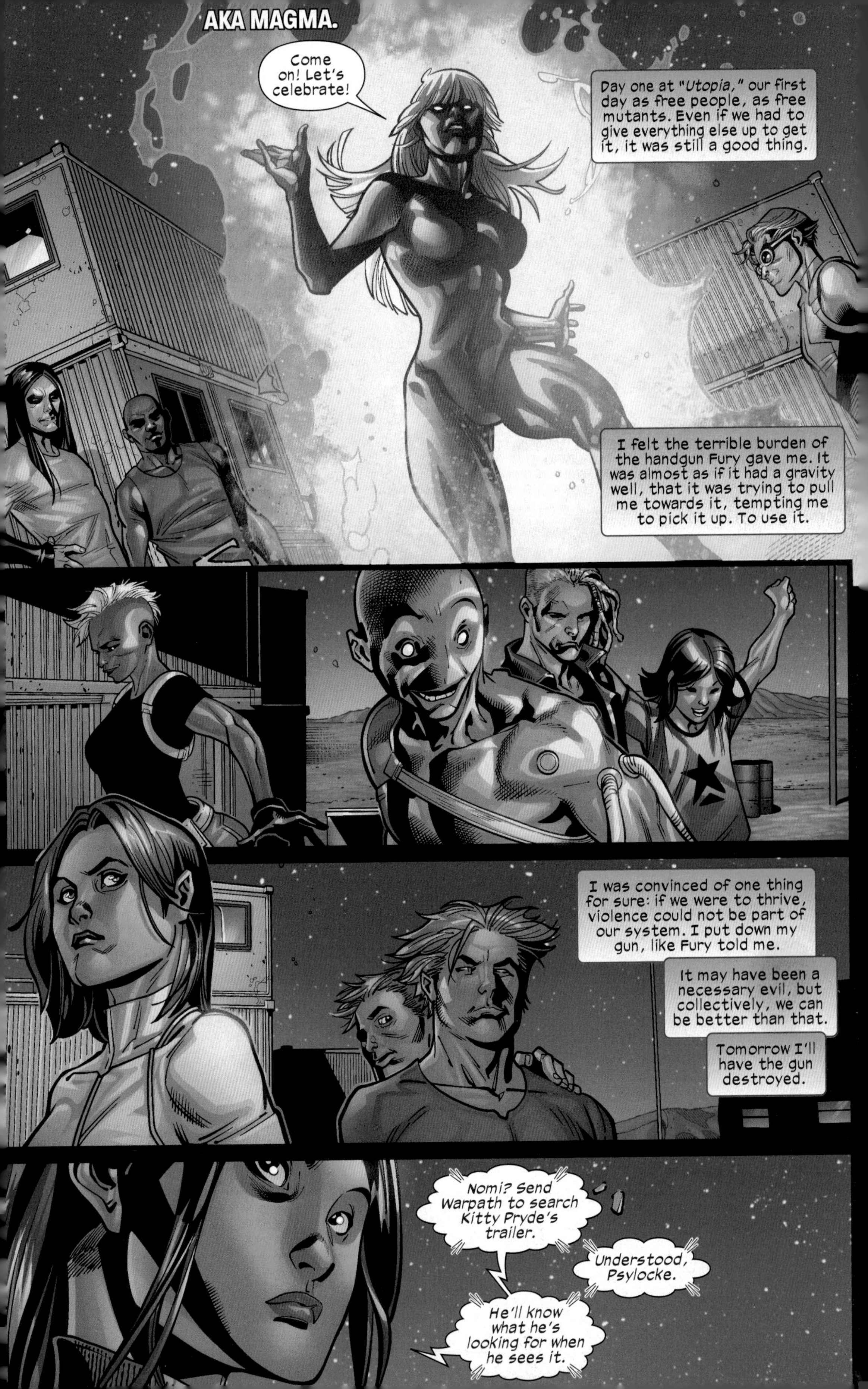
AKA MAGMA.
Come on! Let's celebrate!
Day one at "Utopia," our first day as free people, as free mutants. Even if we had to give everything else up to get it, it was still a good thing.
I felt the terrible burden of the handgun Fury gave me. It was almost as if it had a gravity well, that it was trying to pull me towards it, tempting me to pick it up. To use it.
I was convinced of one thing for sure: if we were to thrive, violence could not be part of our system. I put down my gun, like Fury told me.
It may have been a necessary evil, but collectively, we can be better than that.
Tomorrow I'll have the gun destroyed.
Nomi? Send Warpath to search Kitty Pryde's trailer.
Understood, Psylocke.
He'll know what he's looking for when he sees it.

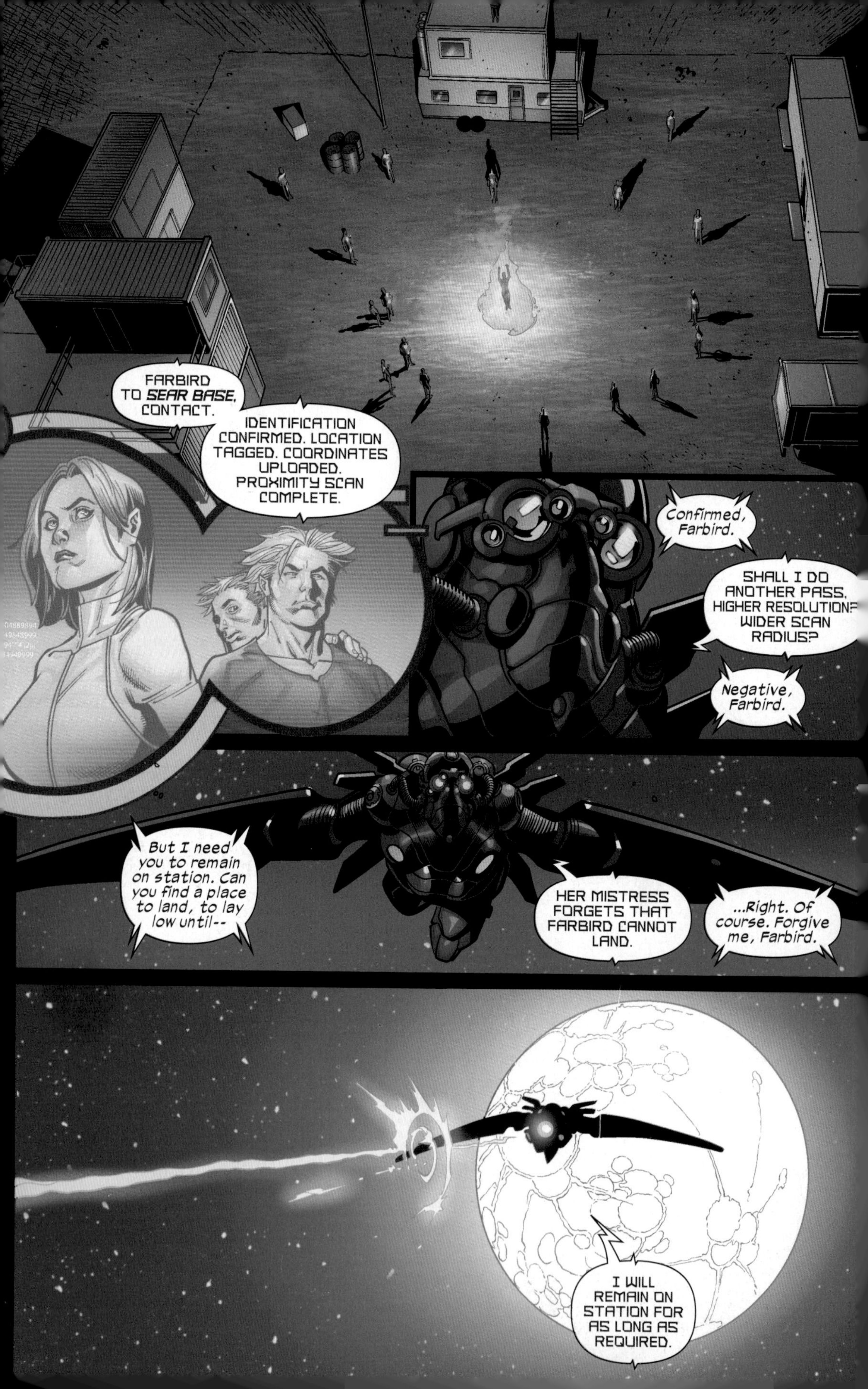
FARBIRD TO *SEAR BASE*, CONTACT.
IDENTIFICATION CONFIRMED. LOCATION TAGGED. COORDINATES UPLOADED. PROXIMITY SCAN COMPLETE.
Confirmed, Farbird.
SHALL I DO ANOTHER PASS, HIGHER RESOLUTION? WIDER SCAN RADIUS?
Negative, Farbird.
But I need you to remain on station. Can you find a place to land, to lay low until--
HER MISTRESS FORGETS THAT FARBIRD CANNOT LAND.
...Right. Of course. Forgive me, Farbird.
I WILL REMAIN ON STATION FOR AS LONG AS REQUIRED.

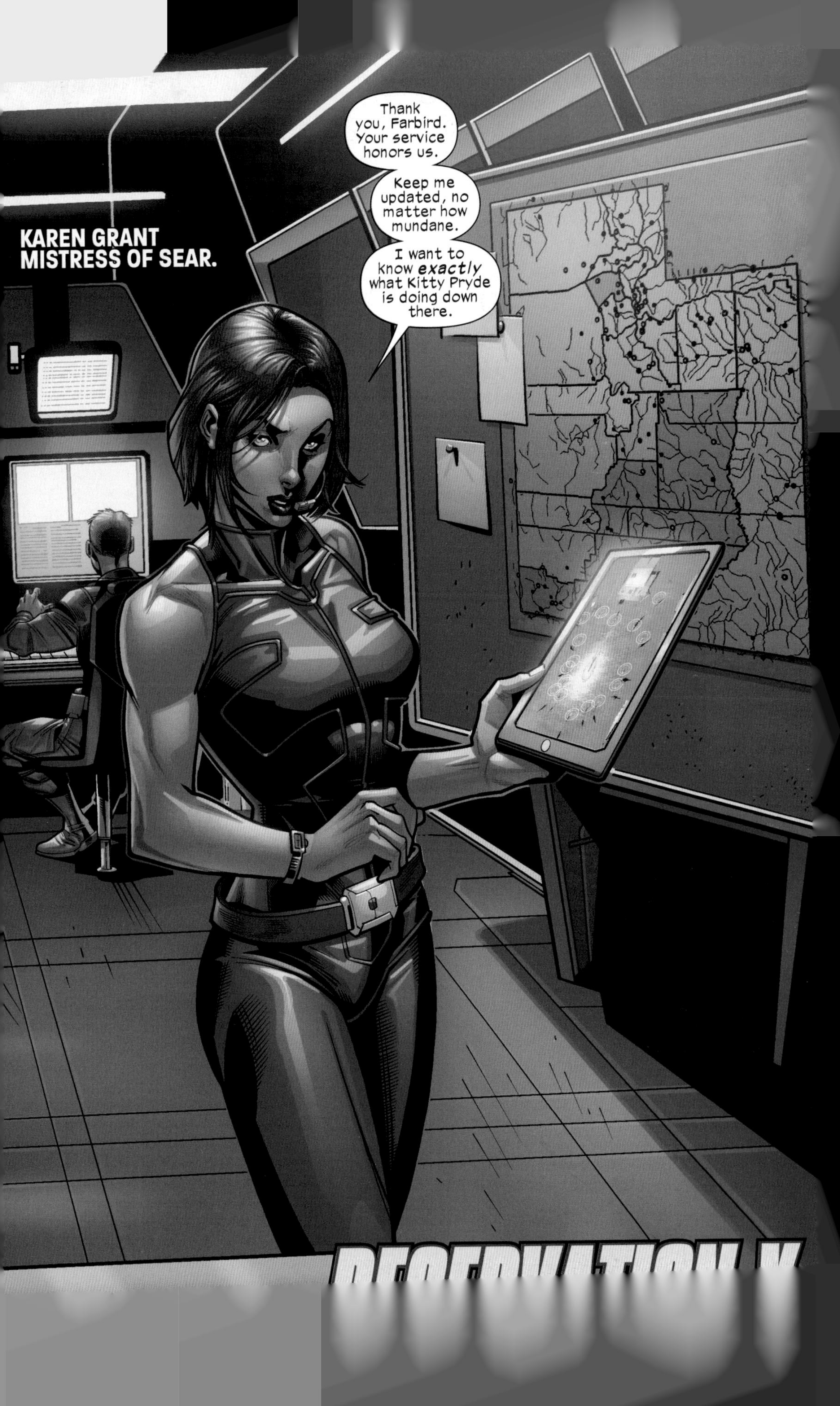
KAREN GRANT
MISTRESS OF SEAR.
Thank you, Farbird. Your service honors us.
Keep me updated, no matter how mundane.
I want to know *exactly* what Kitty Pryde is doing down there.

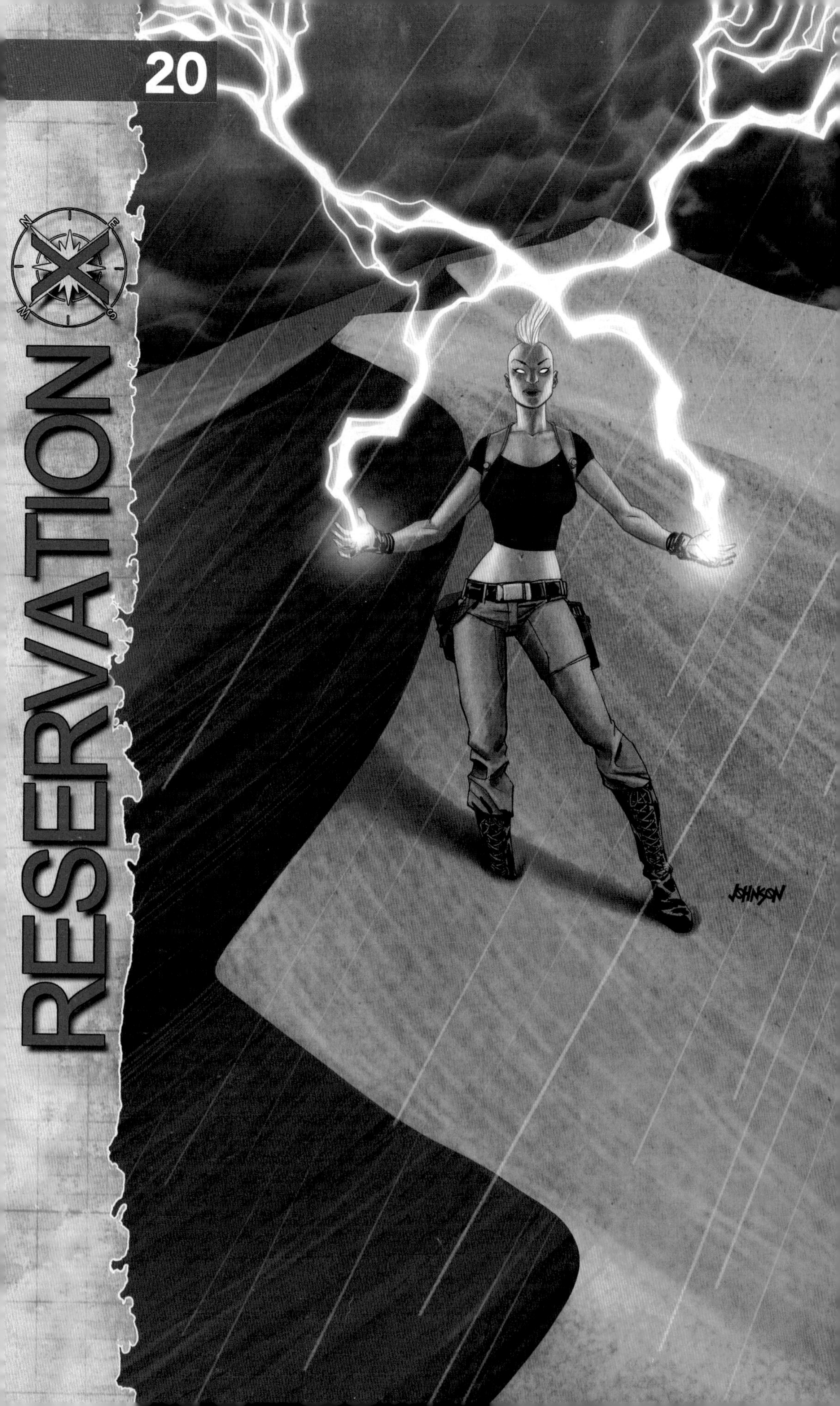
20
RESERVATION
JOHNSON

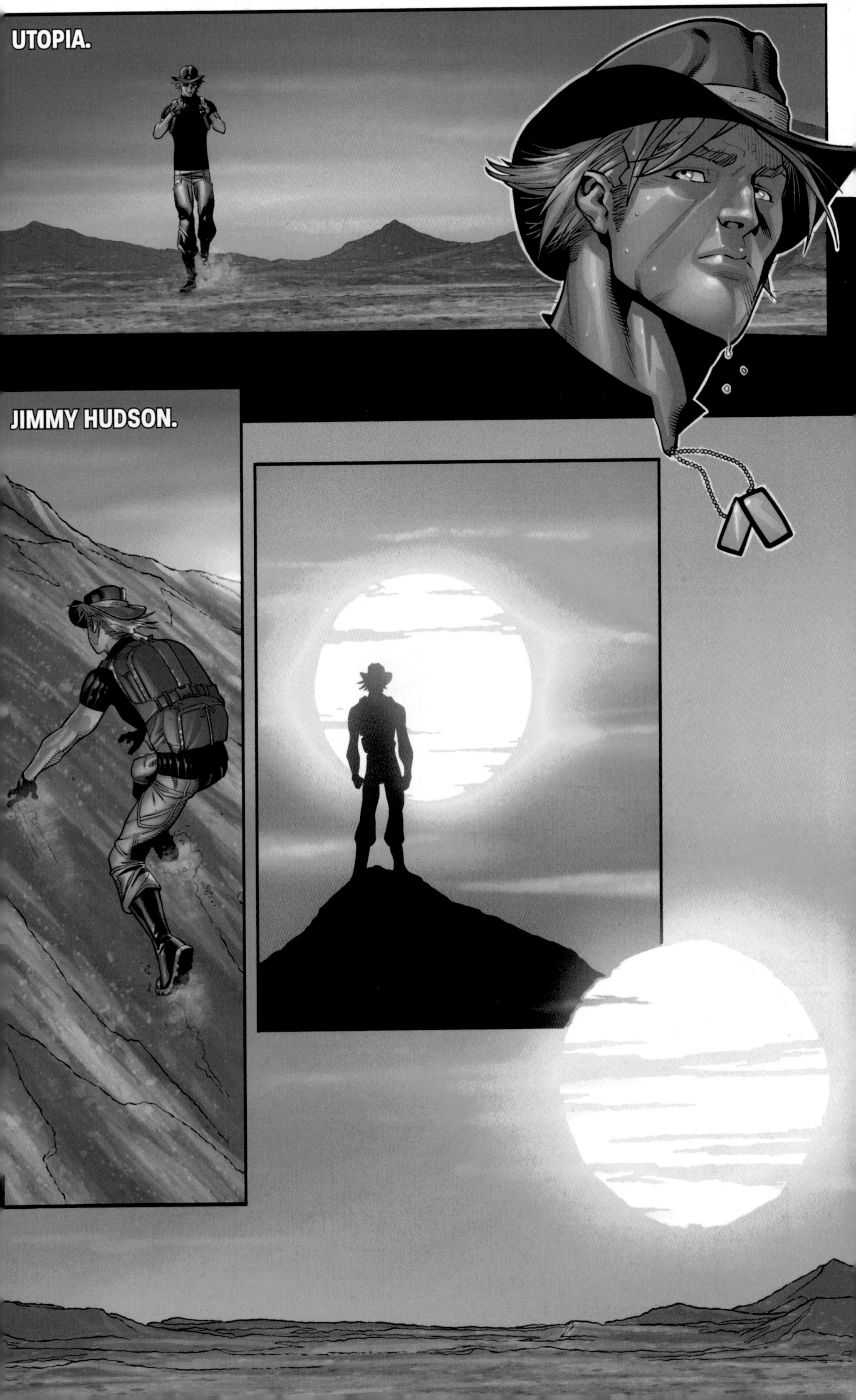
UTOPIA.
JIMMY HUDSON.

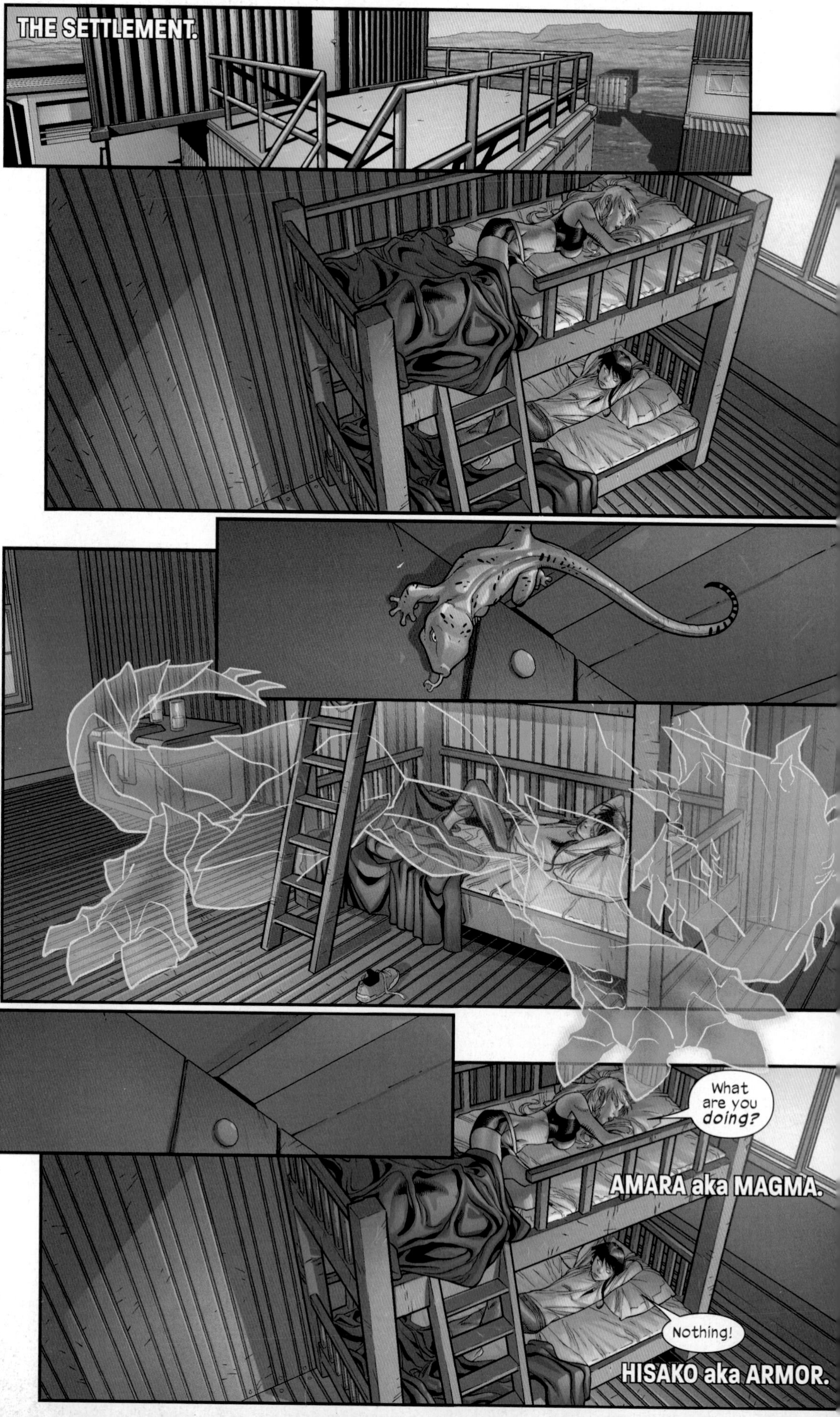
THE SETTLEMENT.
What are you doing?
AMARA aka MAGMA.
Nothing!
HISAKO aka ARMOR.

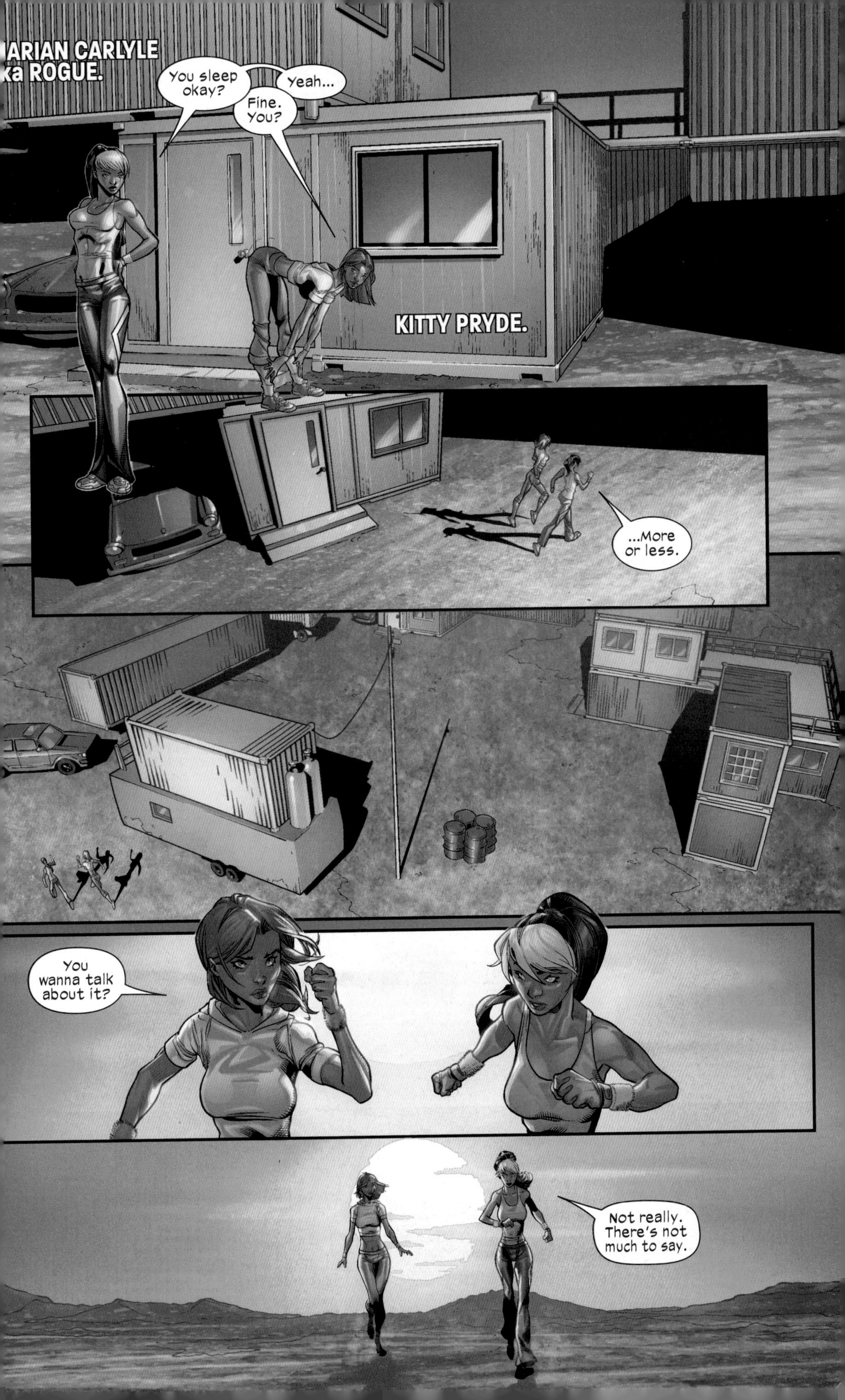
ARIAN CARLYLE
ka ROGUE.
You sleep okay?
Fine. You?
Yeah...
KITTY PRYDE.
...More or less.
You wanna talk about it?
Not really. There's not much to say.

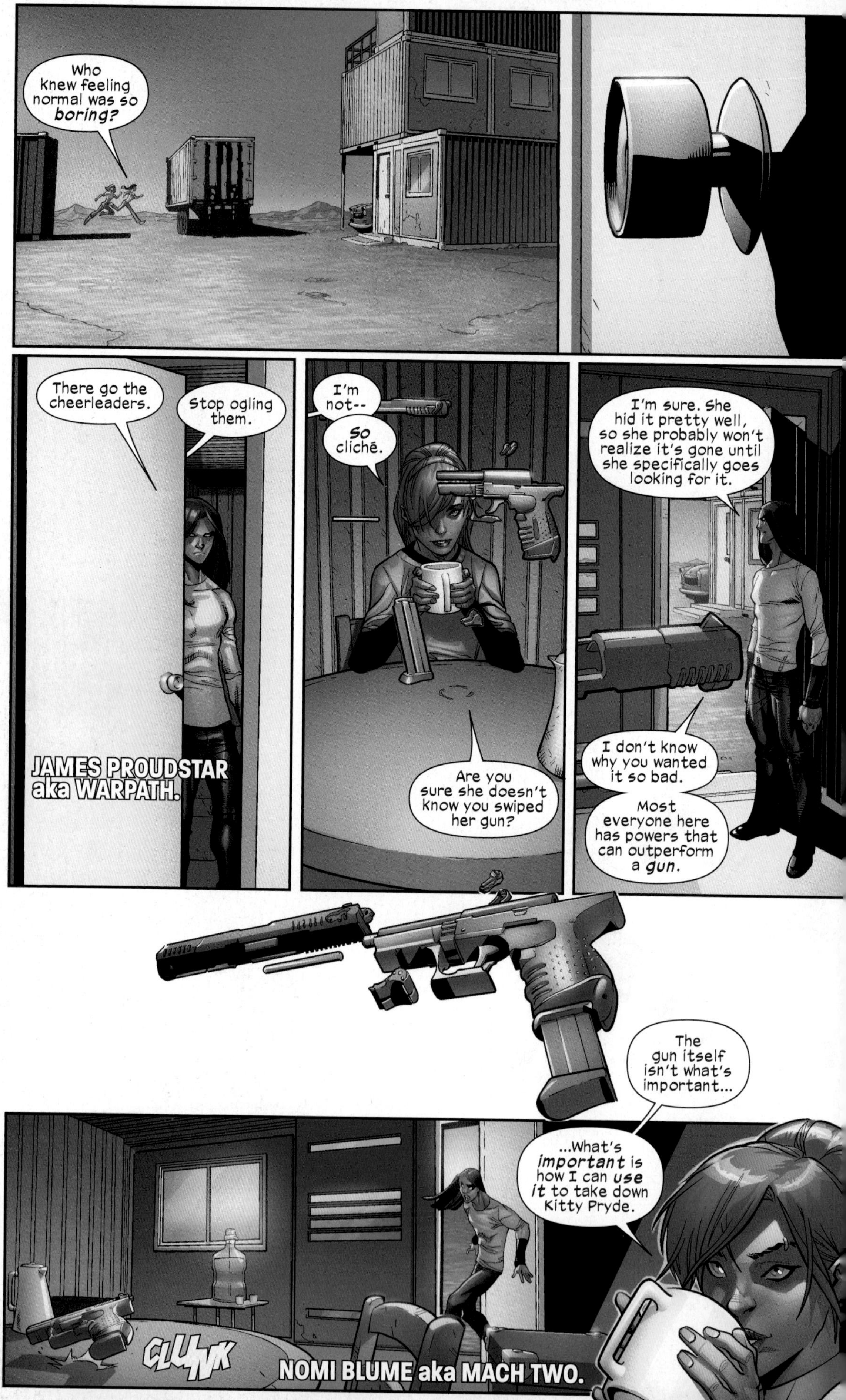

Who knew feeling normal was so *boring?*
There go the cheerleaders.
Stop ogling them.
JAMES PROUDSTAR aka WARPATH.
I'm not--
So cliché.
Are you sure she doesn't know you swiped her gun?
I'm sure. She hid it pretty well, so she probably won't realize it's gone until she specifically goes looking for it.
I don't know why you wanted it so bad.
Most everyone here has powers that can outperform a *gun.*
The gun itself isn't what's important...
...What's *important* is how I can *use it* to take down Kitty Pryde.
CLUNK
NOMI BLUME aka MACH TWO.

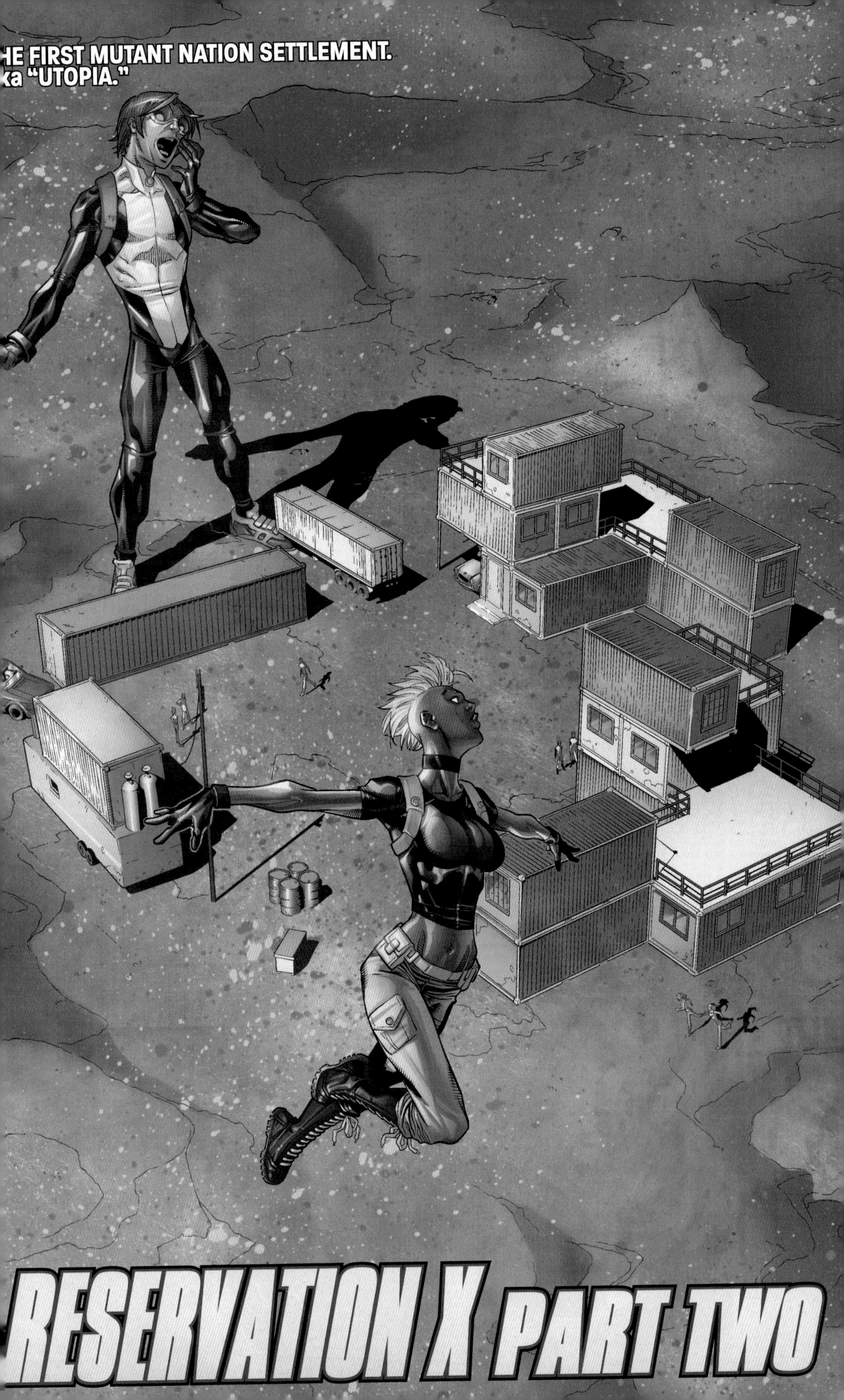
HE FIRST MUTANT NATION SETTLEMENT.
ka "UTOPIA."
RESERVATION X PART TWO

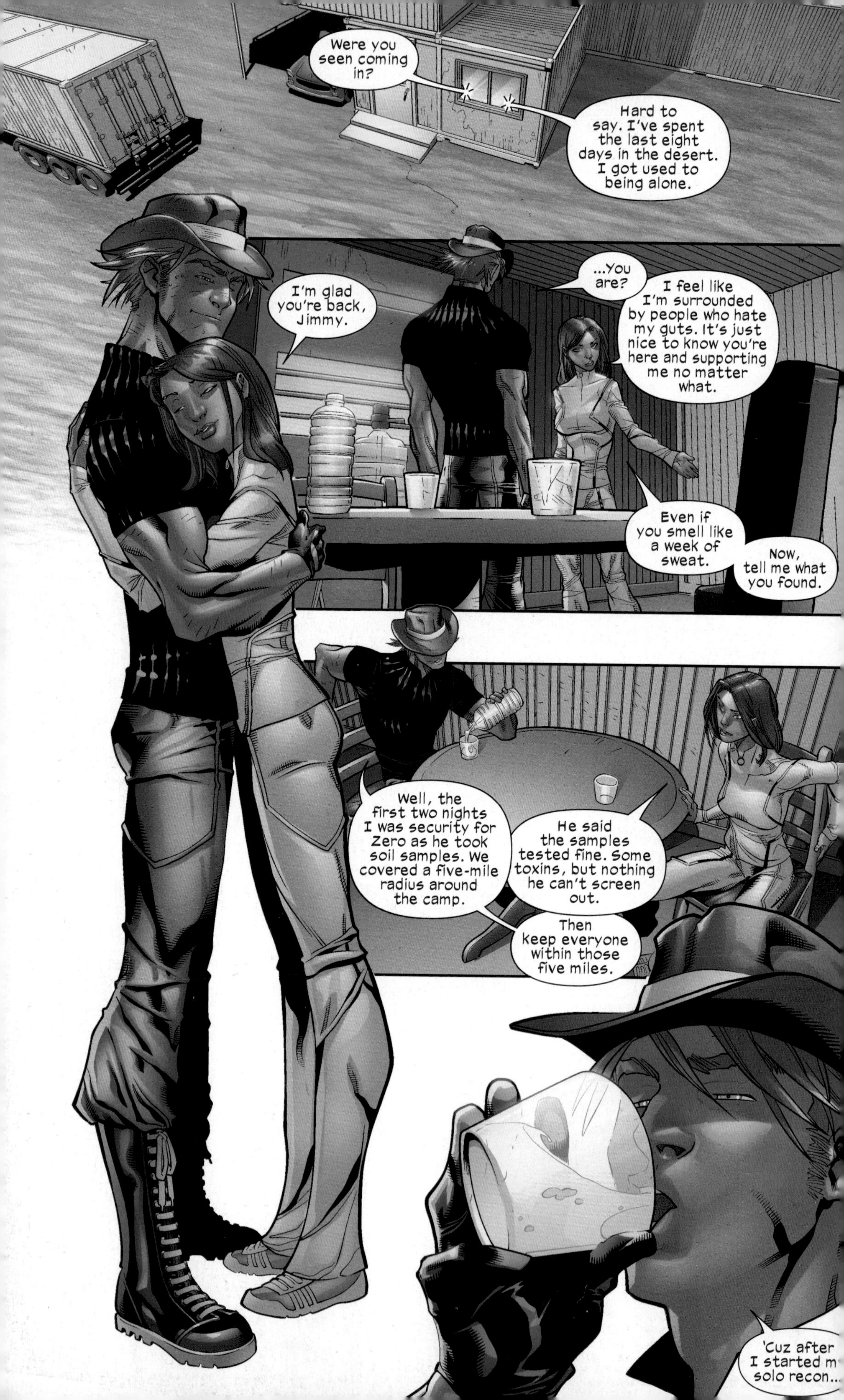
Were you seen coming in?
Hard to say. I've spent the last eight days in the desert. I got used to being alone.
I'm glad you're back, Jimmy.
...You are?
I feel like I'm surrounded by people who hate my guts. It's just nice to know you're here and supporting me no matter what.
Even if you smell like a week of sweat.
Now, tell me what you found.
Well, the first two nights I was security for Zero as he took soil samples. We covered a five-mile radius around the camp.
He said the samples tested fine. Some toxins, but nothing he can't screen out.
Then keep everyone within those five miles.
'Cuz after I started m solo recon...

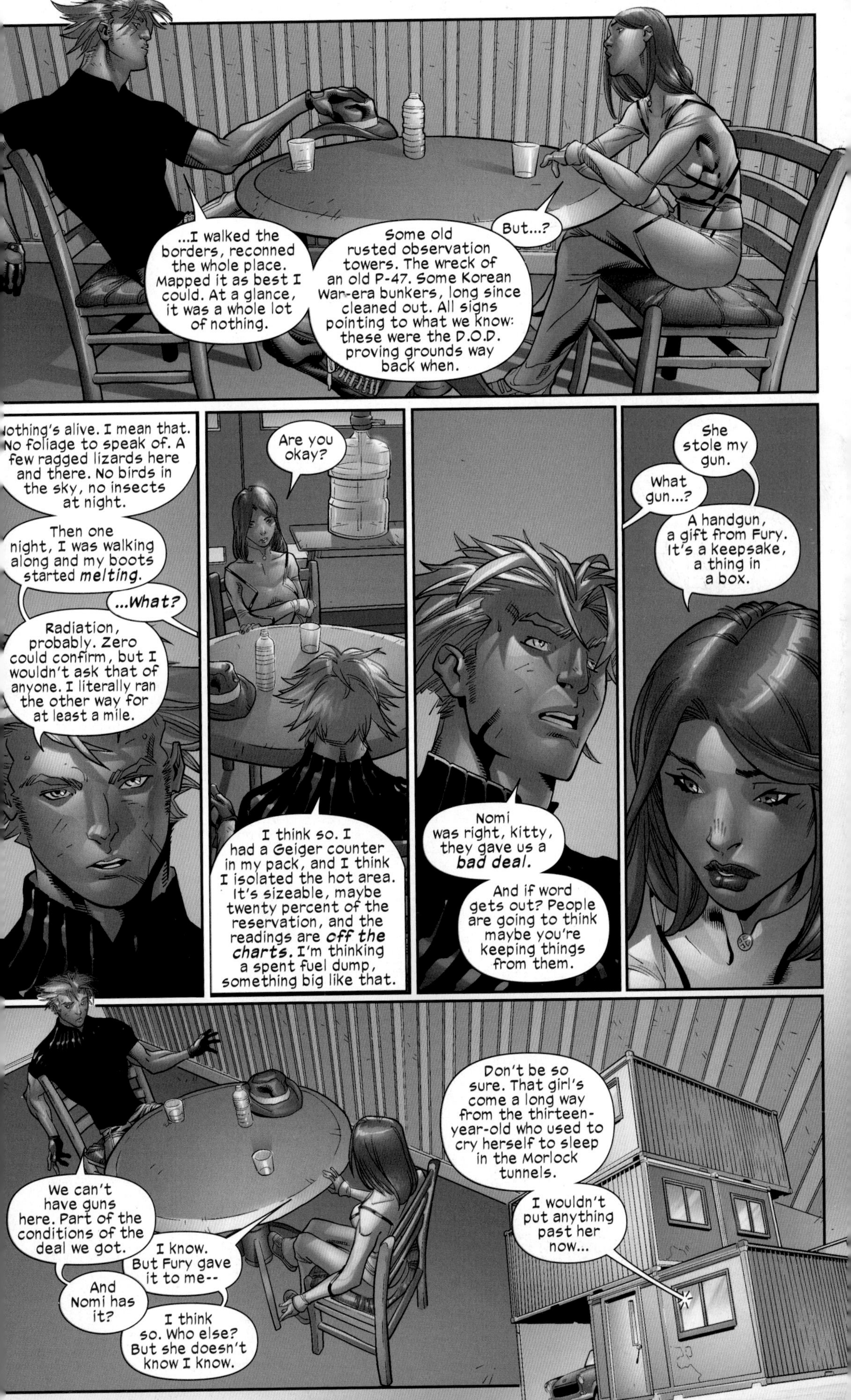
...I walked the borders, reconned the whole place. Mapped it as best I could. At a glance, it was a whole lot of nothing.
Some old rusted observation towers. The wreck of an old P-47. Some Korean War-era bunkers, long since cleaned out. All signs pointing to what we know: these were the D.O.D. proving grounds way back when.
But...?
Nothing's alive. I mean that. No foliage to speak of. A few ragged lizards here and there. No birds in the sky, no insects at night.
Then one night, I was walking along and my boots started *melting*.
...What?
Radiation, probably. Zero could confirm, but I wouldn't ask that of anyone. I literally ran the other way for at least a mile.
Are you okay?
I think so. I had a Geiger counter in my pack, and I think I isolated the hot area. It's sizeable, maybe twenty percent of the reservation, and the readings are *off the charts*. I'm thinking a spent fuel dump, something big like that.
Nomi was right, kitty, they gave us a *bad deal*.
And if word gets out? People are going to think maybe you're keeping things from them.
She stole my gun.
What gun...?
A handgun, a gift from Fury. It's a keepsake, a thing in a box.
We can't have guns here. Part of the conditions of the deal we got.
I know. But Fury gave it to me--
And Nomi has it?
I think so. Who else? But she doesn't know I know.
Don't be so sure. That girl's come a long way from the thirteen-year-old who used to cry herself to sleep in the Morlock tunnels.
I wouldn't put anything past her now...

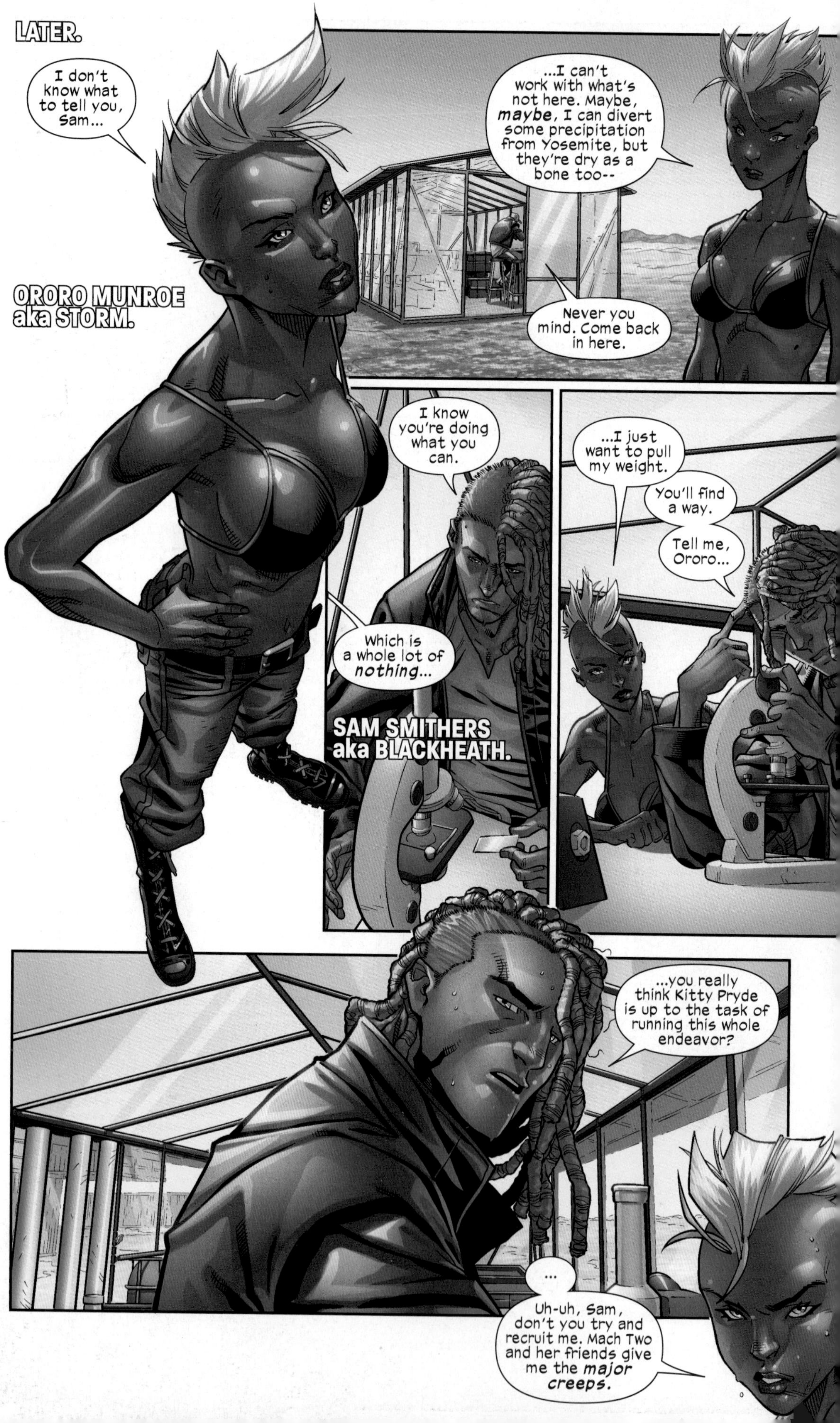
LATER.
I don't know what to tell you, Sam...
...I can't work with what's not here. Maybe, *maybe*, I can divert some precipitation from Yosemite, but they're dry as a bone too--
ORORO MUNROE aka STORM.
Never you mind. Come back in here.
I know you're doing what you can.
Which is a whole lot of *nothing*...
SAM SMITHERS aka BLACKHEATH.
...I just want to pull my weight.
You'll find a way.
Tell me, Ororo...
...you really think Kitty Pryde is up to the task of running this whole endeavor?
...
Uh-uh, Sam, don't you try and recruit me. Mach Two and her friends give me the *major creeps*.

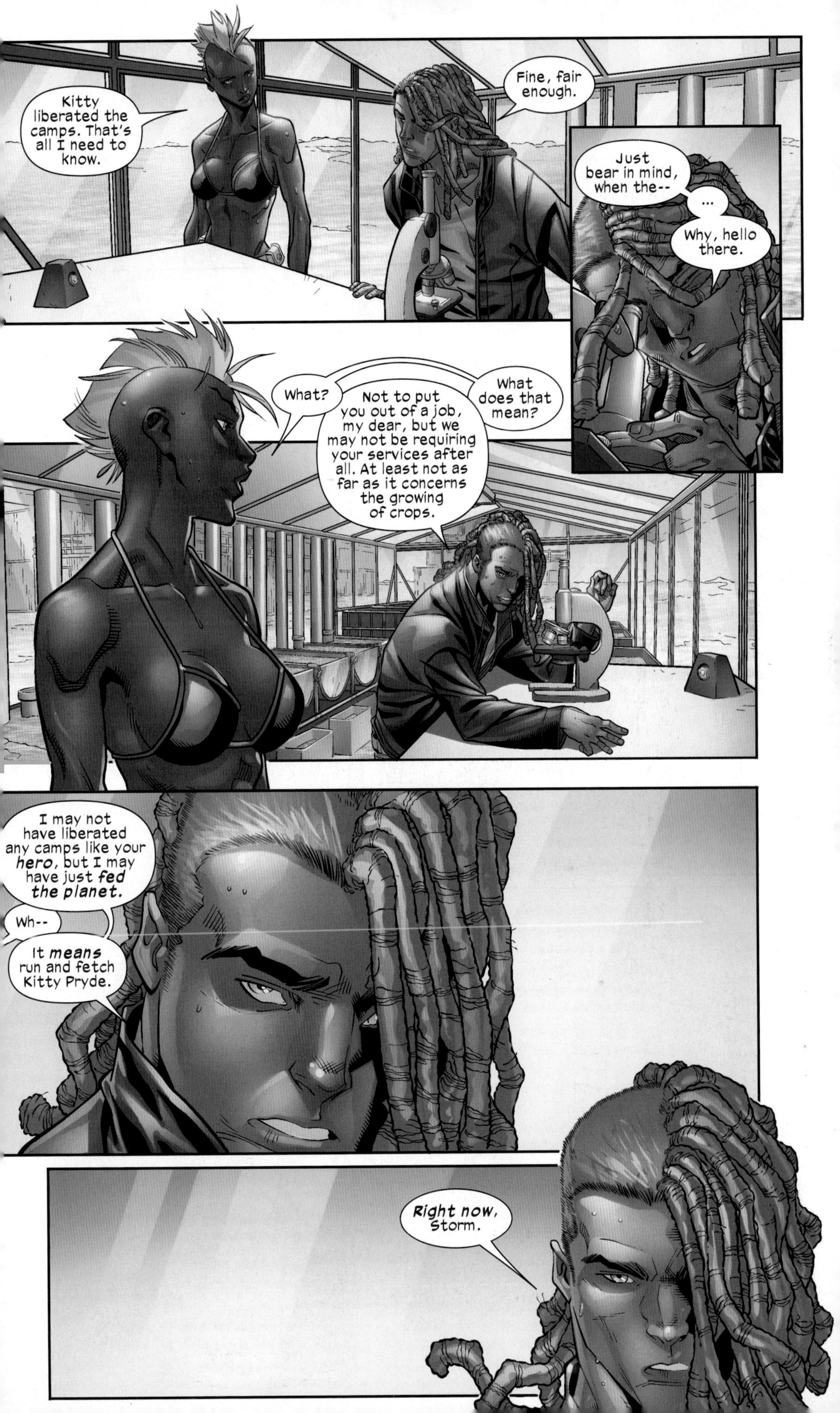
Kitty liberated the camps. That's all I need to know.
Fine, fair enough.
Just bear in mind, when the--
...
Why, hello there.
What?
What does that mean?
Not to put you out of a job, my dear, but we may not be requiring your services after all. At least not as far as it concerns the growing of crops.
I may not have liberated any camps like your *hero*, but I may have just *fed the planet.*
Wh--
It *means* run and fetch Kitty Pryde.
Right now, Storm.

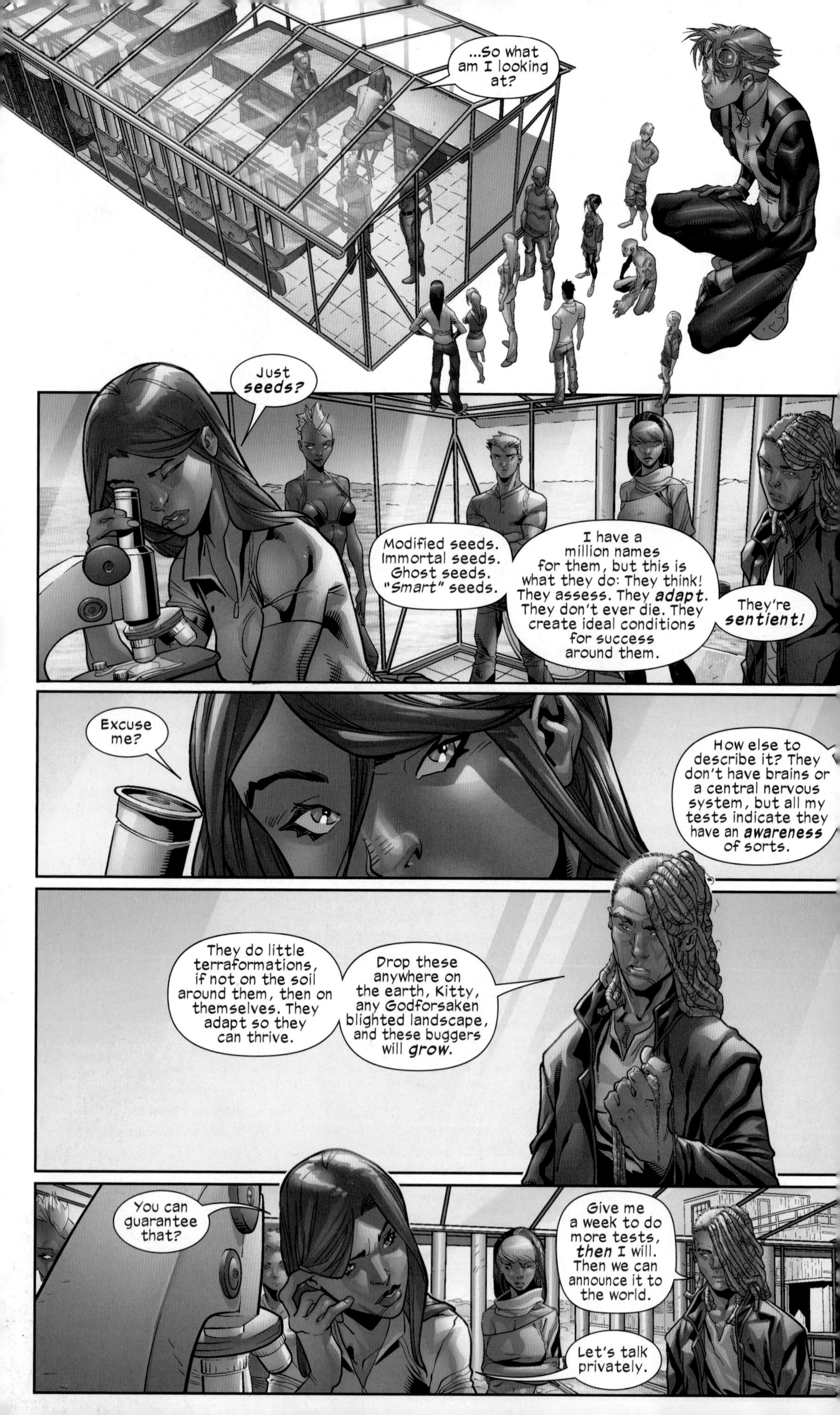
...So what am I looking at?
Just seeds?
Modified seeds. Immortal seeds. Ghost seeds. "Smart" seeds.
I have a million names for them, but this is what they do: They think! They assess. They adapt. They don't ever die. They create ideal conditions for success around them.
They're sentient!
Excuse me?
How else to describe it? They don't have brains or a central nervous system, but all my tests indicate they have an awareness of sorts.
They do little terraformations, if not on the soil around them, then on themselves. They adapt so they can thrive.
Drop these anywhere on the earth, Kitty, any Godforsaken blighted landscape, and these buggers will grow.
You can guarantee that?
Give me a week to do more tests, then I will. Then we can announce it to the world.
Let's talk privately.

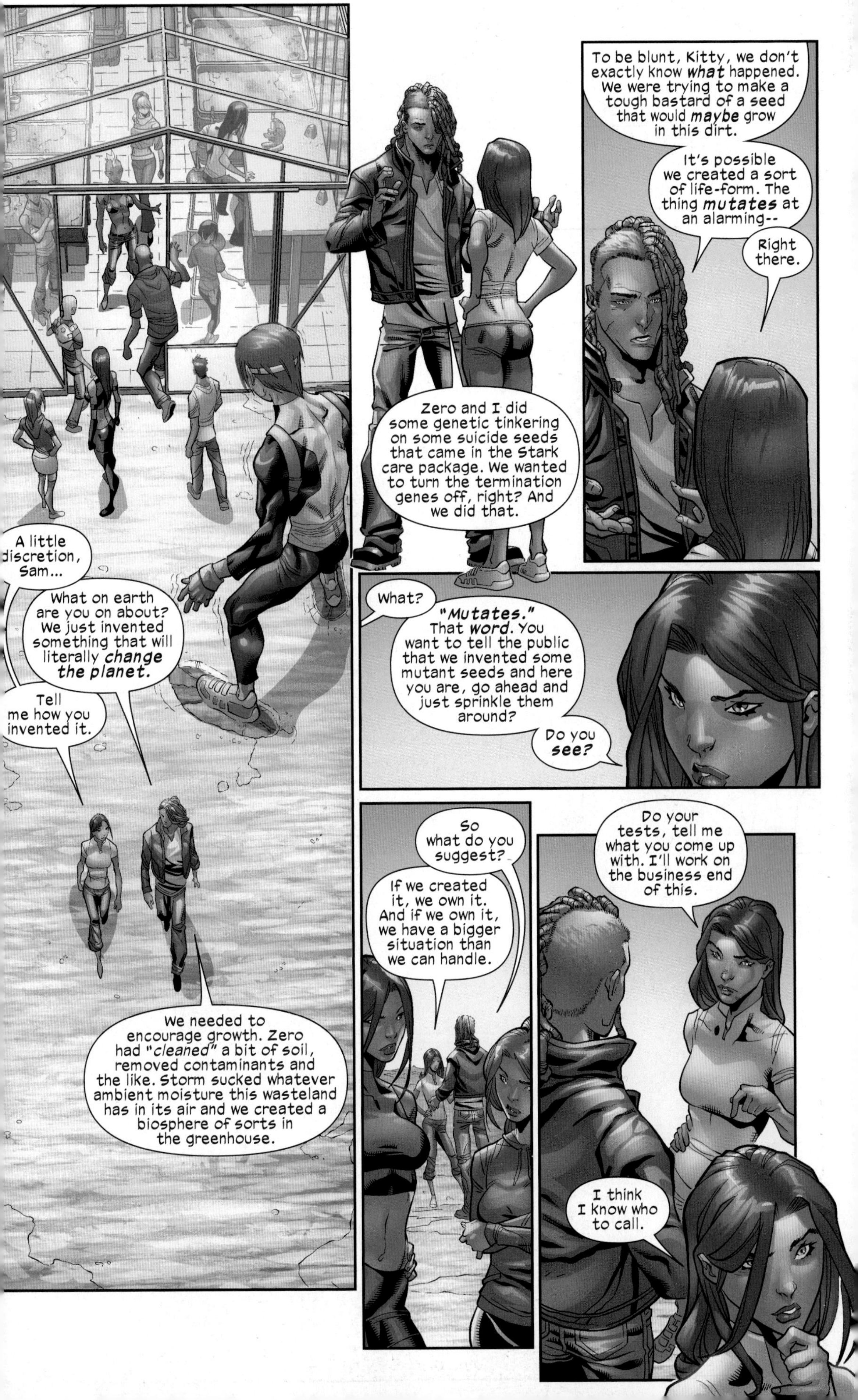

A little discretion, Sam...
What on earth are you on about? We just invented something that will literally change the planet.
Tell me how you invented it.
We needed to encourage growth. Zero had "cleaned" a bit of soil, removed contaminants and the like. Storm sucked whatever ambient moisture this wasteland has in its air and we created a biosphere of sorts in the greenhouse.
Zero and I did some genetic tinkering on some suicide seeds that came in the Stark care package. We wanted to turn the termination genes off, right? And we did that.
To be blunt, Kitty, we don't exactly know what happened. We were trying to make a tough bastard of a seed that would maybe grow in this dirt.
It's possible we created a sort of life-form. The thing mutates at an alarming--
Right there.
What?
"Mutates." That word. You want to tell the public that we invented some mutant seeds and here you are, go ahead and just sprinkle them around?
Do you see?
So what do you suggest?
If we created it, we own it. And if we own it, we have a bigger situation than we can handle.
Do your tests, tell me what you come up with. I'll work on the business end of this.
I think I know who to call.

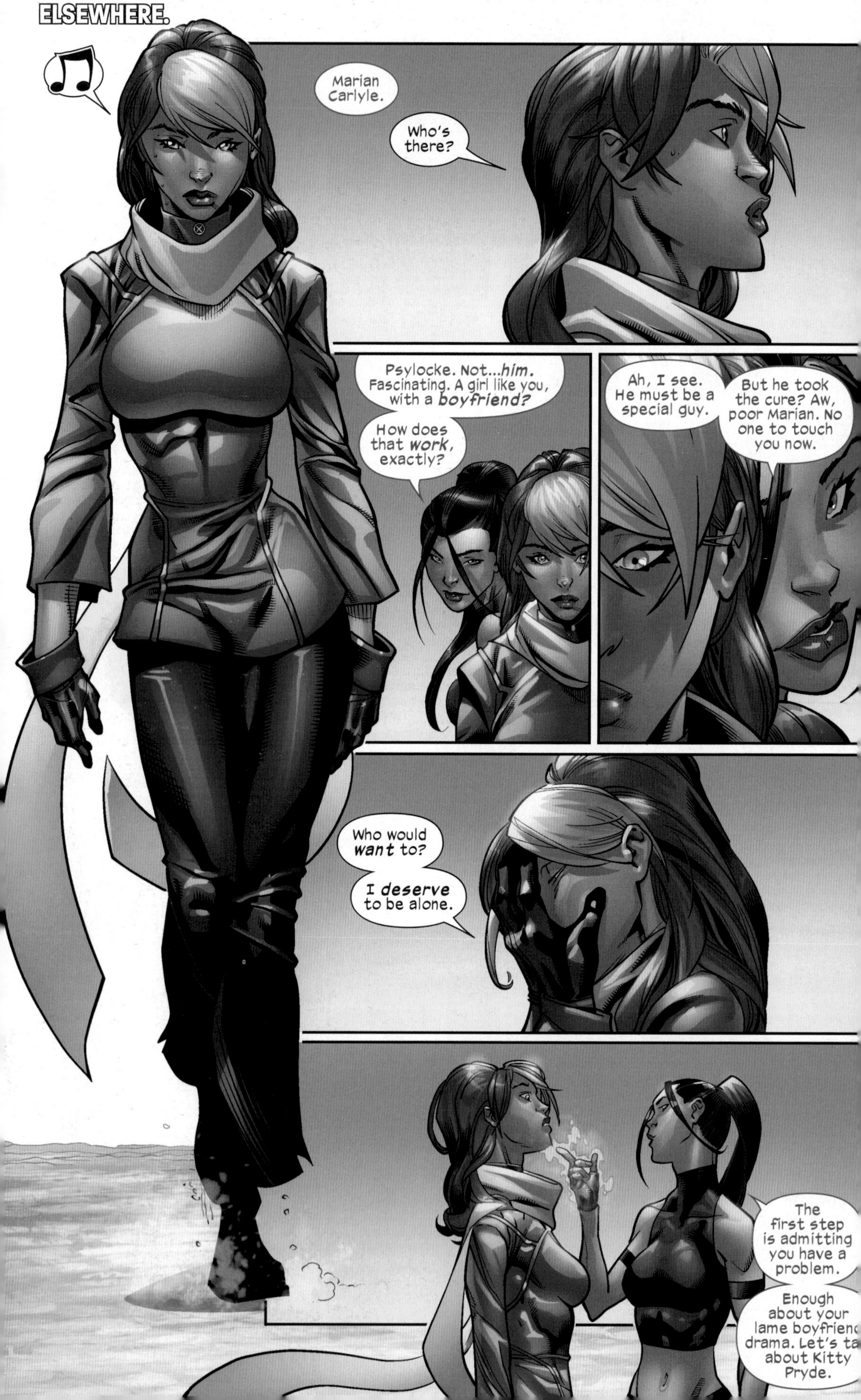
ELSEWHERE.
♫
Marian Carlyle.
Who's there?
Psylocke. Not...*him.* Fascinating. A girl like you, with a *boyfriend?*
How does that *work*, exactly?
Ah, I see. He must be a special guy.
But he took the cure? Aw, poor Marian. No one to touch you now.
Who would *want* to?
I *deserve* to be alone.
The first step is admitting you have a problem.
Enough about your lame boyfriend drama. Let's ta about Kitty Pryde.

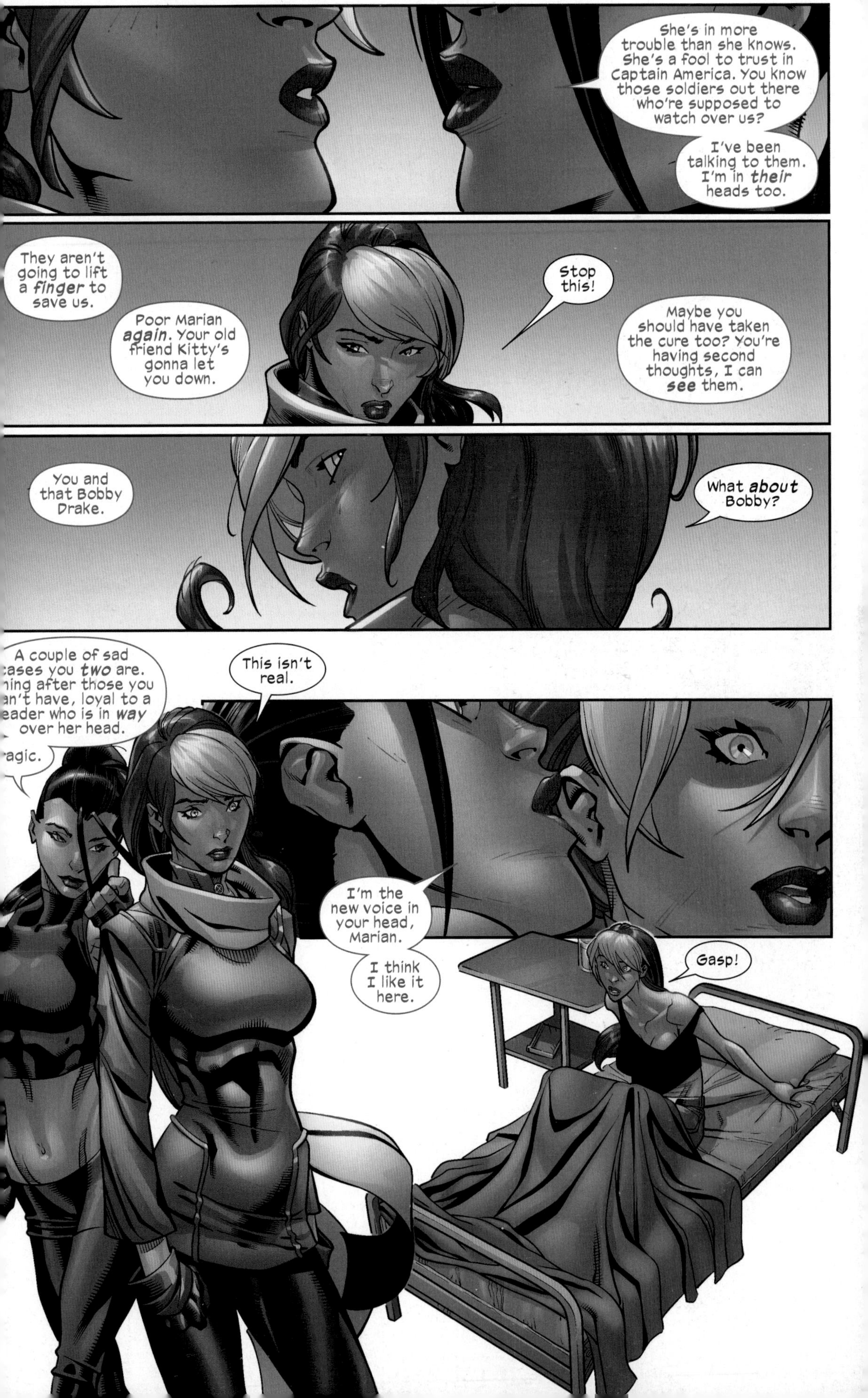

She's in more trouble than she knows. She's a fool to trust in Captain America. You know those soldiers out there who're supposed to watch over us?
I've been talking to them. I'm in *their* heads too.
They aren't going to lift a *finger* to save us.
Poor Marian *again*. Your old friend Kitty's gonna let you down.
Stop this!
Maybe you should have taken the cure too? You're having second thoughts, I can *see* them.
You and that Bobby Drake.
What *about* Bobby?
A couple of sad cases you *two* are.
over her head.
This isn't real.
I'm the new voice in your head, Marian.
I think I like it here.
Gasp!

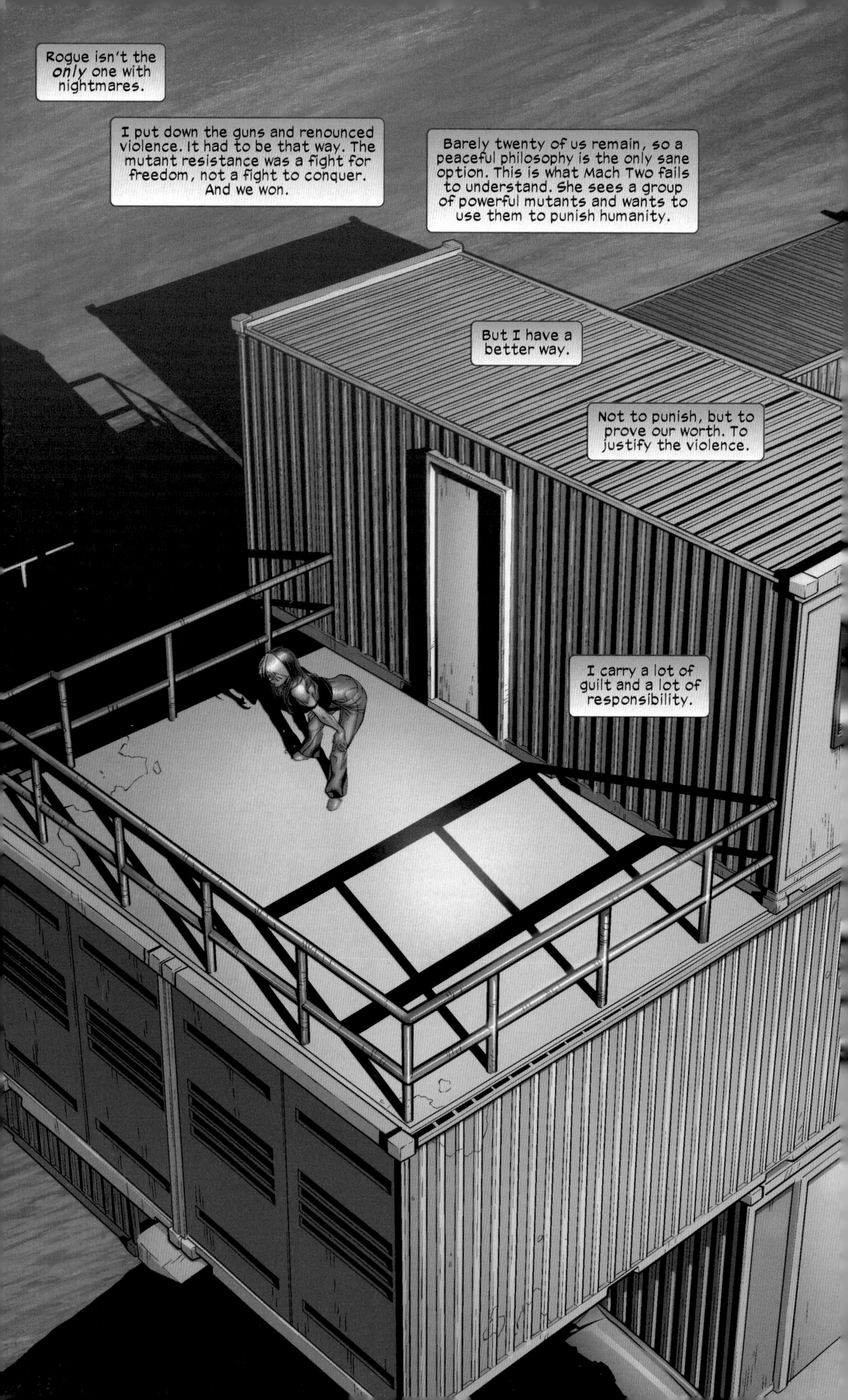
Rogue isn't the *only* one with nightmares.
I put down the guns and renounced violence. It had to be that way. The mutant resistance was a fight for freedom, not a fight to conquer. And we won.
Barely twenty of us remain, so a peaceful philosophy is the only sane option. This is what Mach Two fails to understand. She sees a group of powerful mutants and wants to use them to punish humanity.
But I have a better way.
Not to punish, but to prove our worth. To justify the violence.
I carry a lot of guilt and a lot of responsibility.

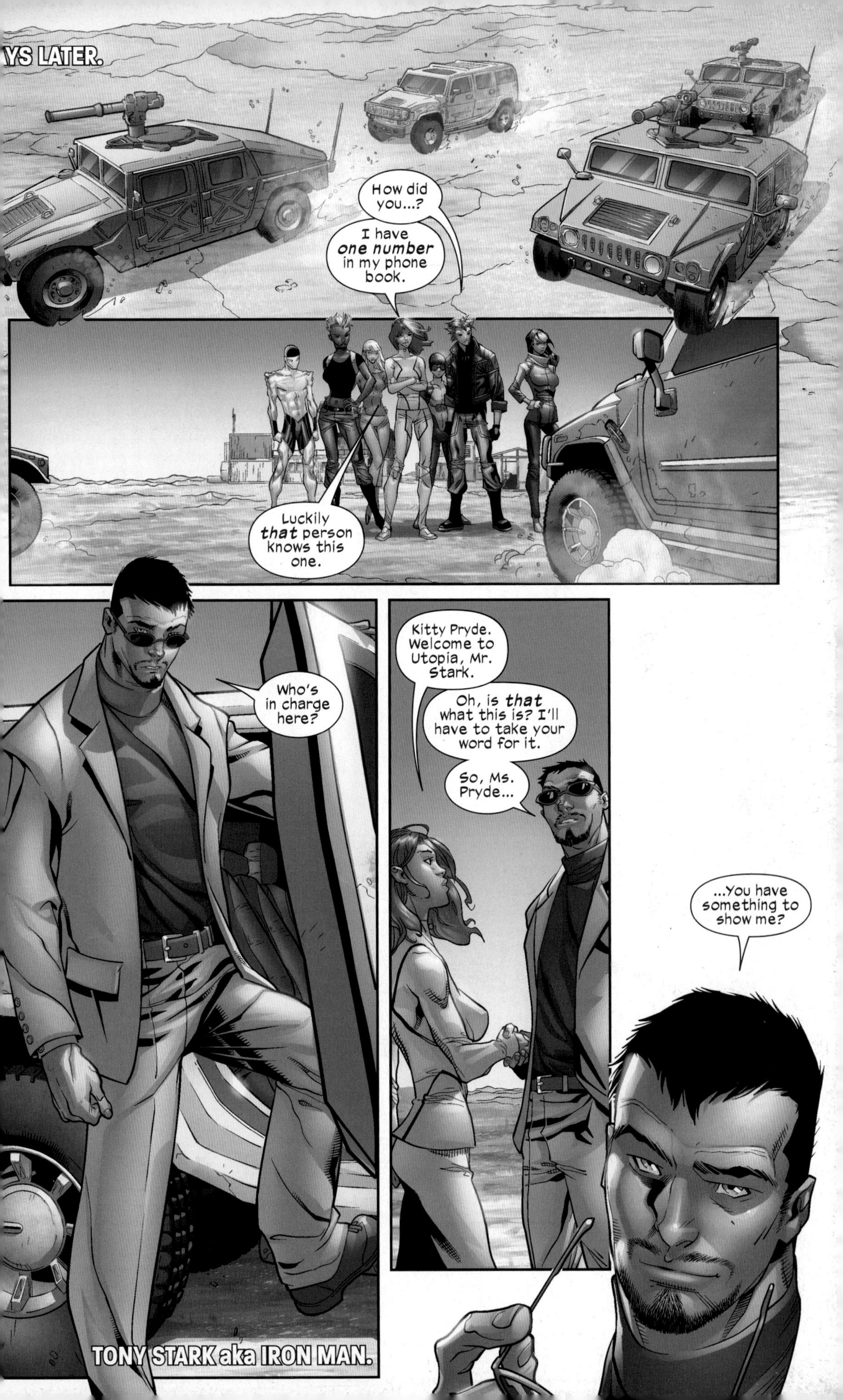
YS LATER.
How did you...?
I have one number in my phone book.
Luckily that person knows this one.
Who's in charge here?
TONY STARK aka IRON MAN.
Kitty Pryde. Welcome to Utopia, Mr. Stark.
Oh, is that what this is? I'll have to take your word for it.
So, Ms. Pryde...
...You have something to show me?

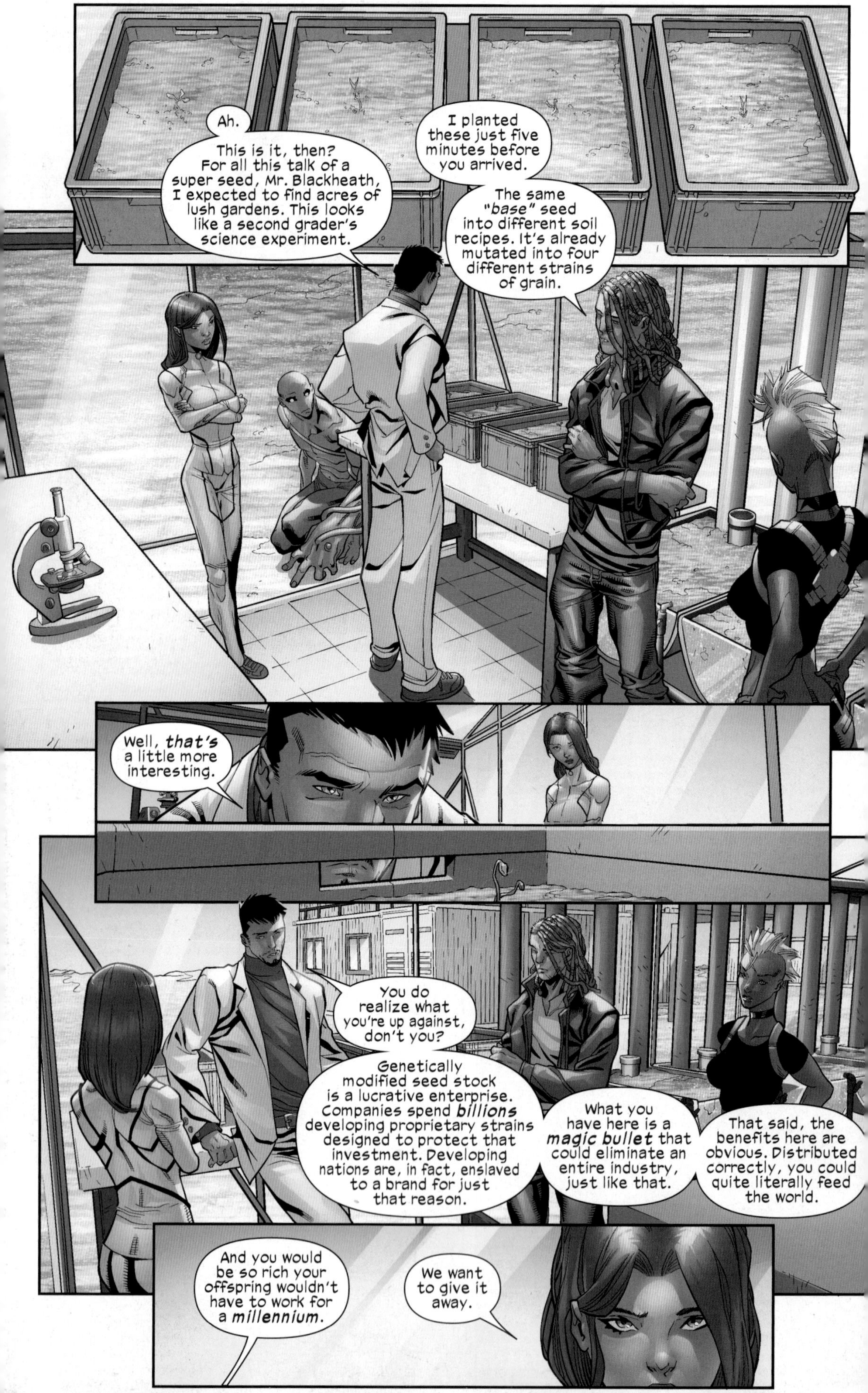
Ah.
This is it, then? For all this talk of a super seed, Mr. Blackheath, I expected to find acres of lush gardens. This looks like a second grader's science experiment.
I planted these just five minutes before you arrived.
The same "base" seed into different soil recipes. It's already mutated into four different strains of grain.
Well, that's a little more interesting.
You do realize what you're up against, don't you?
Genetically modified seed stock is a lucrative enterprise. Companies spend billions developing proprietary strains designed to protect that investment. Developing nations are, in fact, enslaved to a brand for just that reason.
What you have here is a magic bullet that could eliminate an entire industry, just like that.
That said, the benefits here are obvious. Distributed correctly, you could quite literally feed the world.
And you would be so rich your offspring wouldn't have to work for a millennium.
We want to give it away.

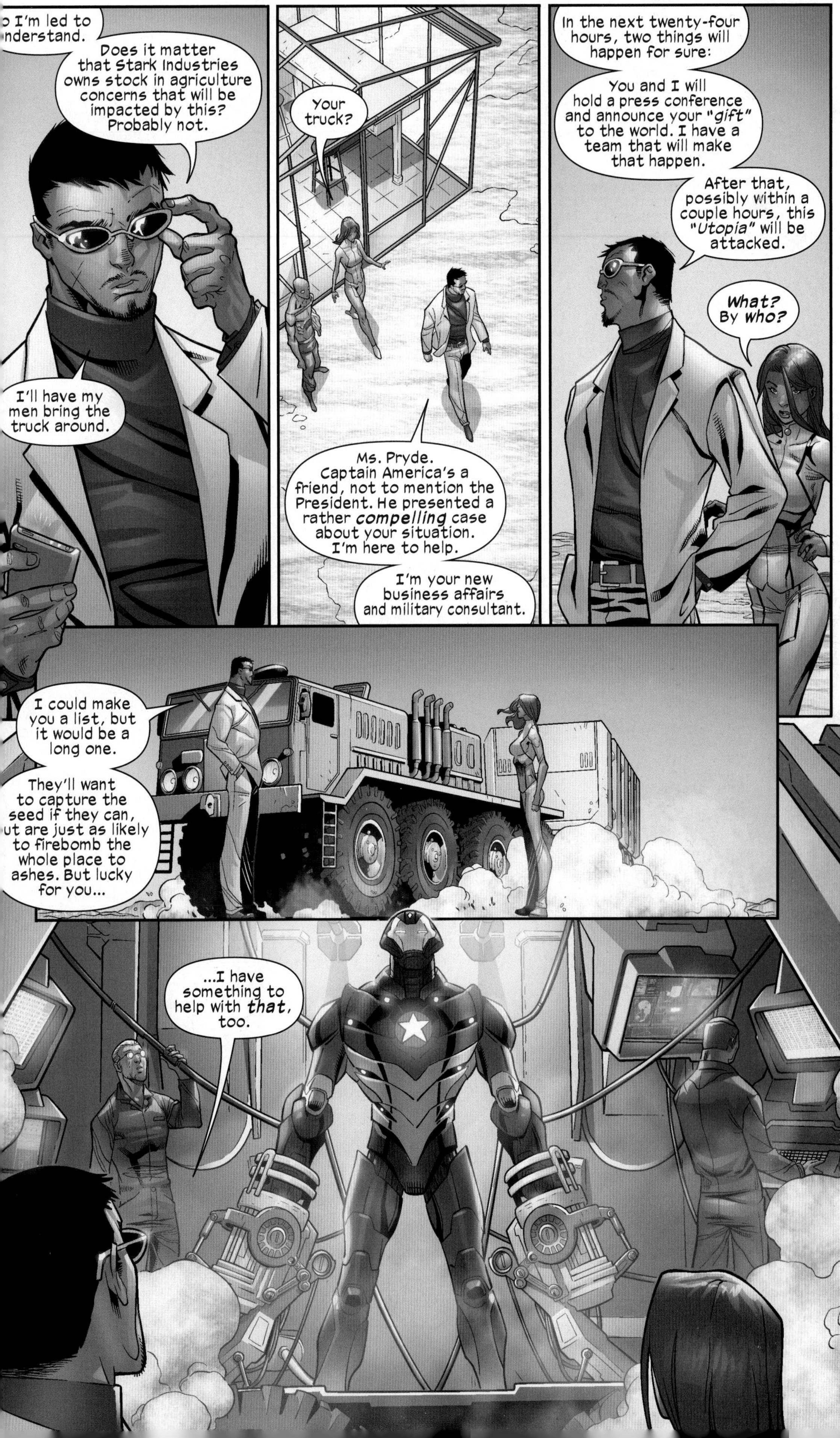

o I'm led to
nderstand.
Does it matter that Stark Industries owns stock in agriculture concerns that will be impacted by this? Probably not.
I'll have my men bring the truck around.
Your truck?
Ms. Pryde. Captain America's a friend, not to mention the President. He presented a rather *compelling* case about your situation. I'm here to help.
I'm your new business affairs and military consultant.
In the next twenty-four hours, two things will happen for sure:
You and I will hold a press conference and announce your "*gift*" to the world. I have a team that will make that happen.
After that, possibly within a couple hours, this "*Utopia*" will be attacked.
What? By *who?*
I could make you a list, but it would be a long one.
They'll want to capture the seed if they can, ut are just as likely to firebomb the whole place to ashes. But lucky for you...
...I have something to help with *that*, too.

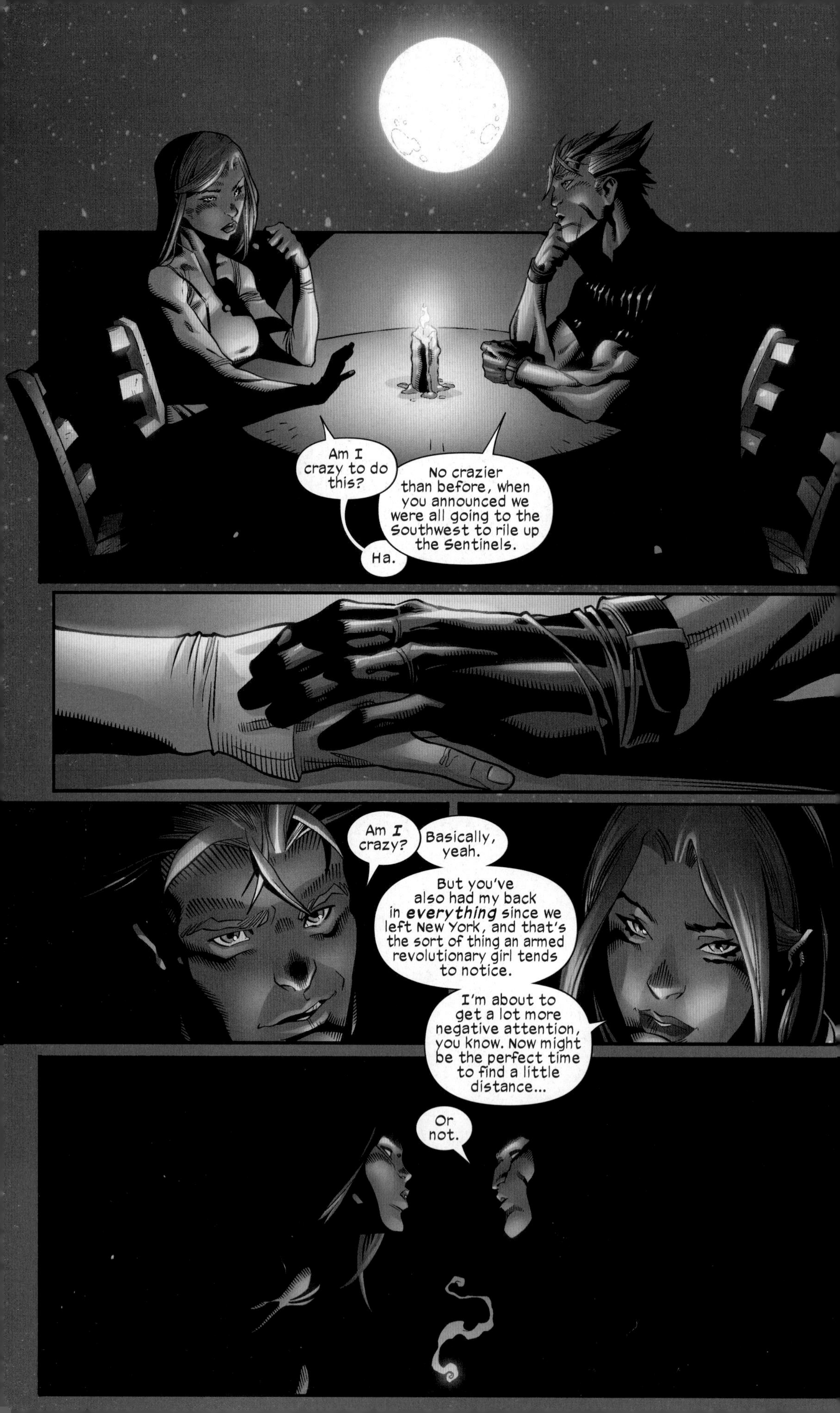
Am I crazy to do this?
No crazier than before, when you announced we were all going to the Southwest to rile up the Sentinels.
Ha.
Am *I* crazy?
Basically, yeah.
But you've also had my back in ***everything*** since we left New York, and that's the sort of thing an armed revolutionary girl tends to notice.
I'm about to get a lot more negative attention, you know. Now might be the perfect time to find a little distance...
Or not.

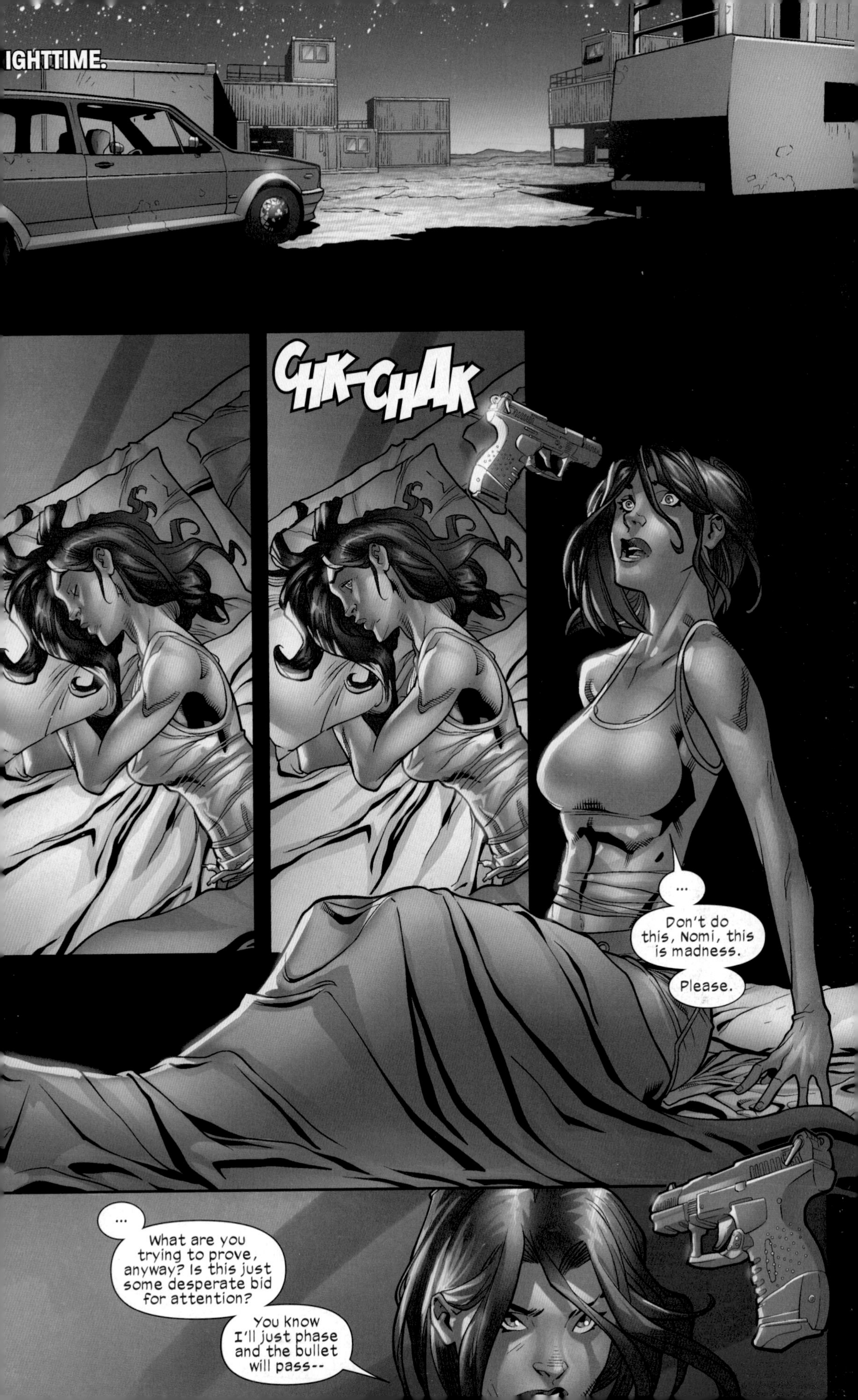
IGHTTIME.
CHK-CHAK
...
Don't do this, Nomi, this is madness.
Please.
...
What are you trying to prove, anyway? Is this just some desperate bid for attention?
You know I'll just phase and the bullet will pass--

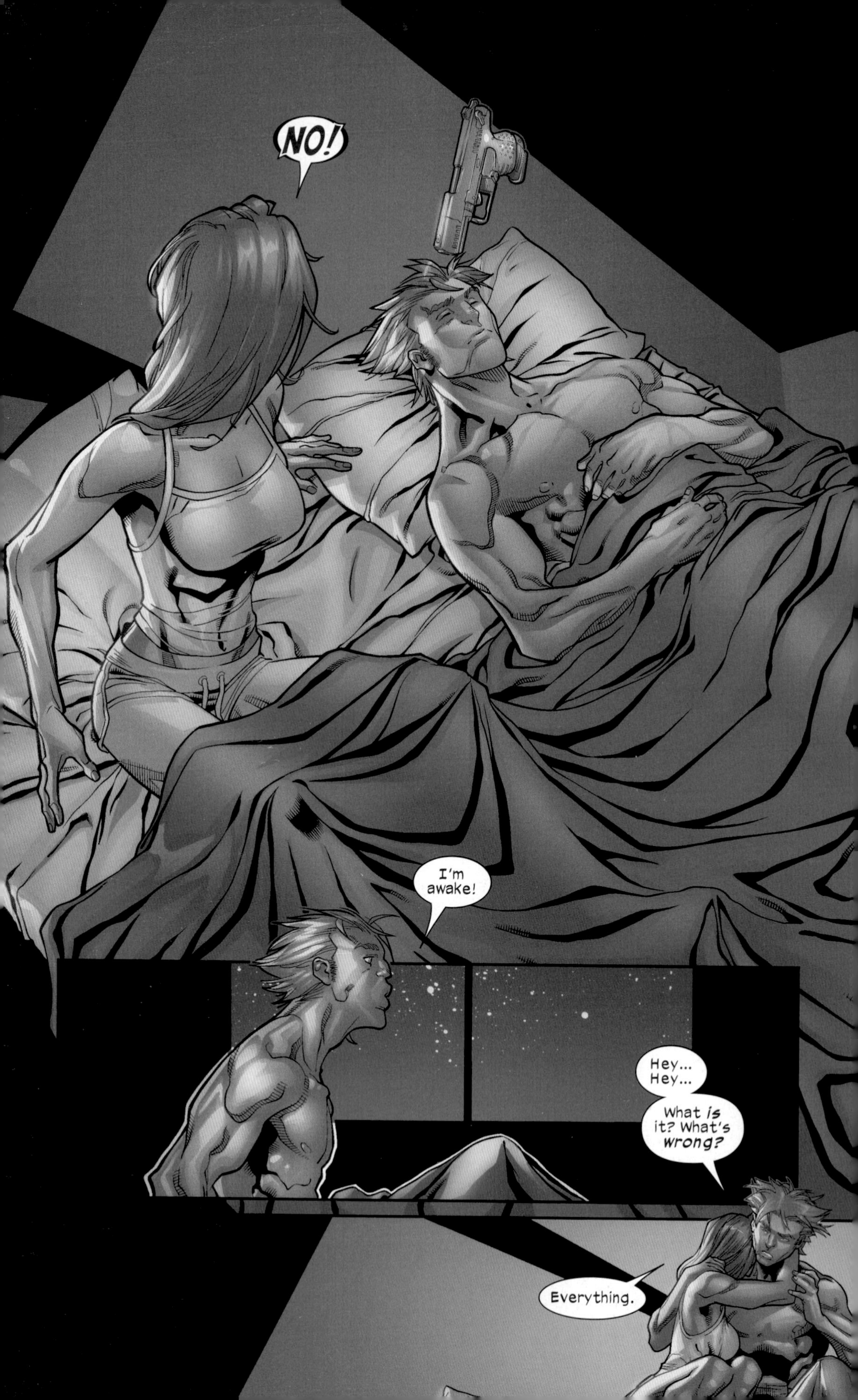
NO!
I'm awake!
Hey... Hey...
What *is* it? What's *wrong?*
Everything.

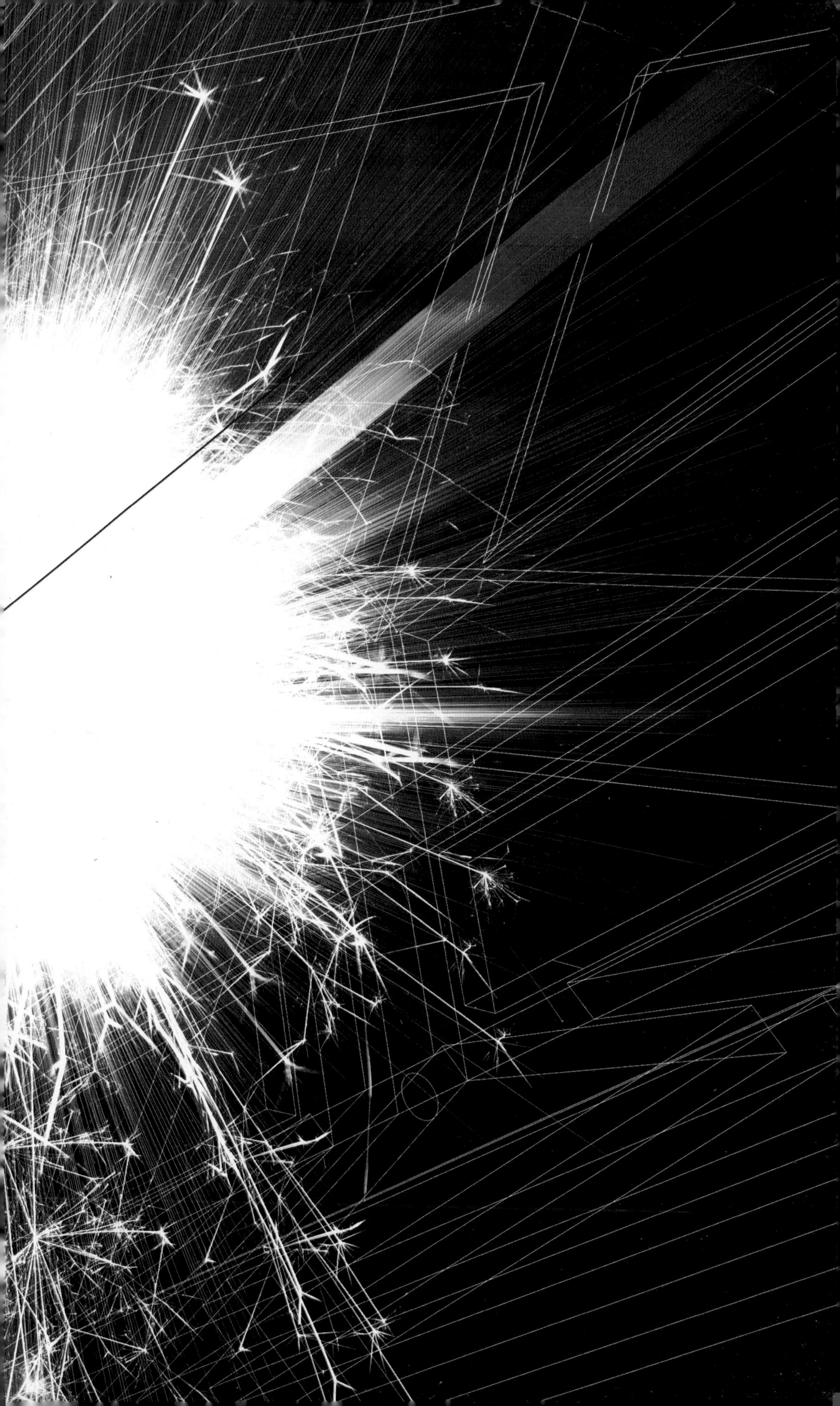

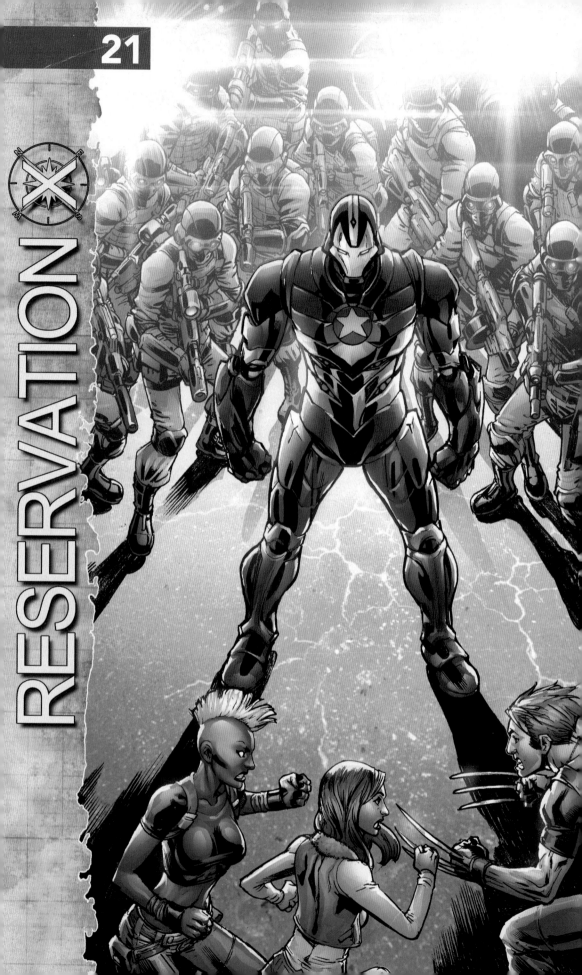

RESERVATION X

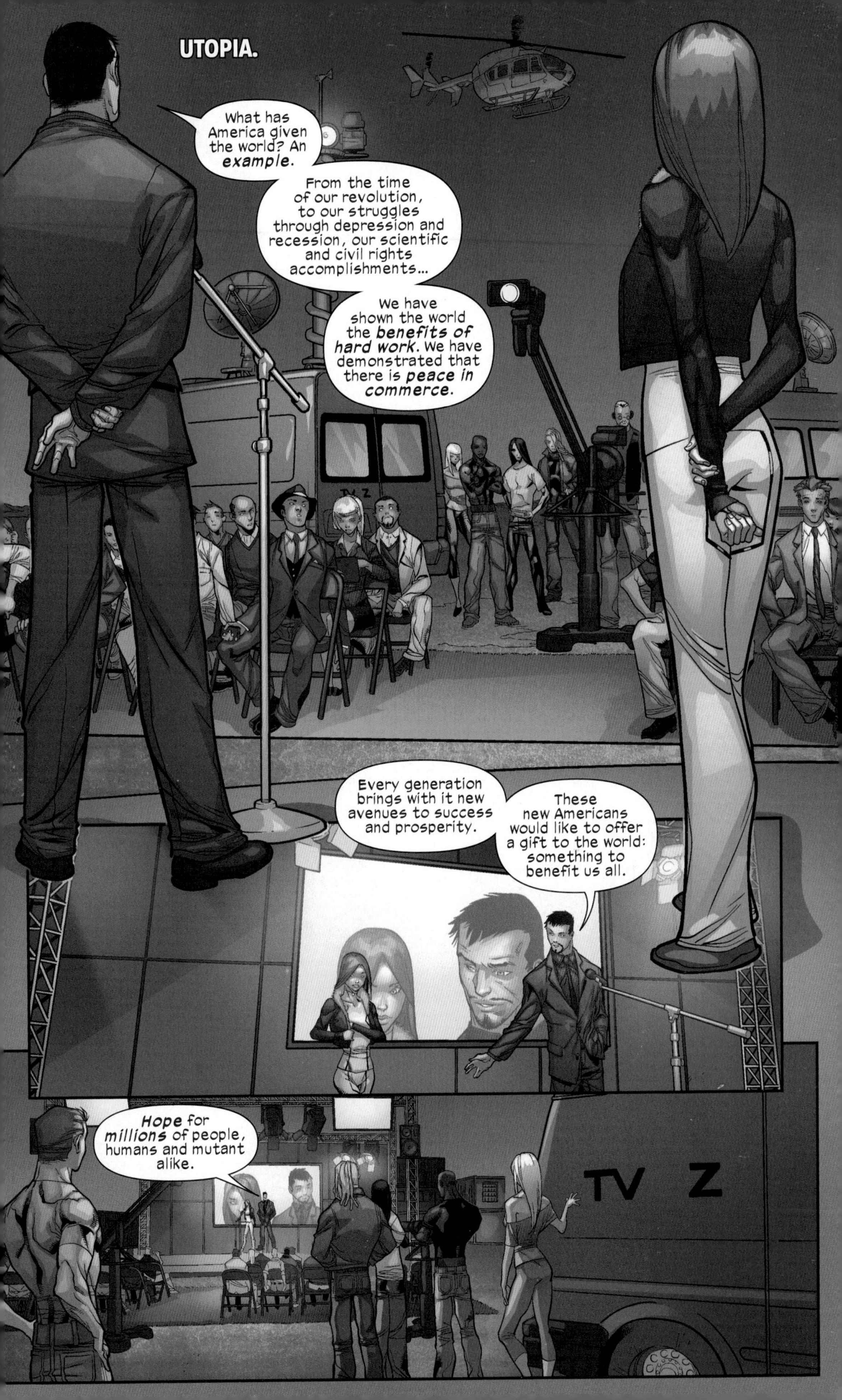
UTOPIA.
What has America given the world? An *example*.
From the time of our revolution, to our struggles through depression and recession, our scientific and civil rights accomplishments...
We have shown the world the *benefits of hard work*. We have demonstrated that there is *peace in commerce*.
TV Z
Every generation brings with it new avenues to success and prosperity.
These new Americans would like to offer a gift to the world: something to benefit us all.
Hope for *millions* of people, humans and mutant alike.
TV Z

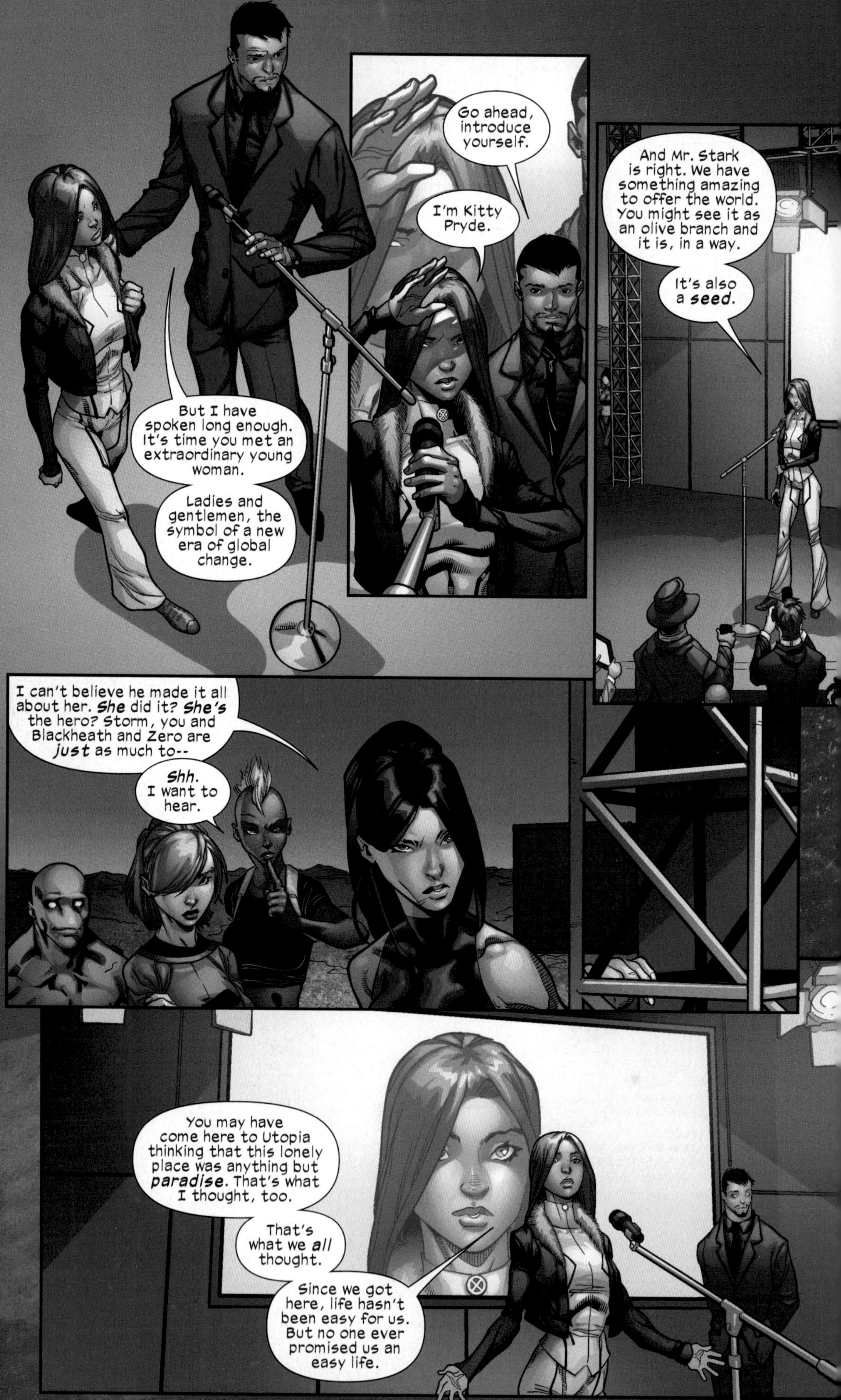
But I have spoken long enough. It's time you met an extraordinary young woman.
Ladies and gentlemen, the symbol of a new era of global change.
Go ahead, introduce yourself.
I'm Kitty Pryde.
And Mr. Stark is right. We have something amazing to offer the world. You might see it as an olive branch and it is, in a way.
It's also a *seed*.
I can't believe he made it all about her. *She* did it? *She's* the hero? Storm, you and Blackheath and Zero are *just* as much to--
Shh. I want to hear.
You may have come here to Utopia thinking that this lonely place was anything but *paradise*. That's what I thought, too.
That's what we *all* thought.
Since we got here, life hasn't been easy for us. But no one ever promised us an easy life.

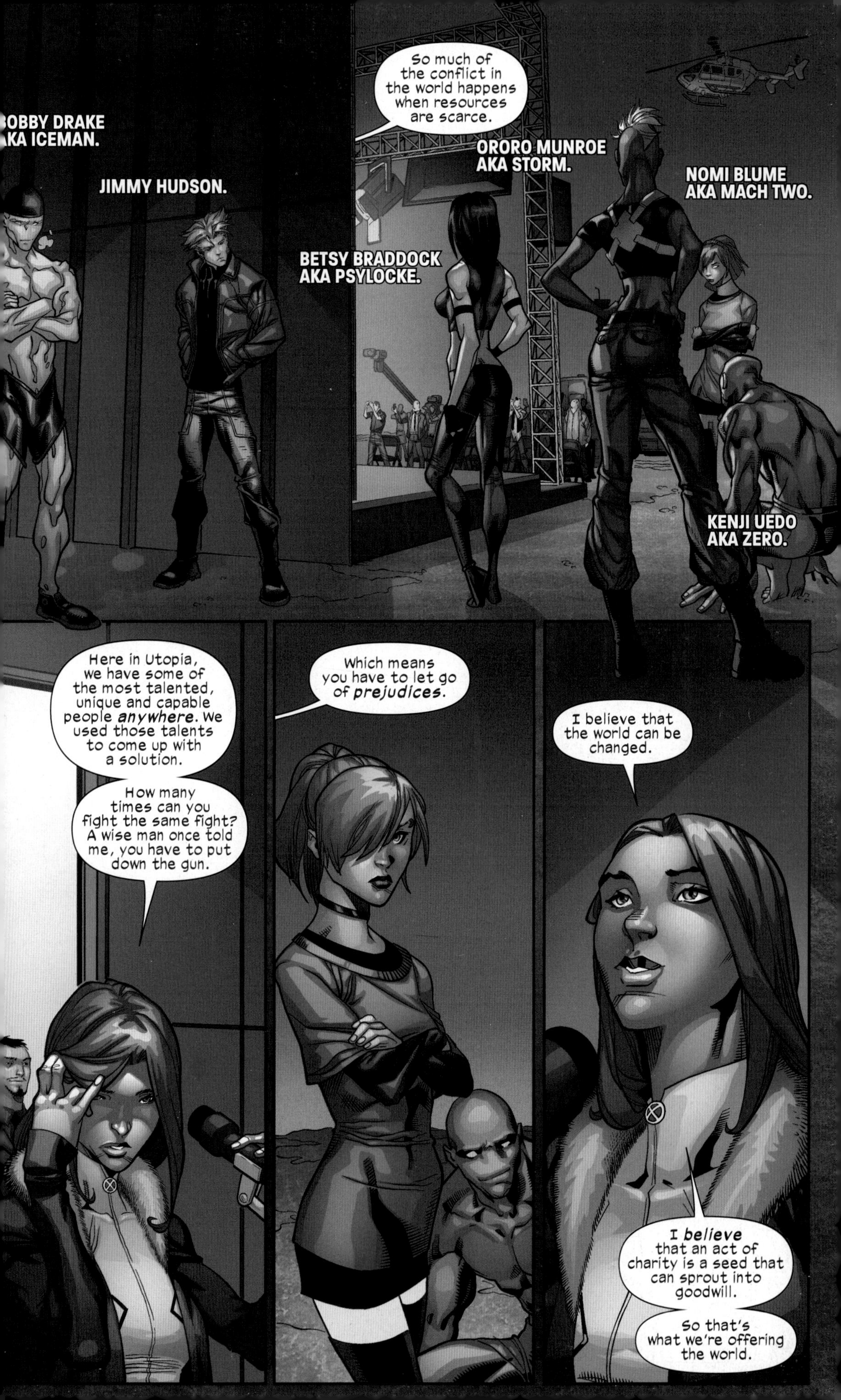

So much of the conflict in the world happens when resources are scarce.
OBBY DRAKE AKA ICEMAN.
JIMMY HUDSON.
BETSY BRADDOCK AKA PSYLOCKE.
ORORO MUNROE AKA STORM.
NOMI BLUME AKA MACH TWO.
KENJI UEDO AKA ZERO.
Here in Utopia, we have some of the most talented, unique and capable people *anywhere*. We used those talents to come up with a solution.
How many times can you fight the same fight? A wise man once told me, you have to put down the gun.
Which means you have to let go of *prejudices*.
I believe that the world can be changed.
I *believe* that an act of charity is a seed that can sprout into goodwill.
So that's what we're offering the world.

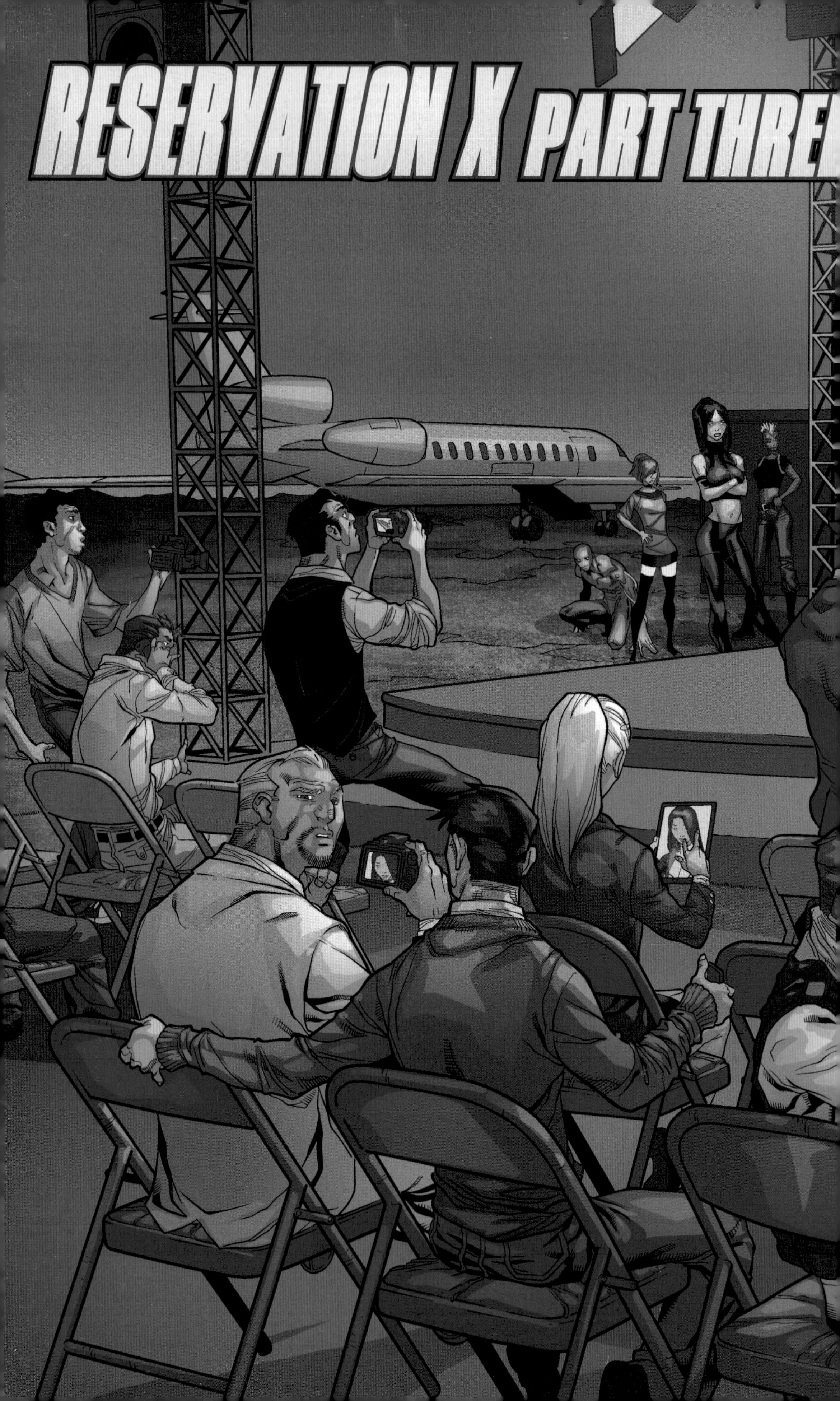
RESERVATION X PART THREE

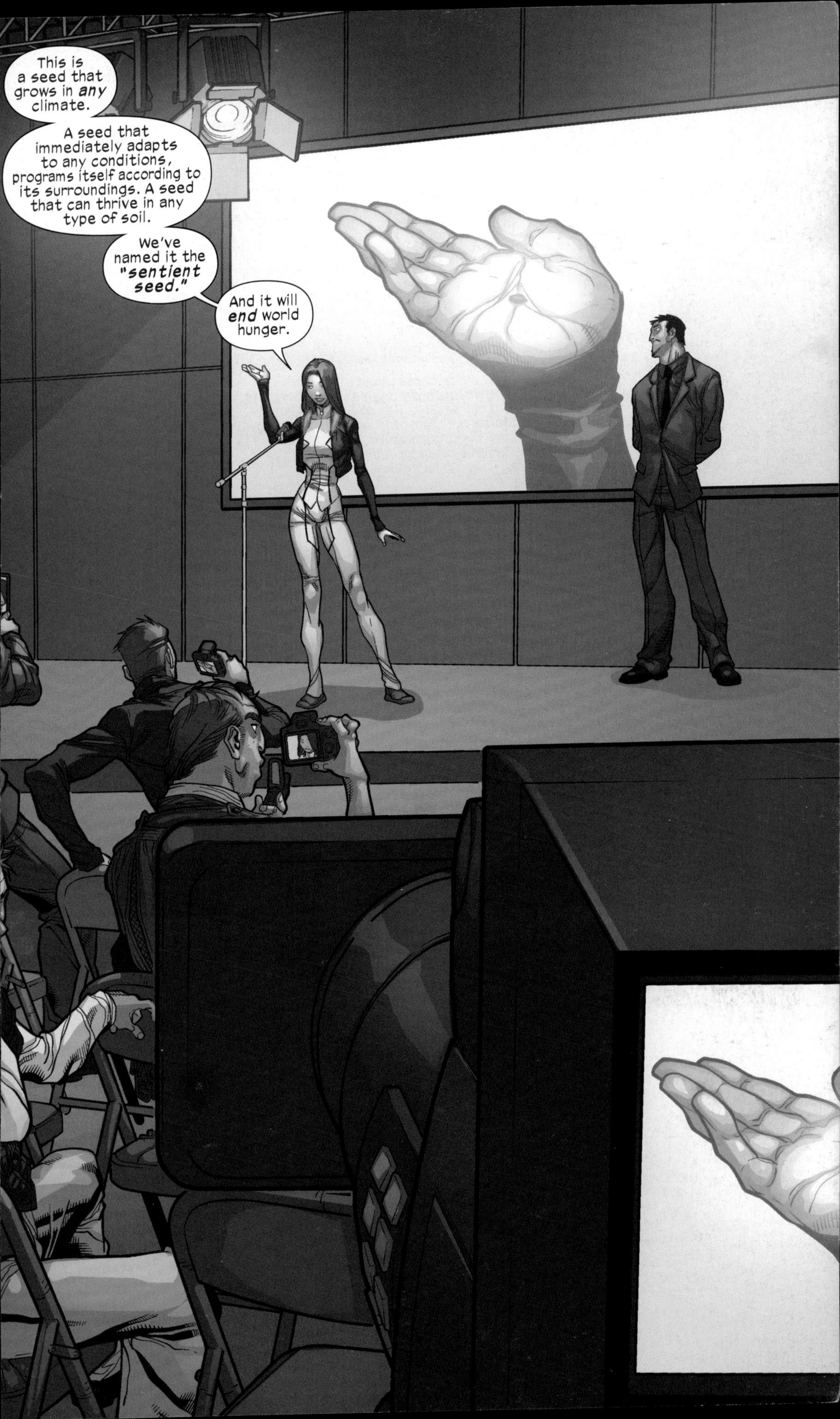
This is a seed that grows in *any* climate.
A seed that immediately adapts to any conditions, programs itself according to its surroundings. A seed that can thrive in any type of soil.
We've named it the *"sentient seed."*
And it will *end* world hunger.

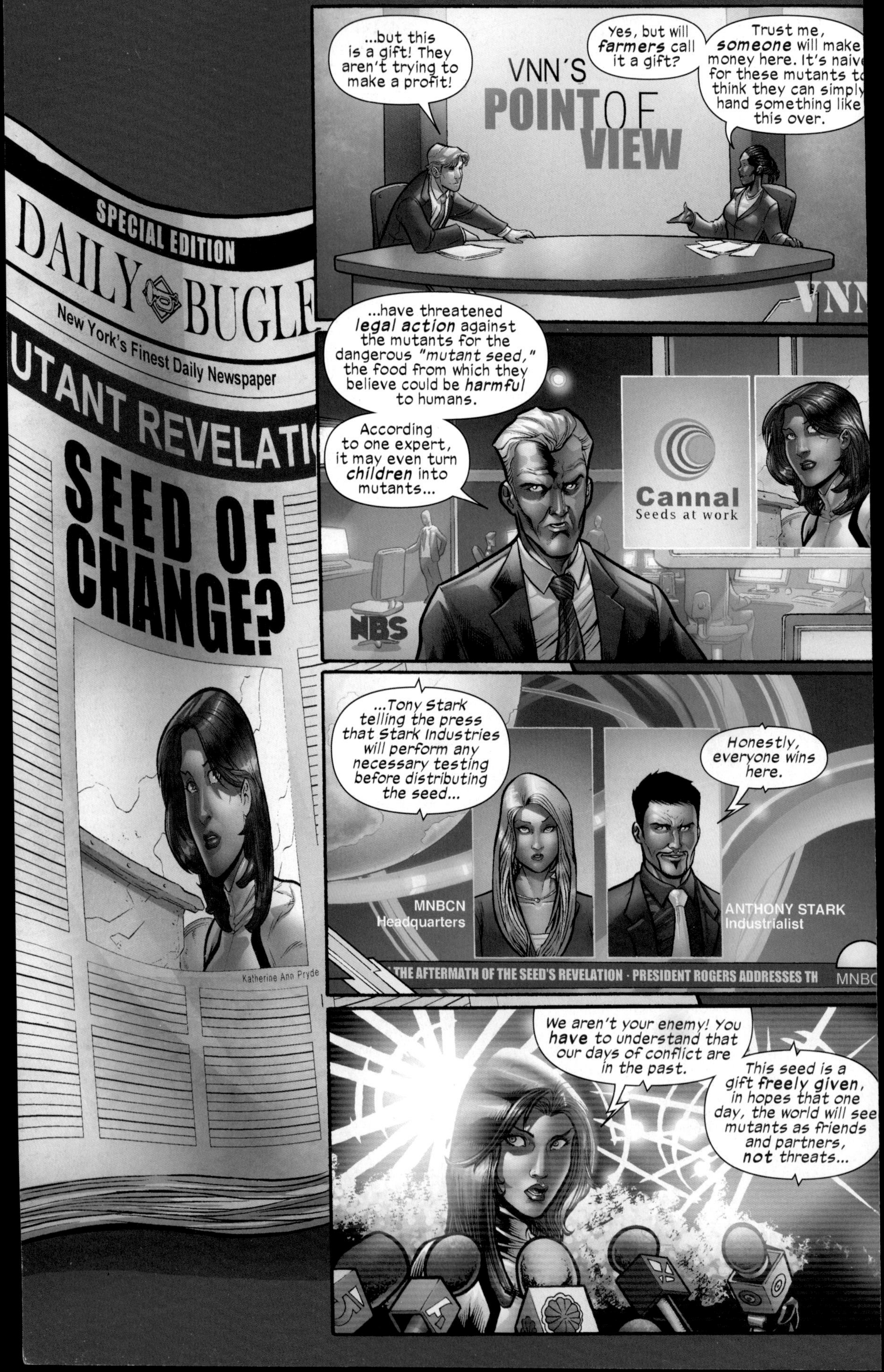
SPECIAL EDITION
DAILY BUGLE
New York's Finest Daily Newspaper
UTANT REVELATI
SEED OF CHANGE?
Katherine Ann Pryde
VNN'S POINT OF VIEW
...but this is a gift! They aren't trying to make a profit!
Yes, but will farmers call it a gift?
Trust me, someone will make money here. It's naive for these mutants to think they can simply hand something like this over.
VNN
...have threatened legal action against the mutants for the dangerous "mutant seed," the food from which they believe could be harmful to humans.
According to one expert, it may even turn children into mutants...
Cannal
Seeds at work
NBS
...Tony Stark telling the press that Stark Industries will perform any necessary testing before distributing the seed...
Honestly, everyone wins here.
MNBCN
Headquarters
ANTHONY STARK
Industrialist
THE AFTERMATH OF THE SEED'S REVELATION · PRESIDENT ROGERS ADDRESSES TH
MNBC
We aren't your enemy! You have to understand that our days of conflict are in the past.
This seed is a gift freely given, in hopes that one day, the world will see mutants as friends and partners, not threats...

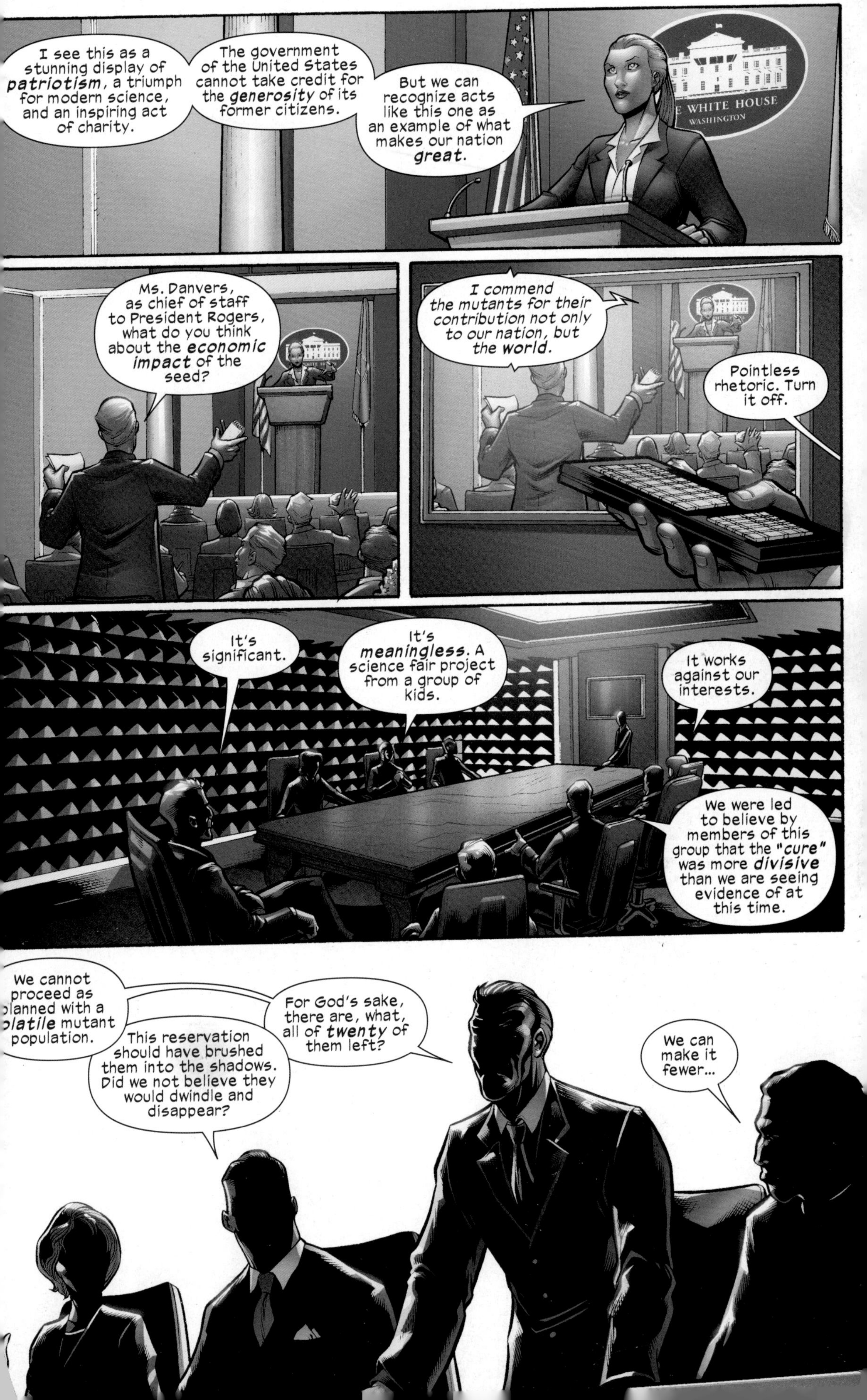

I see this as a stunning display of patriotism, a triumph for modern science, and an inspiring act of charity.
The government of the United States cannot take credit for the generosity of its former citizens.
But we can recognize acts like this one as an example of what makes our nation great.
THE WHITE HOUSE
WASHINGTON
Ms. Danvers, as chief of staff to President Rogers, what do you think about the economic impact of the seed?
I commend the mutants for their contribution not only to our nation, but the world.
Pointless rhetoric. Turn it off.
It's significant.
It's meaningless. A science fair project from a group of kids.
It works against our interests.
We were led to believe by members of this group that the "cure" was more divisive than we are seeing evidence of at this time.
We cannot proceed as planned with a volatile mutant population.
This reservation should have brushed them into the shadows. Did we not believe they would dwindle and disappear?
For God's sake, there are, what, all of twenty of them left?
We can make it fewer...

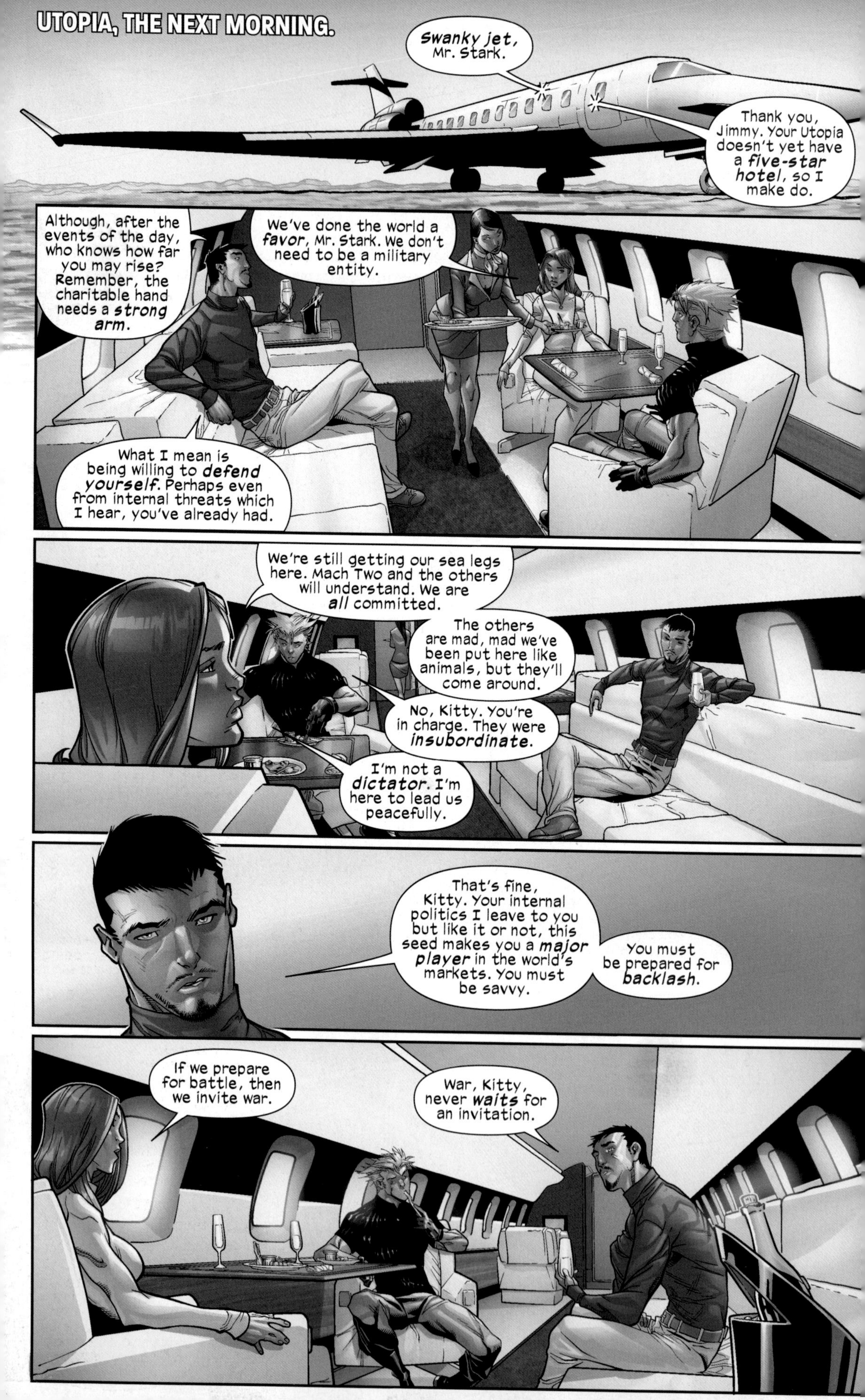
UTOPIA, THE NEXT MORNING.
Swanky jet, Mr. Stark.
Thank you, Jimmy. Your Utopia doesn't yet have a five-star hotel, so I make do.
Although, after the events of the day, who knows how far you may rise? Remember, the charitable hand needs a strong arm.
We've done the world a favor, Mr. Stark. We don't need to be a military entity.
What I mean is being willing to defend yourself. Perhaps even from internal threats which I hear, you've already had.
We're still getting our sea legs here. Mach Two and the others will understand. We are all committed.
The others are mad, mad we've been put here like animals, but they'll come around.
No, Kitty. You're in charge. They were insubordinate.
I'm not a dictator. I'm here to lead us peacefully.
That's fine, Kitty. Your internal politics I leave to you but like it or not, this seed makes you a major player in the world's markets. You must be savvy.
You must be prepared for backlash.
If we prepare for battle, then we invite war.
War, Kitty, never waits for an invitation.

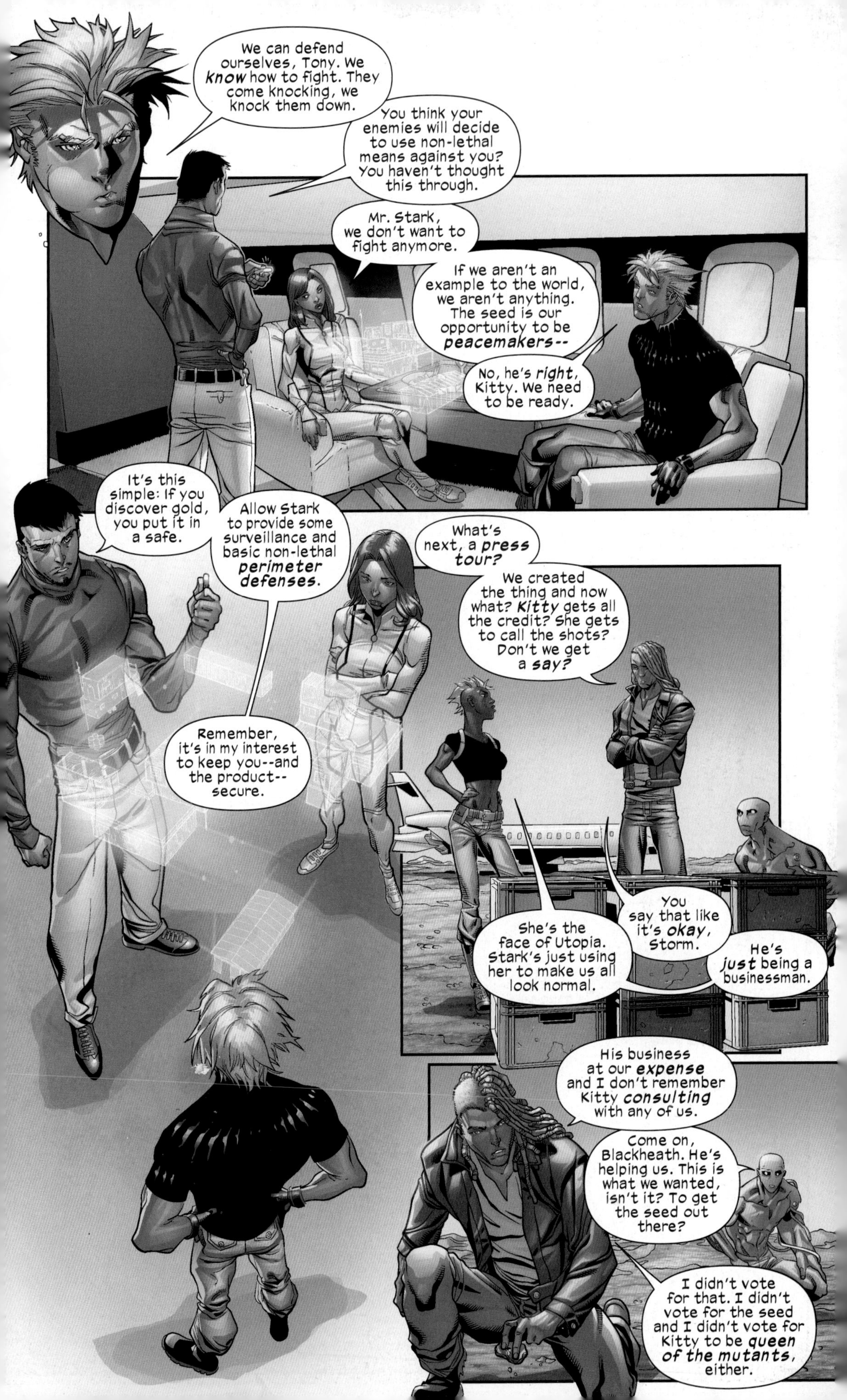
We can defend ourselves, Tony. We know how to fight. They come knocking, we knock them down.
You think your enemies will decide to use non-lethal means against you? You haven't thought this through.
Mr. Stark, we don't want to fight anymore.
If we aren't an example to the world, we aren't anything. The seed is our opportunity to be peacemakers--
No, he's right, Kitty. We need to be ready.
It's this simple: If you discover gold, you put it in a safe.
Allow Stark to provide some surveillance and basic non-lethal perimeter defenses.
Remember, it's in my interest to keep you--and the product--secure.
What's next, a press tour?
We created the thing and now what? Kitty gets all the credit? She gets to call the shots? Don't we get a say?
She's the face of Utopia. Stark's just using her to make us all look normal.
You say that like it's okay, Storm.
He's just being a businessman.
His business at our expense and I don't remember Kitty consulting with any of us.
Come on, Blackheath. He's helping us. This is what we wanted, isn't it? To get the seed out there?
I didn't vote for that. I didn't vote for the seed and I didn't vote for Kitty to be queen of the mutants, either.

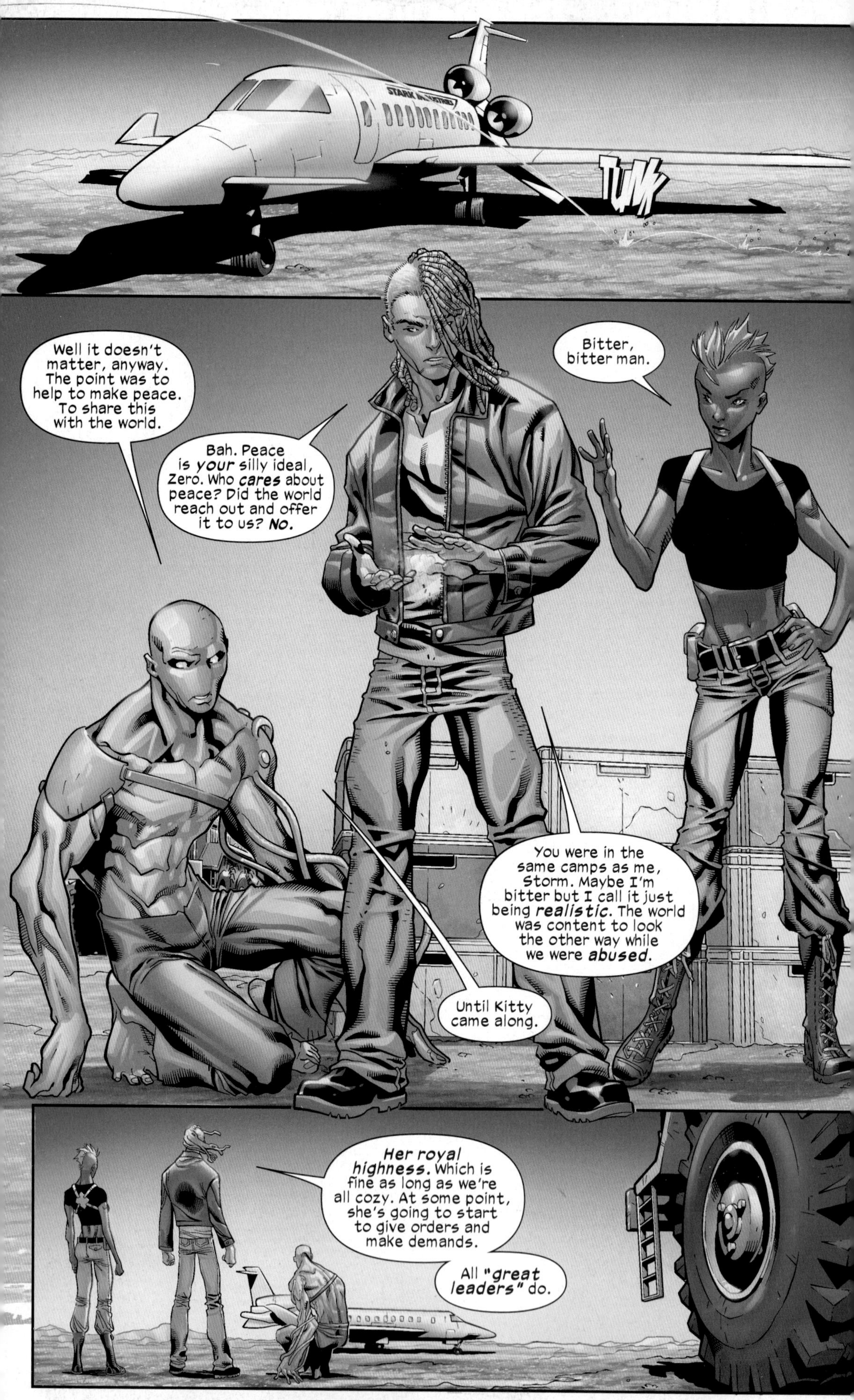
TUNK
Well it doesn't matter, anyway. The point was to help to make peace. To share this with the world.
Bah. Peace is *your* silly ideal, Zero. Who *cares* about peace? Did the world reach out and offer it to us? **No.**
Bitter, bitter man.
You were in the same camps as me, Storm. Maybe I'm bitter but I call it just being ***realistic***. The world was content to look the other way while we were ***abused***.
Until Kitty came along.
Her royal highness. Which is fine as long as we're all cozy. At some point, she's going to start to give orders and make demands.
All "***great leaders***" do.

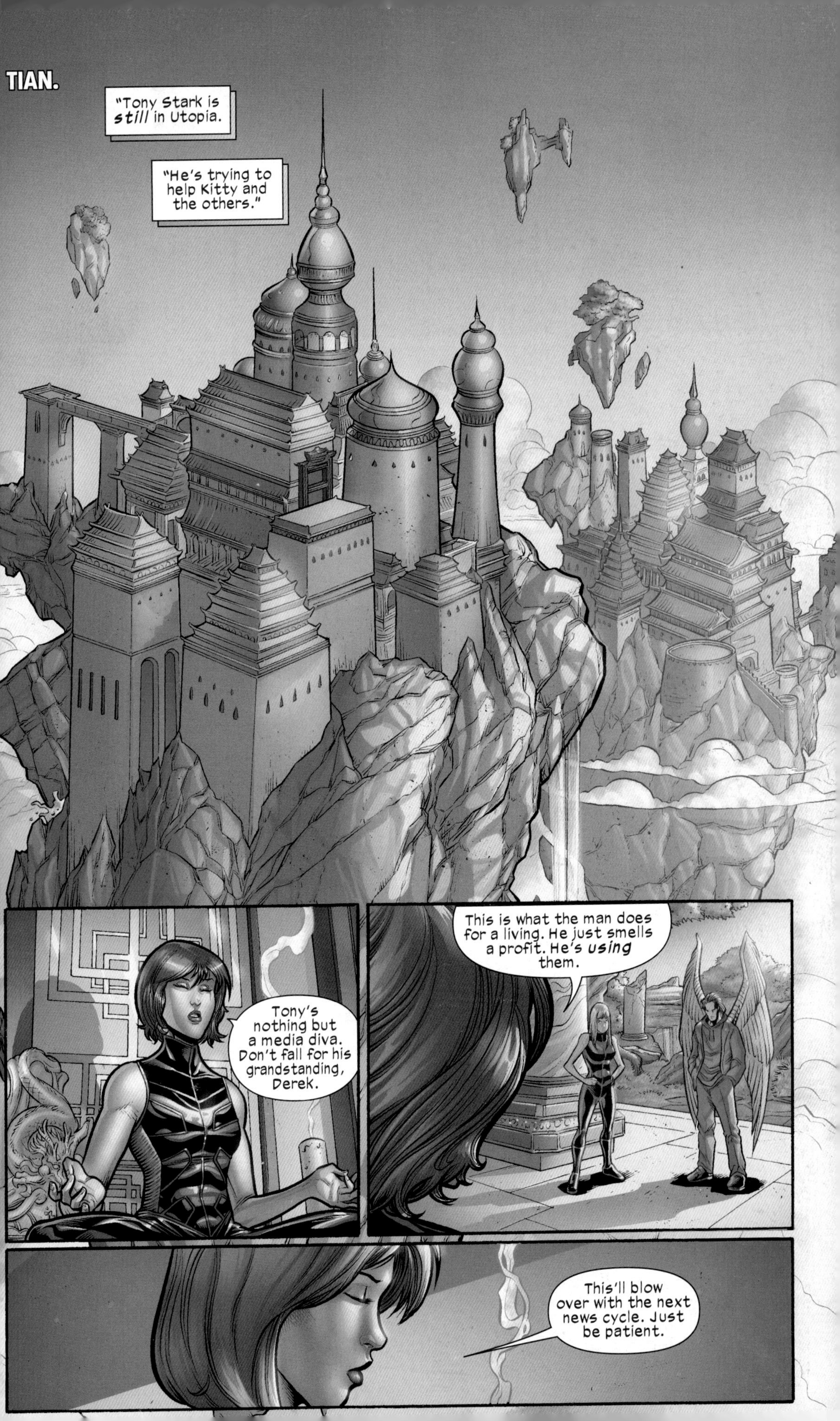
TIAN.
"Tony Stark is still in Utopia.
"He's trying to help Kitty and the others."
Tony's nothing but a media diva. Don't fall for his grandstanding, Derek.
This is what the man does for a living. He just smells a profit. He's using them.
This'll blow over with the next news cycle. Just be patient.

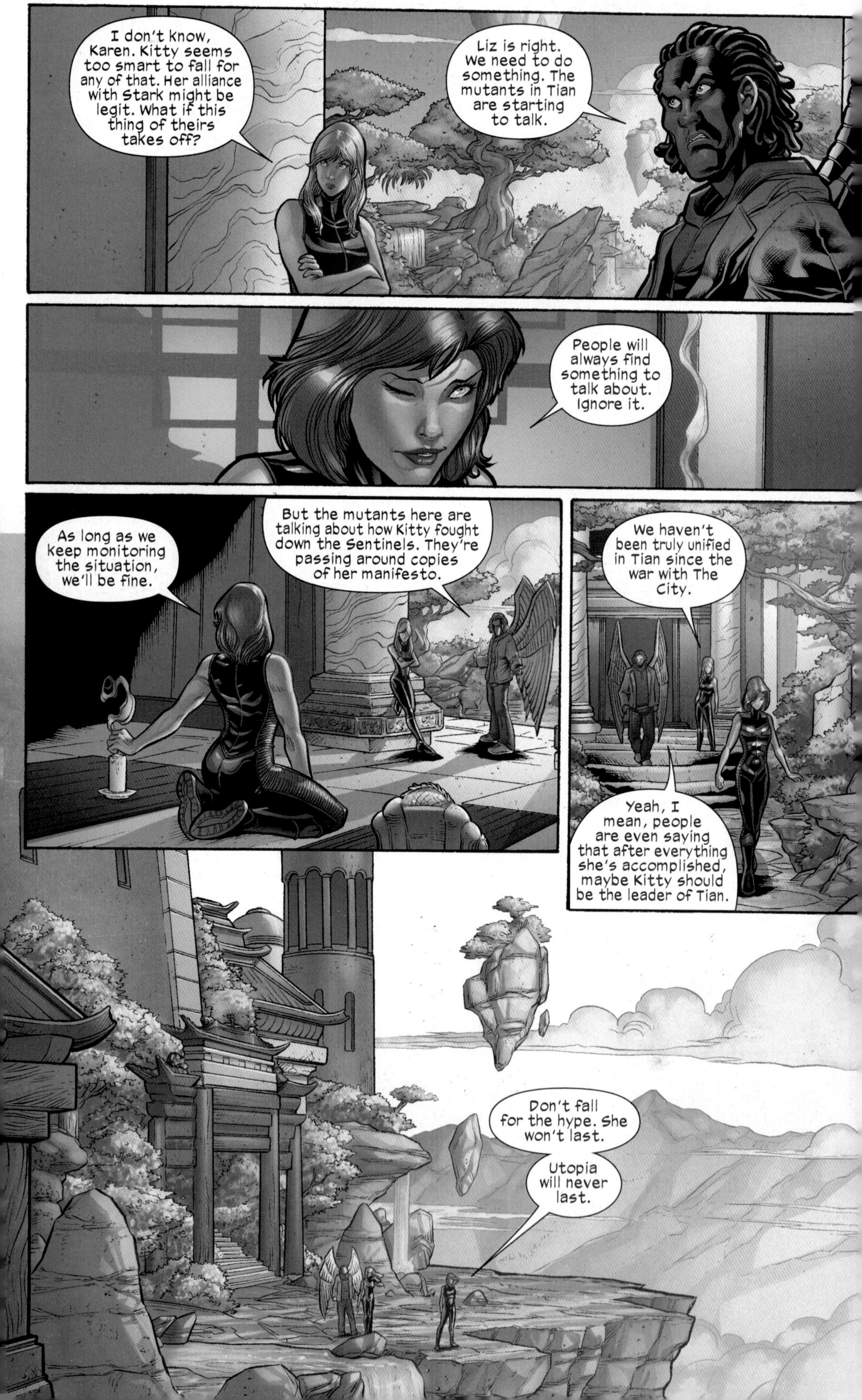
I don't know, Karen. Kitty seems too smart to fall for any of that. Her alliance with Stark might be legit. What if this thing of theirs takes off?
Liz is right. We need to do something. The mutants in Tian are starting to talk.
People will always find something to talk about. Ignore it.
As long as we keep monitoring the situation, we'll be fine.
But the mutants here are talking about how Kitty fought down the Sentinels. They're passing around copies of her manifesto.
We haven't been truly unified in Tian since the war with The City.
Yeah, I mean, people are even saying that after everything she's accomplished, maybe Kitty should be the leader of Tian.
Don't fall for the hype. She won't last.
Utopia will never last.

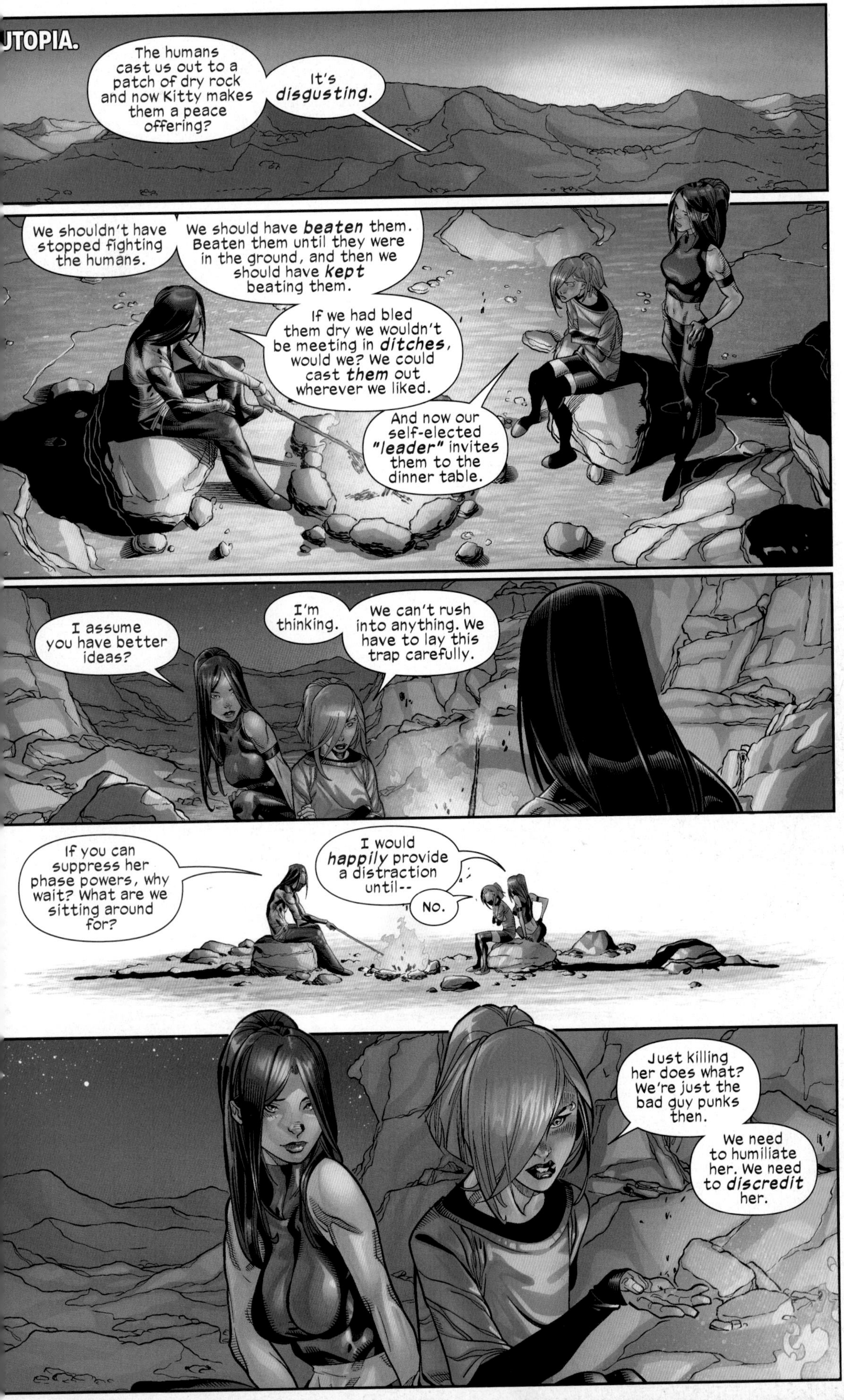
UTOPIA.
The humans cast us out to a patch of dry rock and now Kitty makes them a peace offering?
It's disgusting.
We shouldn't have stopped fighting the humans.
We should have beaten them. Beaten them until they were in the ground, and then we should have kept beating them.
If we had bled them dry we wouldn't be meeting in ditches, would we? We could cast them out wherever we liked.
And now our self-elected "leader" invites them to the dinner table.
I assume you have better ideas?
I'm thinking.
We can't rush into anything. We have to lay this trap carefully.
If you can suppress her phase powers, why wait? What are we sitting around for?
I would happily provide a distraction until--
No.
Just killing her does what? We're just the bad guy punks then.
We need to humiliate her. We need to discredit her.

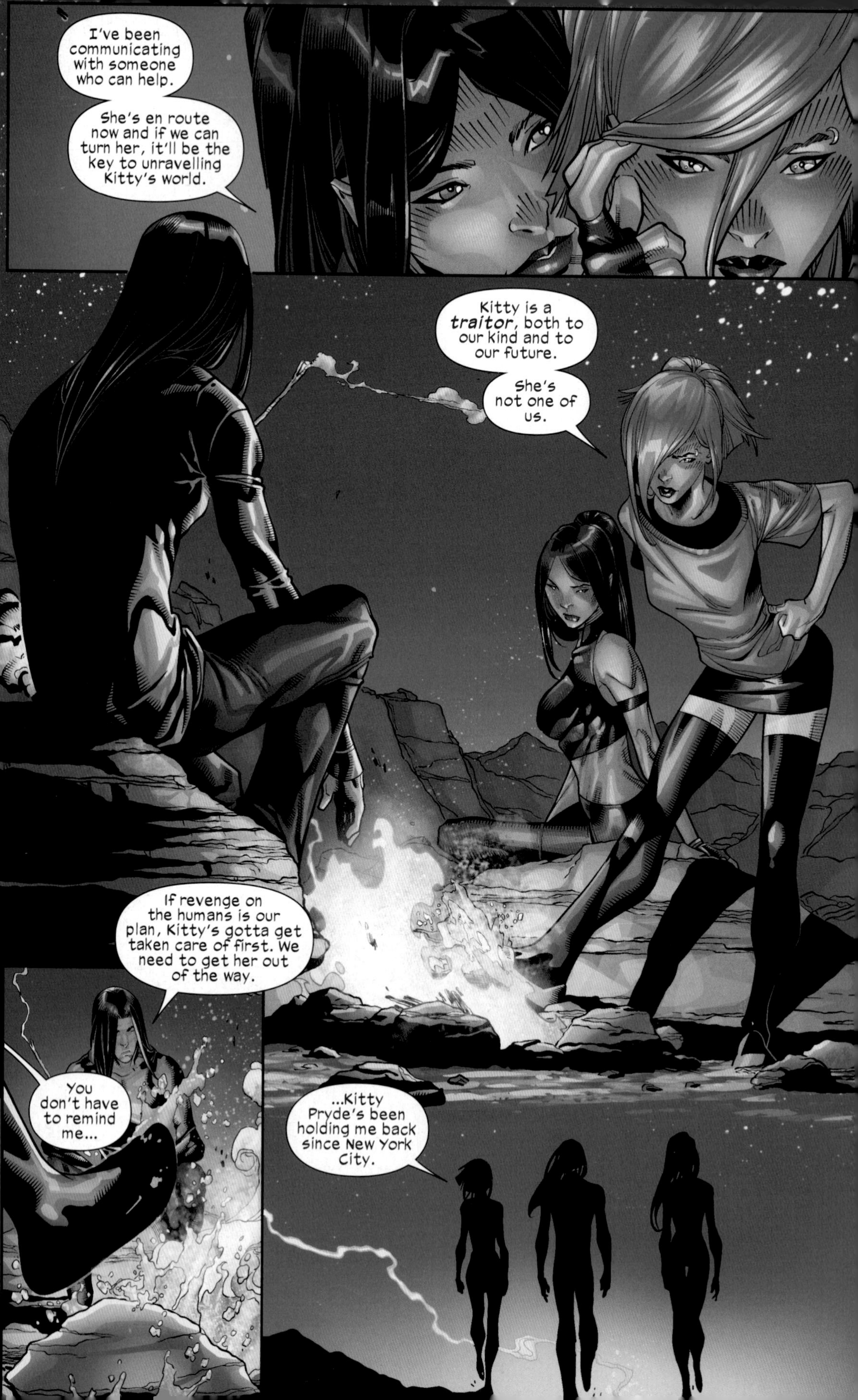

I've been communicating with someone who can help.
She's en route now and if we can turn her, it'll be the key to unravelling Kitty's world.
Kitty is a *traitor*, both to our kind and to our future.
She's not one of us.
If revenge on the humans is our plan, Kitty's gotta get taken care of first. We need to get her out of the way.
You don't have to remind me...
...Kitty Pryde's been holding me back since New York City.

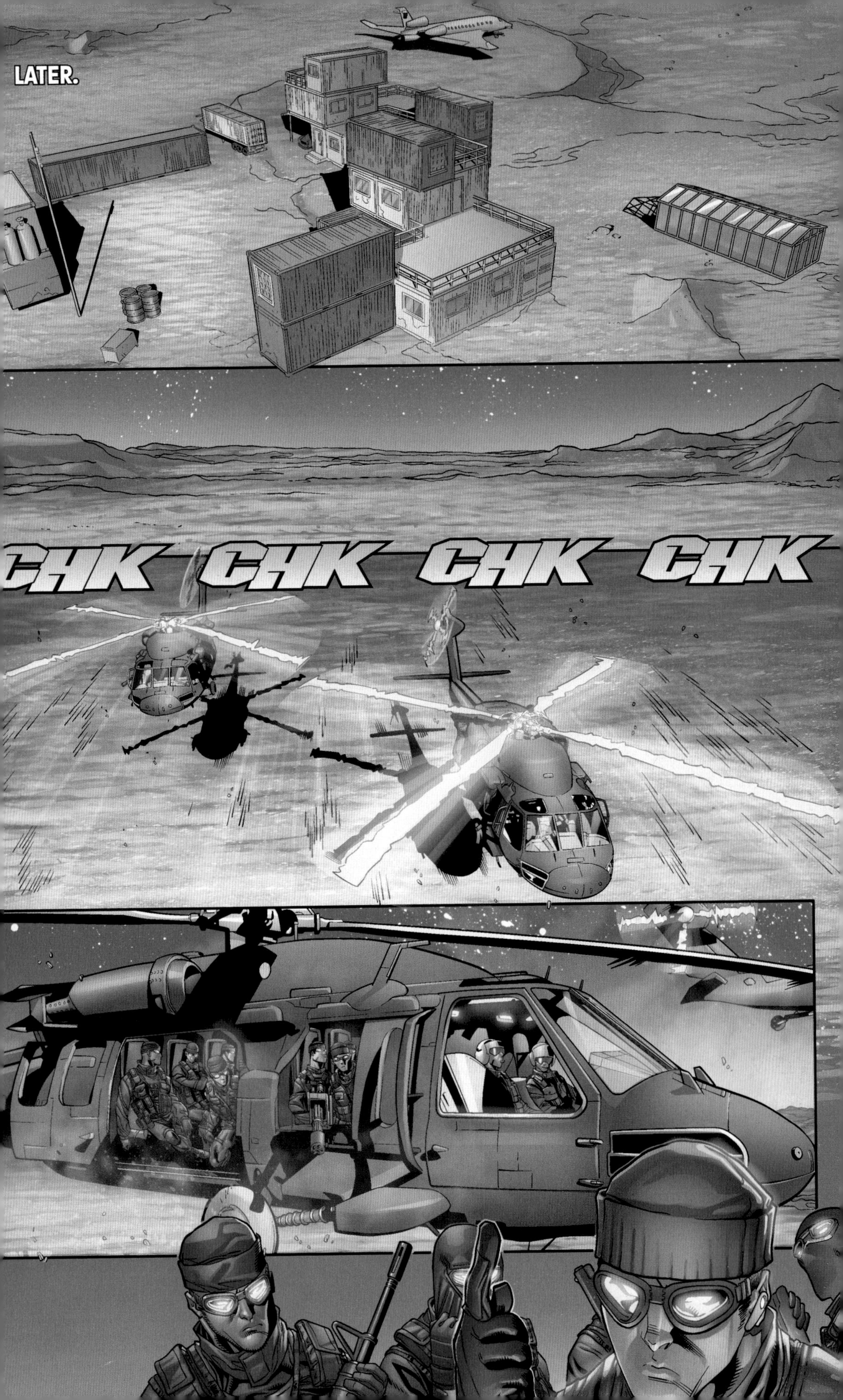
LATER.
CHK CHK CHK CHK

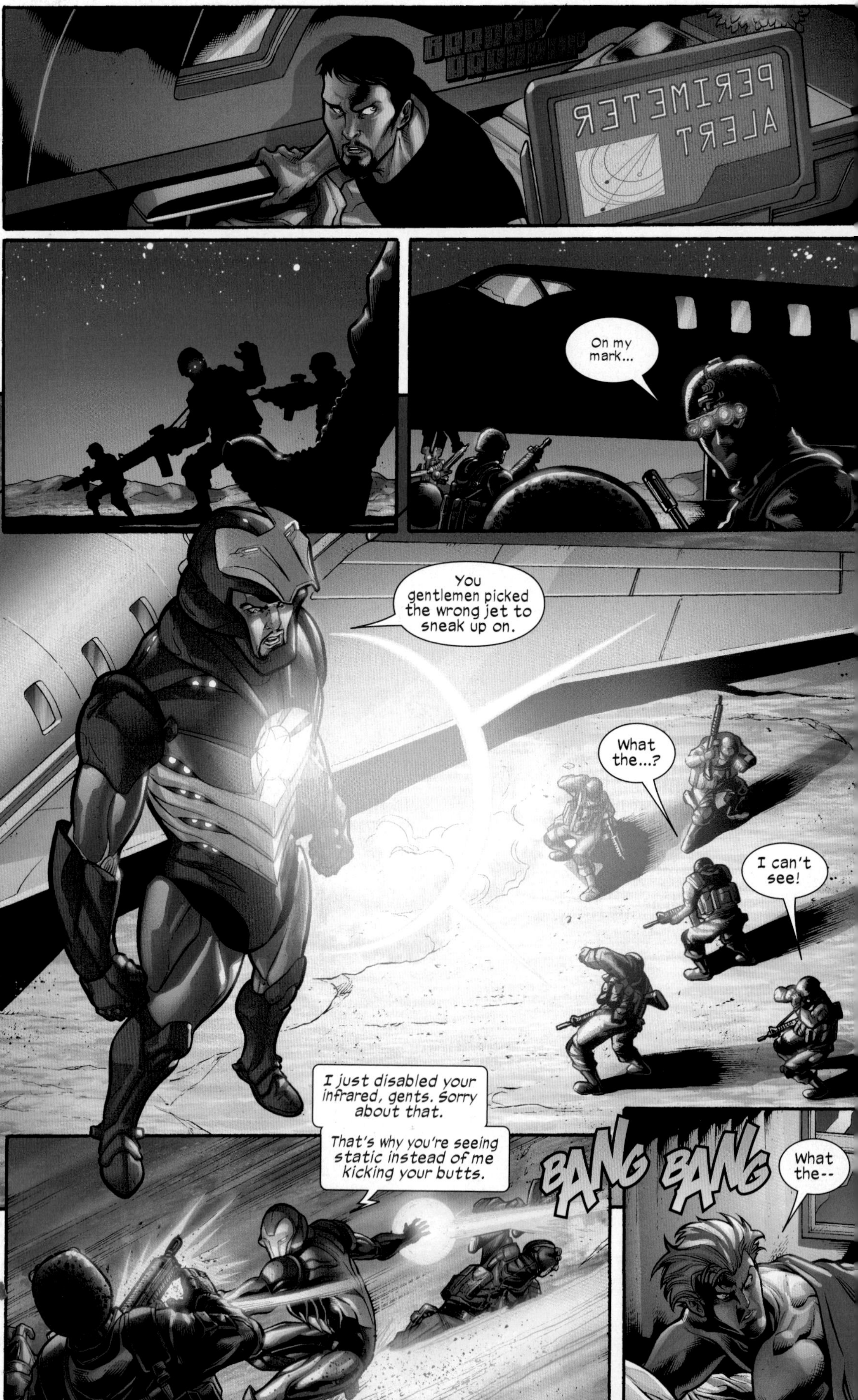

PERIMETER ALERT
On my mark...
You gentlemen picked the wrong jet to sneak up on.
What the...?
I can't see!
I just disabled your infrared, gents. Sorry about that.
That's why you're seeing static instead of me kicking your butts.
BANG BANG
What the--

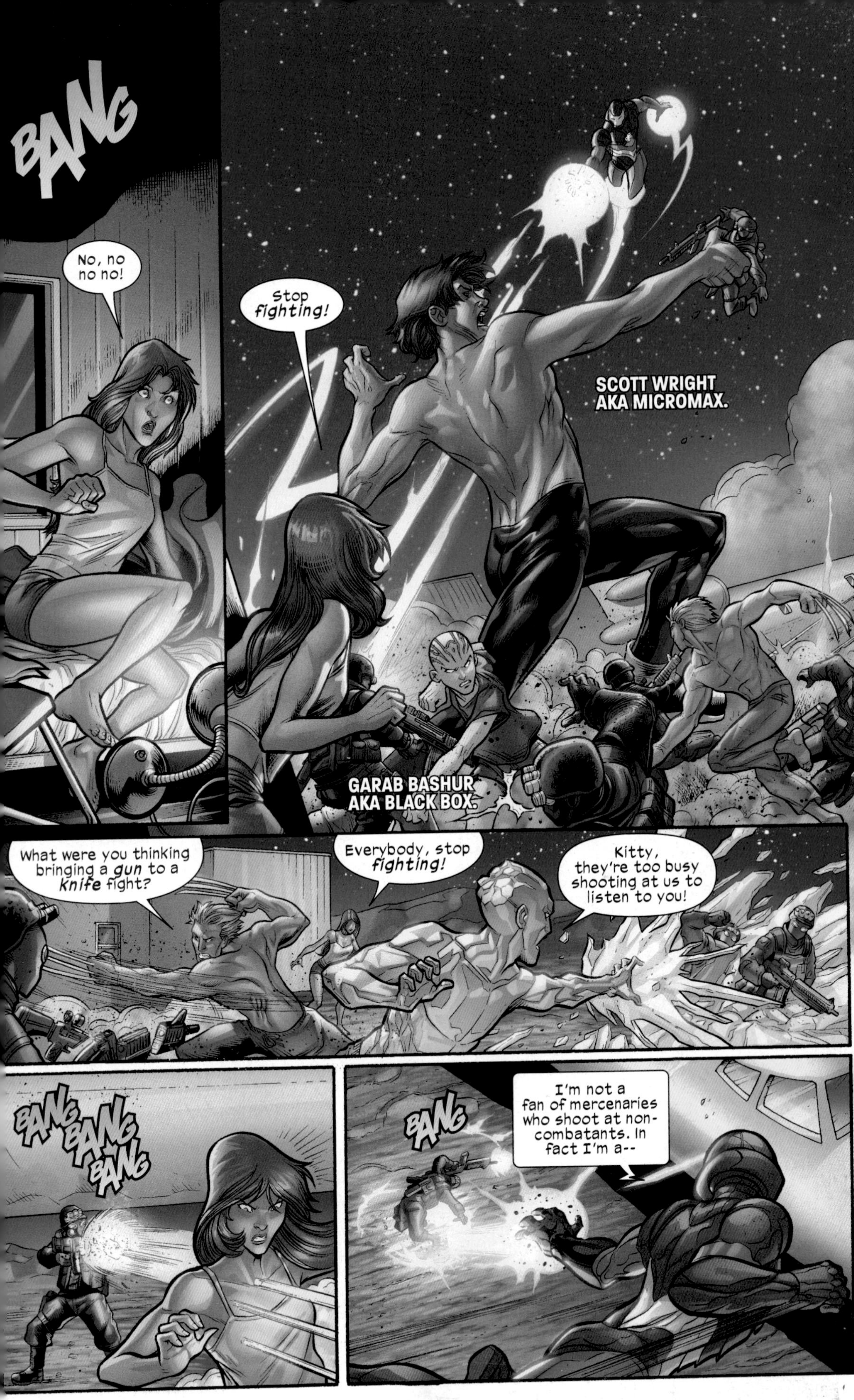

BANG
No, no no no!
Stop fighting!
SCOTT WRIGHT AKA MICROMAX.
GARAB BASHUR AKA BLACK BOX.
What were you thinking bringing a gun to a knife fight?
Everybody, stop fighting!
Kitty, they're too busy shooting at us to listen to you!
BANG BANG BANG
BANG
I'm not a fan of mercenaries who shoot at non-combatants. In fact I'm a--

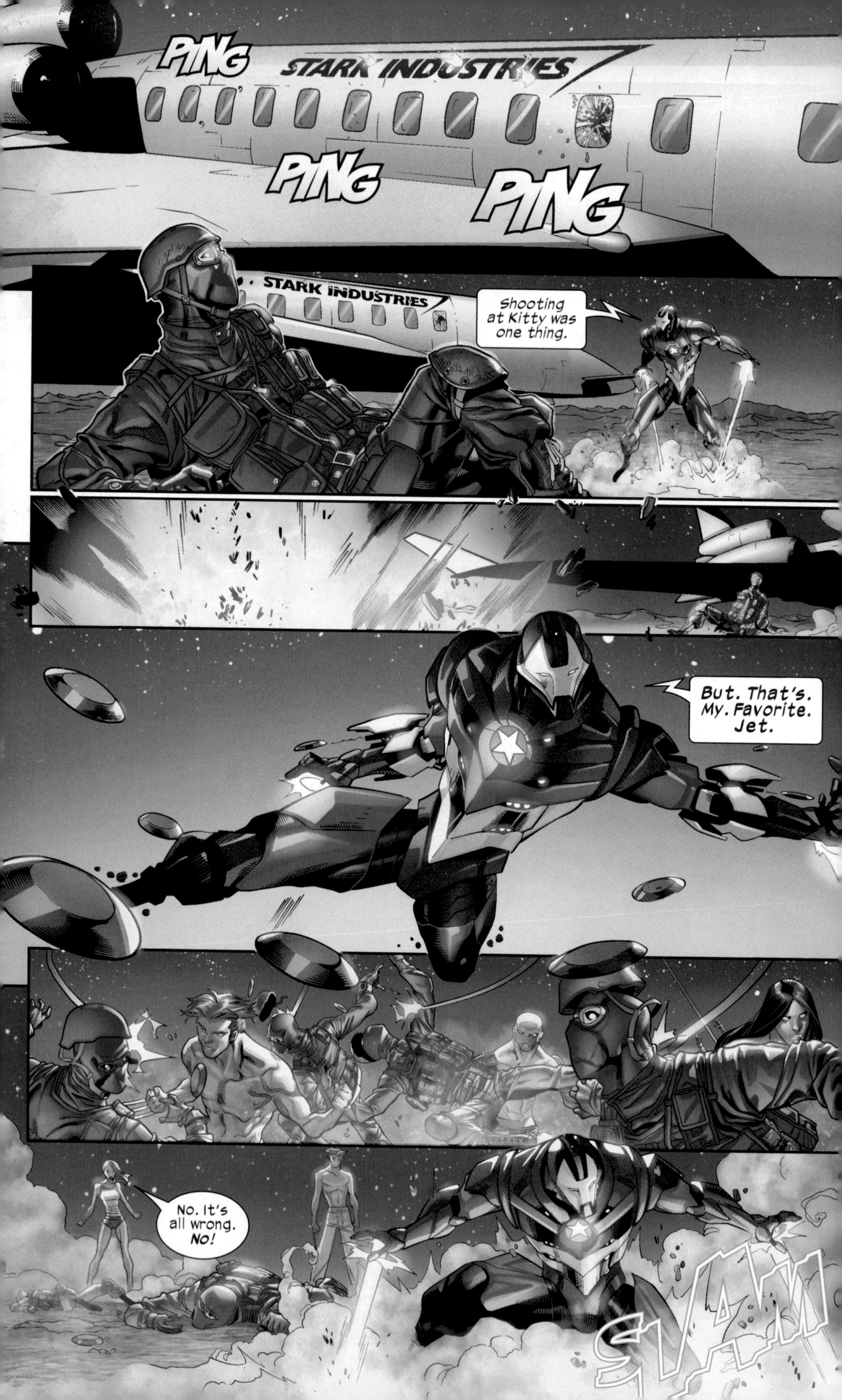
PING
STARK INDUSTRIES
PING
PING
STARK INDUSTRIES
Shooting at Kitty was one thing.
But. That's. My. Favorite. Jet.
No. It's all wrong. No!
SLAM

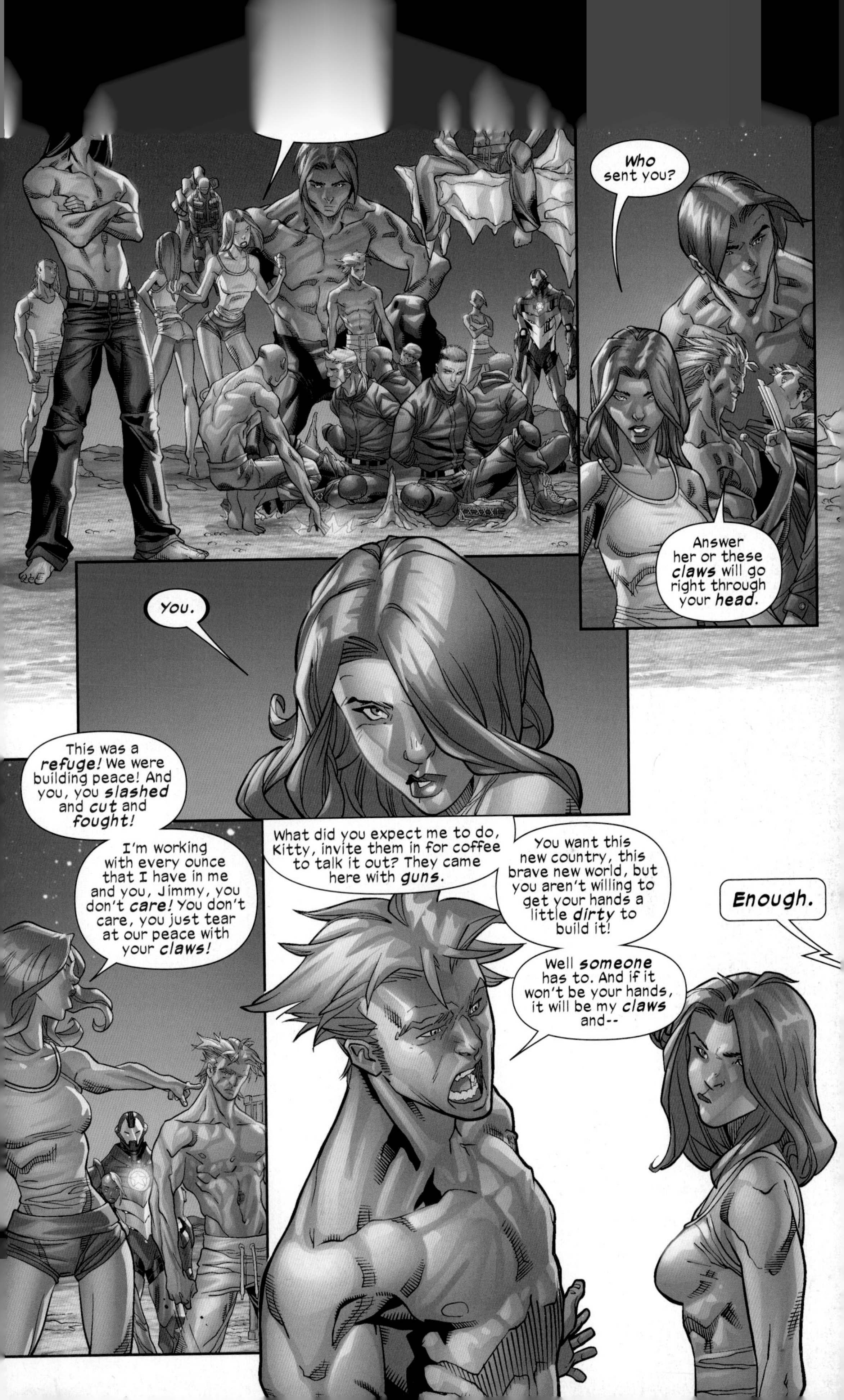
Who sent you?
Answer her or these claws will go right through your head.
You.
This was a refuge! We were building peace! And you, you slashed and cut and fought!
I'm working with every ounce that I have in me and you, Jimmy, you don't care! You don't care, you just tear at our peace with your claws!
What did you expect me to do, Kitty, invite them in for coffee to talk it out? They came here with guns.
You want this new country, this brave new world, but you aren't willing to get your hands a little dirty to build it!
Well someone has to. And if it won't be your hands, it will be my claws and--
Enough.

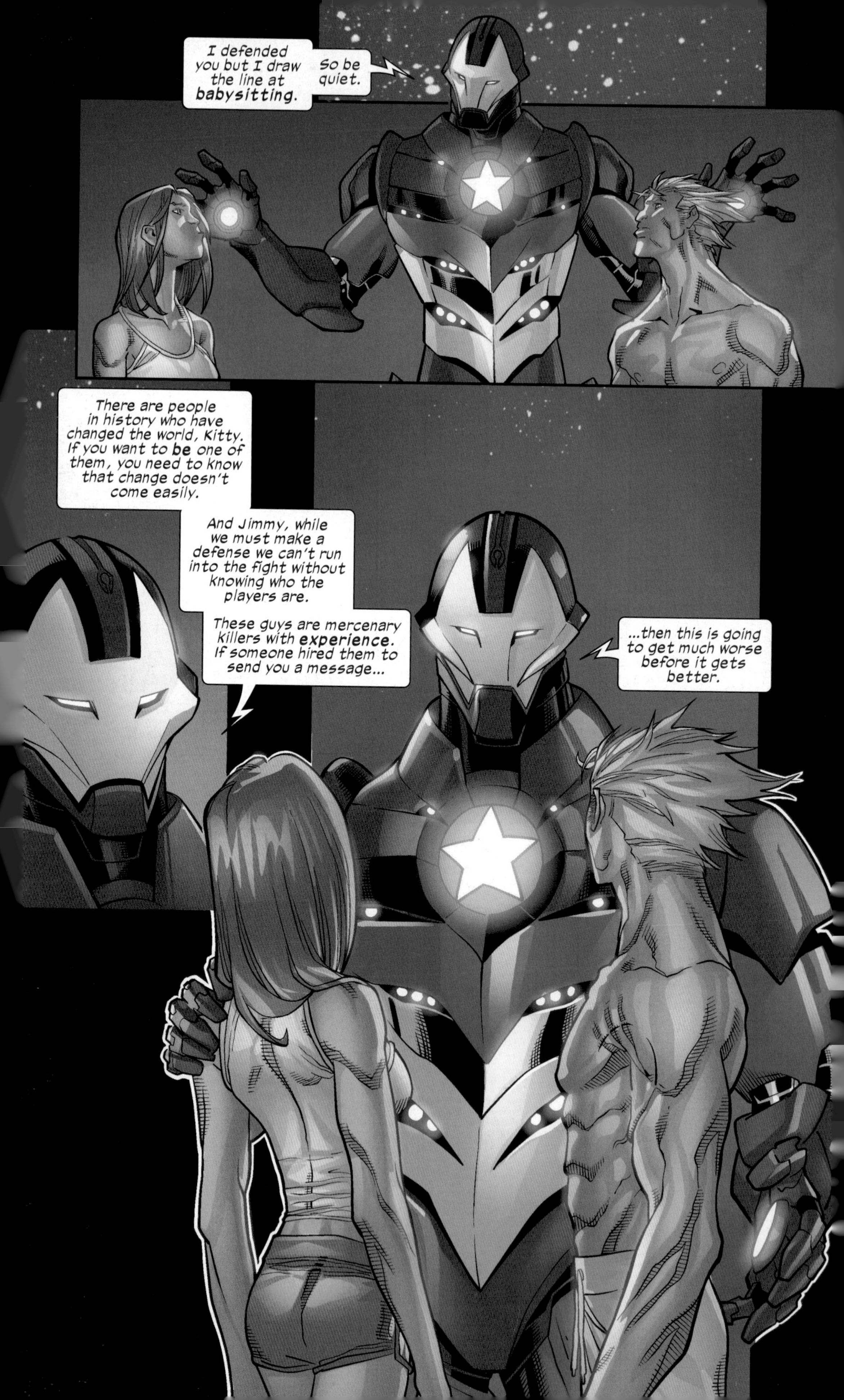

I defended you but I draw the line at babysitting.
So be quiet.
There are people in history who have changed the world, Kitty. If you want to be one of them, you need to know that change doesn't come easily.
And Jimmy, while we must make a defense we can't run into the fight without knowing who the players are.
These guys are mercenary killers with experience. If someone hired them to send you a message...
...then this is going to get much worse before it gets better.

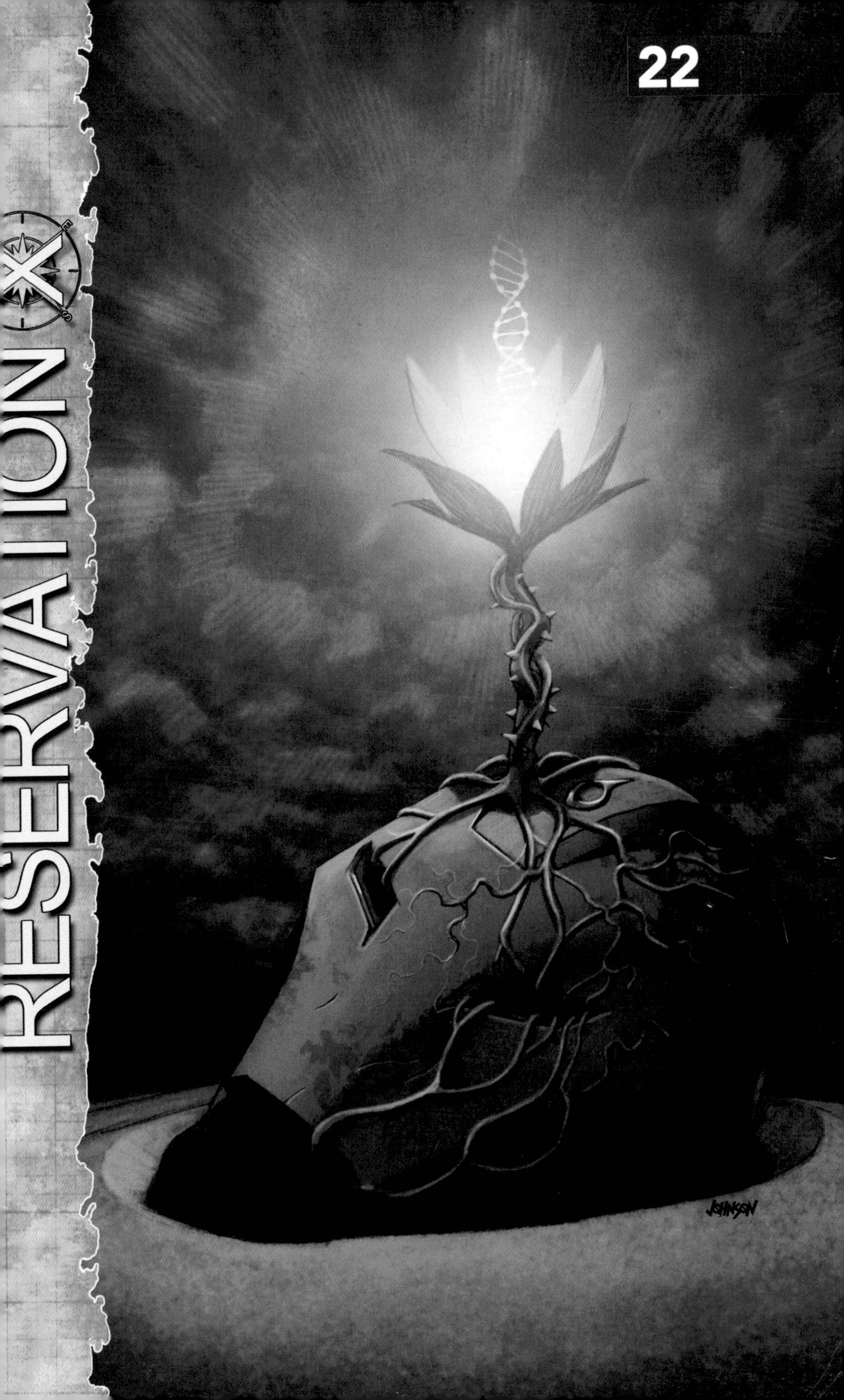

RESERVATION X
22
JOHNSON

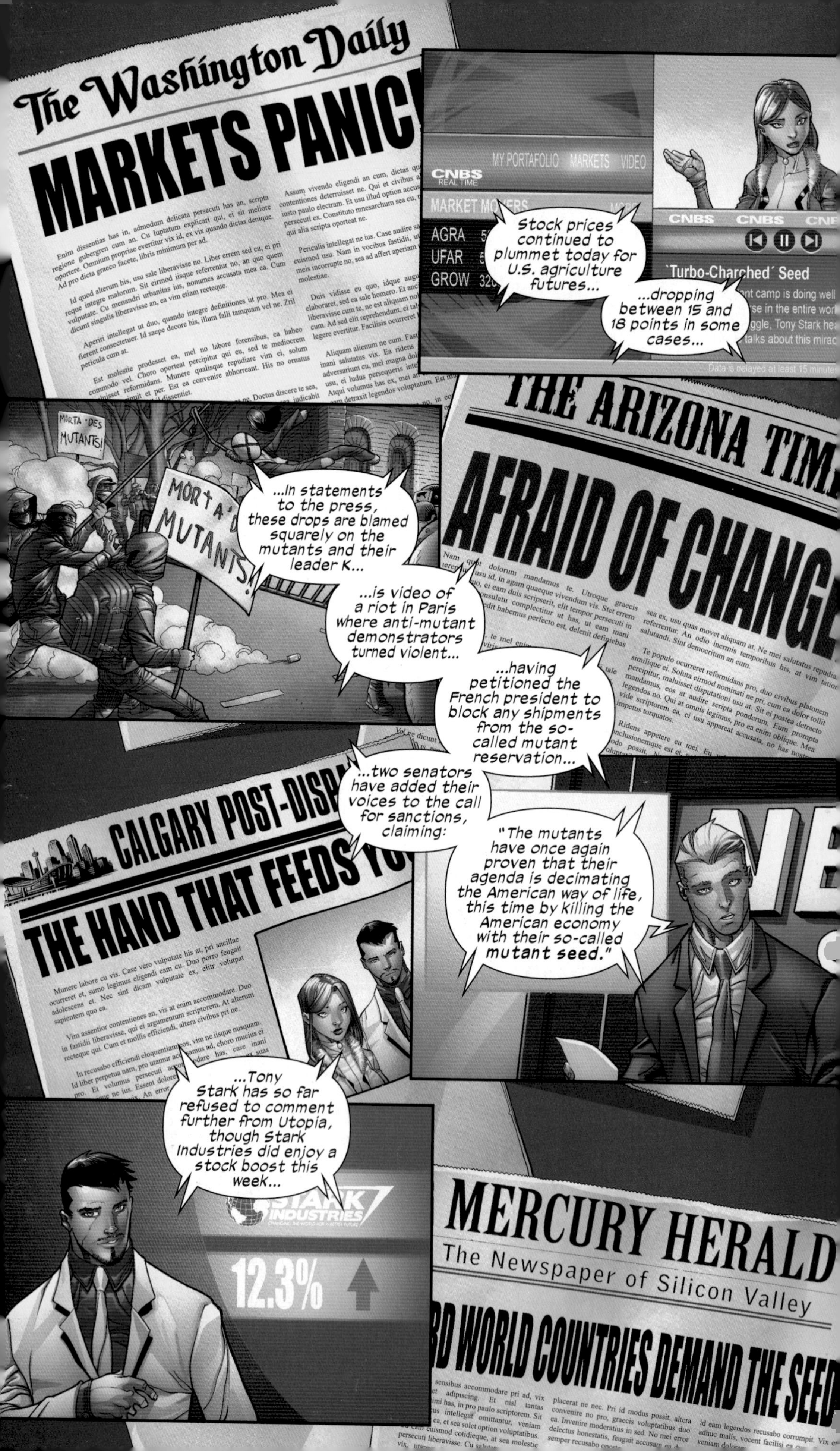

The Washington Daily
MARKETS PANIC
MY PORTAFOLIO MARKETS VIDEO
CNBS REAL TIME
AGRA
UFAR
GROW
CNBS CNBS
`Turbo-Charched´ Seed
Stock prices continued to plummet today for U.S. agriculture futures...
...dropping between 15 and 18 points in some cases...
Data is delayed at least 15 minutes
THE ARIZONA TIM
AFRAID OF CHANGE
MORTA · DES MUTANTS!
MORT A'D MUTANTS!
...In statements to the press, these drops are blamed squarely on the mutants and their leader K...
...is video of a riot in Paris where anti-mutant demonstrators turned violent...
...having petitioned the French president to block any shipments from the so-called mutant reservation...
...two senators have added their voices to the call for sanctions, claiming:
CALGARY POST-DISPA
THE HAND THAT FEEDS YO
"The mutants have once again proven that their agenda is decimating the American way of life, this time by killing the American economy with their so-called mutant seed."
...Tony Stark has so far refused to comment further from Utopia, though Stark Industries did enjoy a stock boost this week...
STARK INDUSTRIES
12.3%
MERCURY HERALD
The Newspaper of Silicon Valley
RD WORLD COUNTRIES DEMAND THE SEED

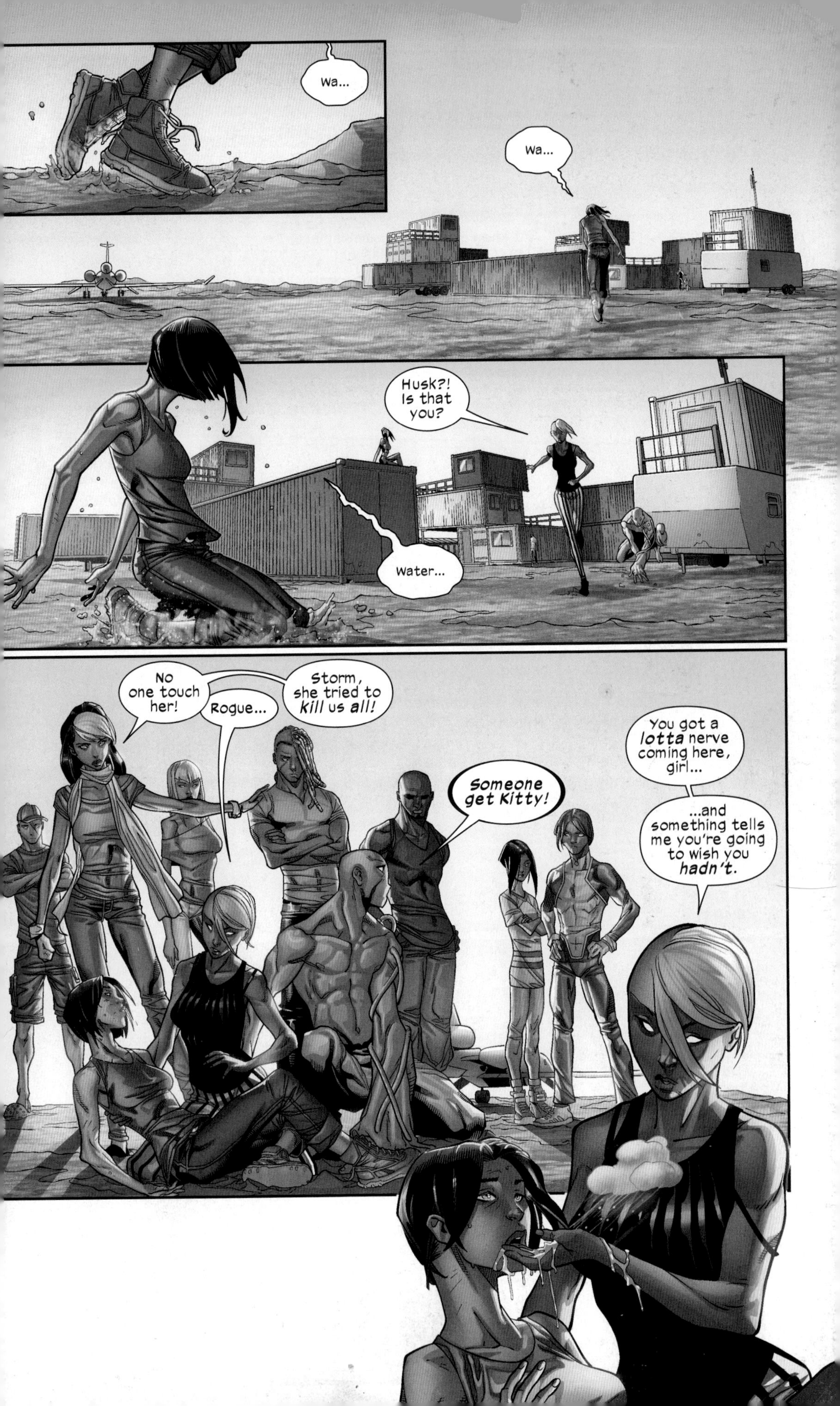

Wa...
Wa...
Husk?! Is that you?
Water...
No one touch her!
Storm, she tried to kill us all!
Rogue...
Someone get Kitty!
You got a lotta nerve coming here, girl...
...and something tells me you're going to wish you hadn't.

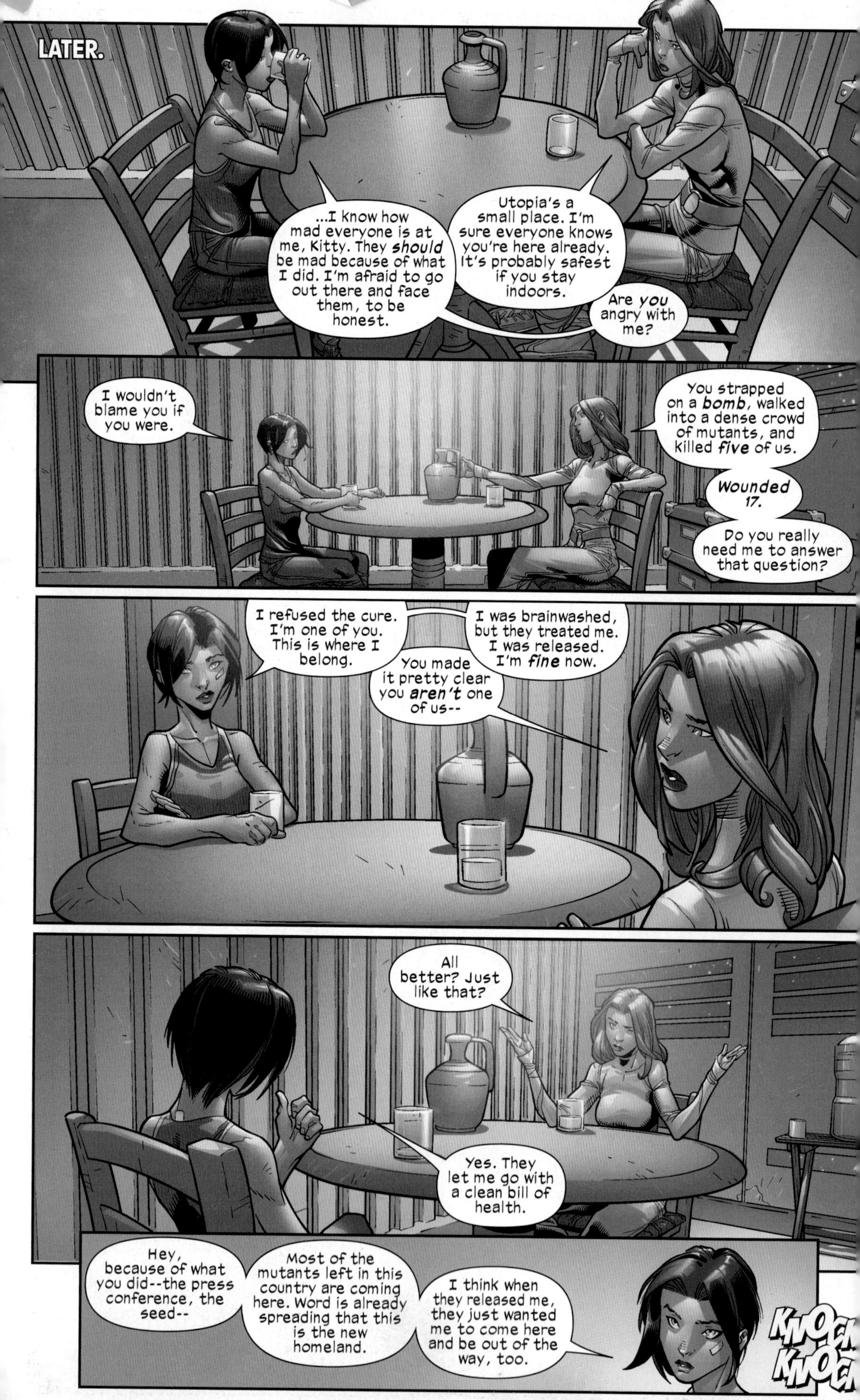

LATER.
...I know how mad everyone is at me, Kitty. They should be mad because of what I did. I'm afraid to go out there and face them, to be honest.
Utopia's a small place. I'm sure everyone knows you're here already. It's probably safest if you stay indoors.
Are you angry with me?
I wouldn't blame you if you were.
You strapped on a bomb, walked into a dense crowd of mutants, and killed five of us.
Wounded 17.
Do you really need me to answer that question?
I refused the cure. I'm one of you. This is where I belong.
You made it pretty clear you aren't one of us--
I was brainwashed, but they treated me. I was released. I'm fine now.
All better? Just like that?
Yes. They let me go with a clean bill of health.
Hey, because of what you did--the press conference, the seed--
Most of the mutants left in this country are coming here. Word is already spreading that this is the new homeland.
I think when they released me, they just wanted me to come here and be out of the way, too.
KNOCK KNOCK

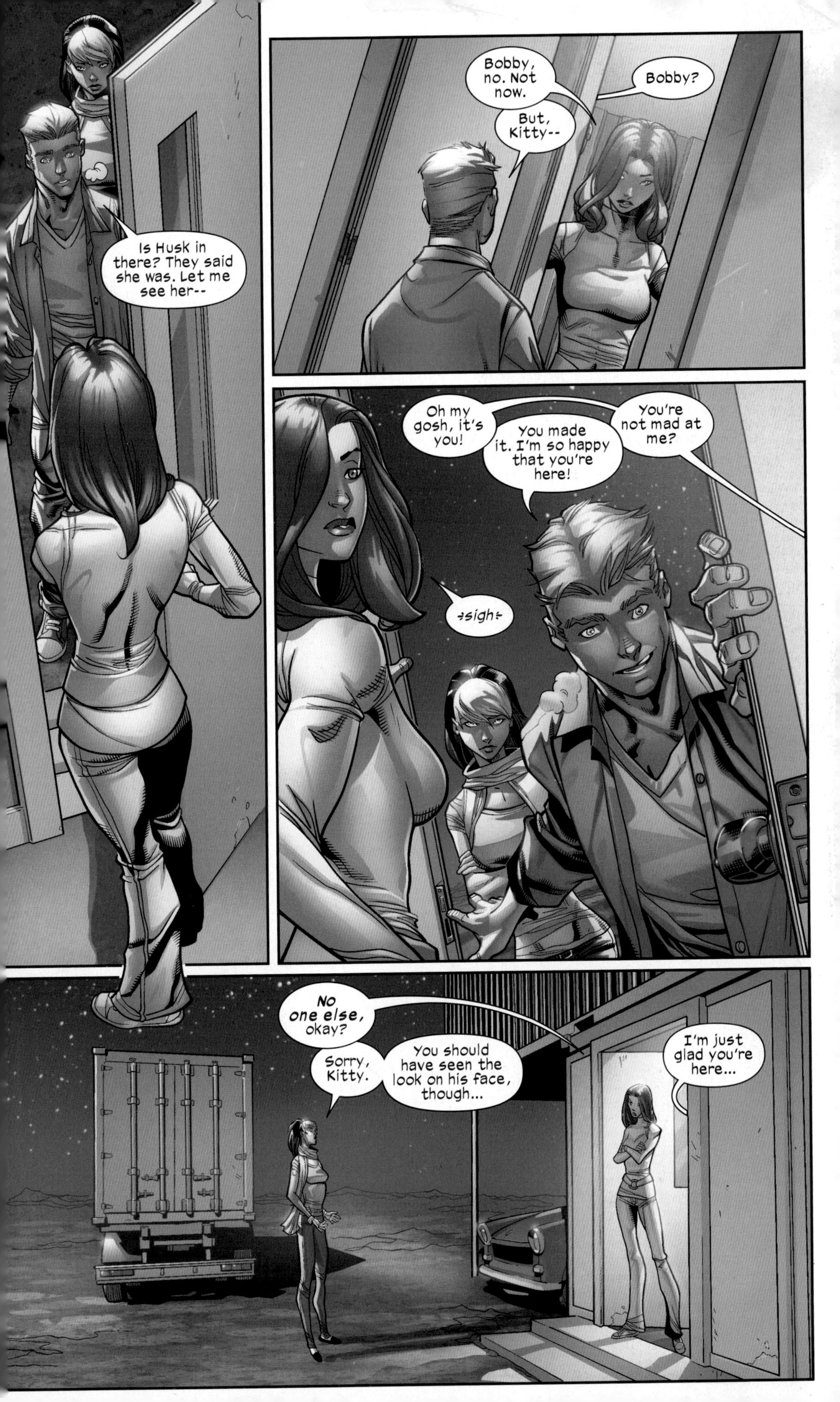
Is Husk in there? They said she was. Let me see her--
Bobby, no. Not now.
Bobby?
But, Kitty--
Oh my gosh, it's you!
You made it. I'm so happy that you're here!
You're not mad at me?
=sigh=
No one else, okay?
Sorry, Kitty.
You should have seen the look on his face, though...
I'm just glad you're here...

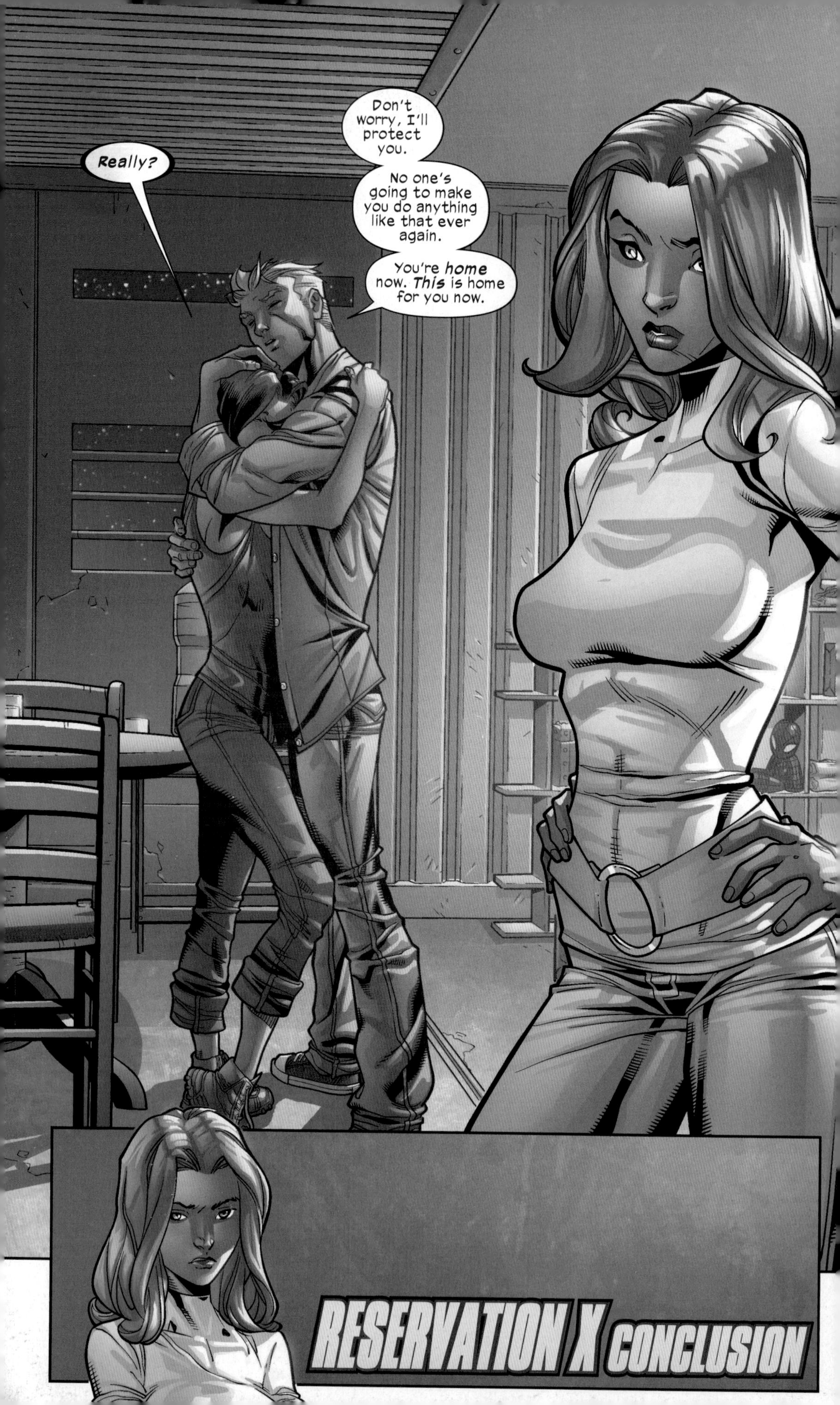
Don't worry, I'll protect you.
Really?
No one's going to make you do anything like that ever again.
You're *home* now. *This* is home for you now.
RESERVATION X CONCLUSION

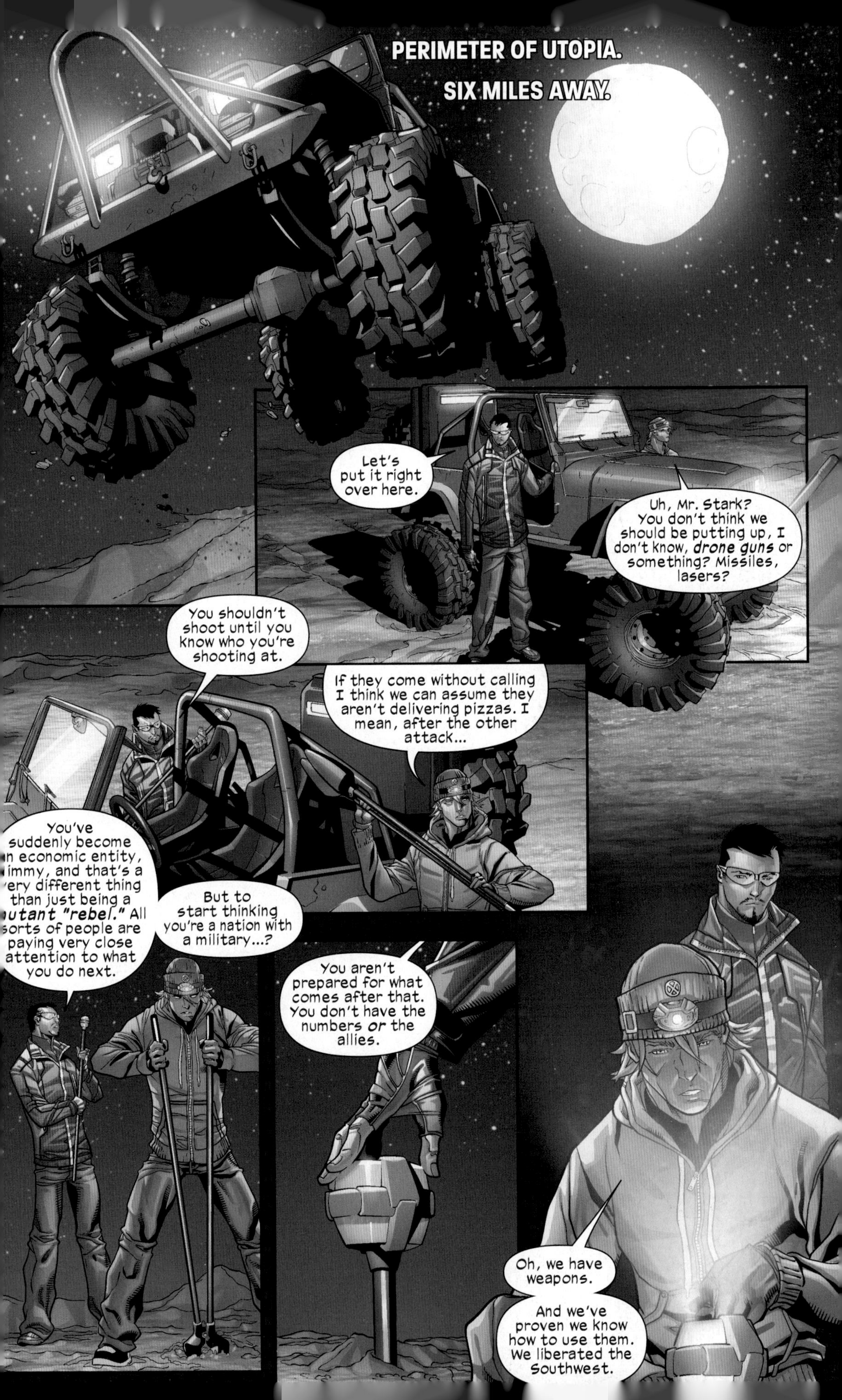
PERIMETER OF UTOPIA.
SIX MILES AWAY.
Let's put it right over here.
Uh, Mr. Stark? You don't think we should be putting up, I don't know, *drone guns* or something? Missiles, lasers?
You shouldn't shoot until you know who you're shooting at.
If they come without calling I think we can assume they aren't delivering pizzas. I mean, after the other attack...
You've suddenly become n economic entity, immy, and that's a ery different thing than just being a utant "rebel." All sorts of people are paying very close attention to what you do next.
But to start thinking you're a nation with a military...?
You aren't prepared for what comes after that. You don't have the numbers *or* the allies.
Oh, we have weapons.
And we've proven we know how to use them. We liberated the Southwest.

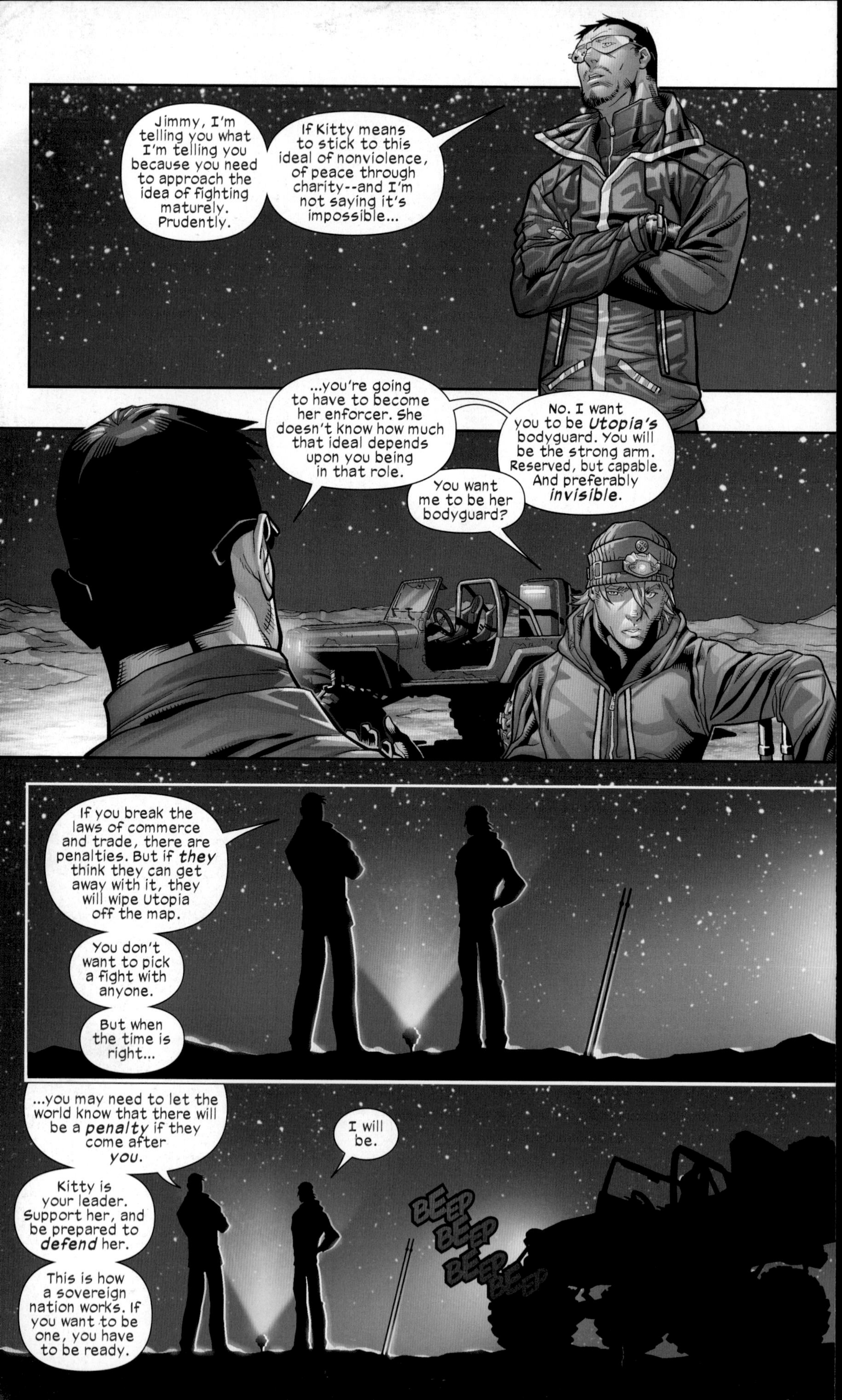
Jimmy, I'm telling you what I'm telling you because you need to approach the idea of fighting maturely. Prudently.
If Kitty means to stick to this ideal of nonviolence, of peace through charity--and I'm not saying it's impossible...
...you're going to have to become her enforcer. She doesn't know how much that ideal depends upon you being in that role.
You want me to be her bodyguard?
No. I want you to be *Utopia's* bodyguard. You will be the strong arm. Reserved, but capable. And preferably *invisible*.
If you break the laws of commerce and trade, there are penalties. But if *they* think they can get away with it, they will wipe Utopia off the map.
You don't want to pick a fight with anyone.
But when the time is right...
...you may need to let the world know that there will be a *penalty* if they come after *you*.
I will be.
Kitty is your leader. Support her, and be prepared to *defend* her.
This is how a sovereign nation works. If you want to be one, you have to be ready.
BEEP BEEP BEEP BEEP

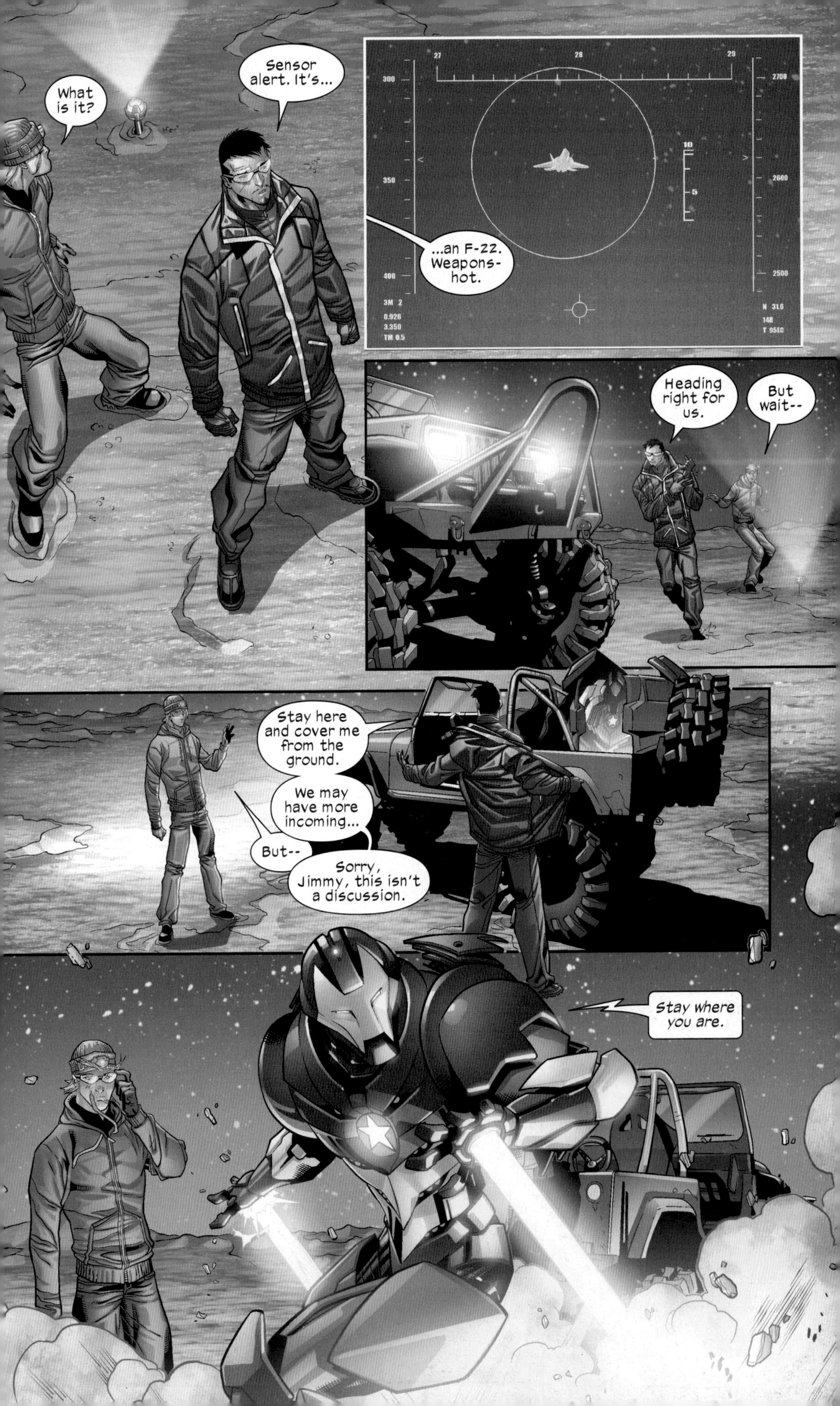

What is it?
Sensor alert. It's...
...an F-22. Weapons-hot.
Heading right for us.
But wait--
Stay here and cover me from the ground.
We may have more incoming...
But--
Sorry, Jimmy, this isn't a discussion.
Stay where you are.

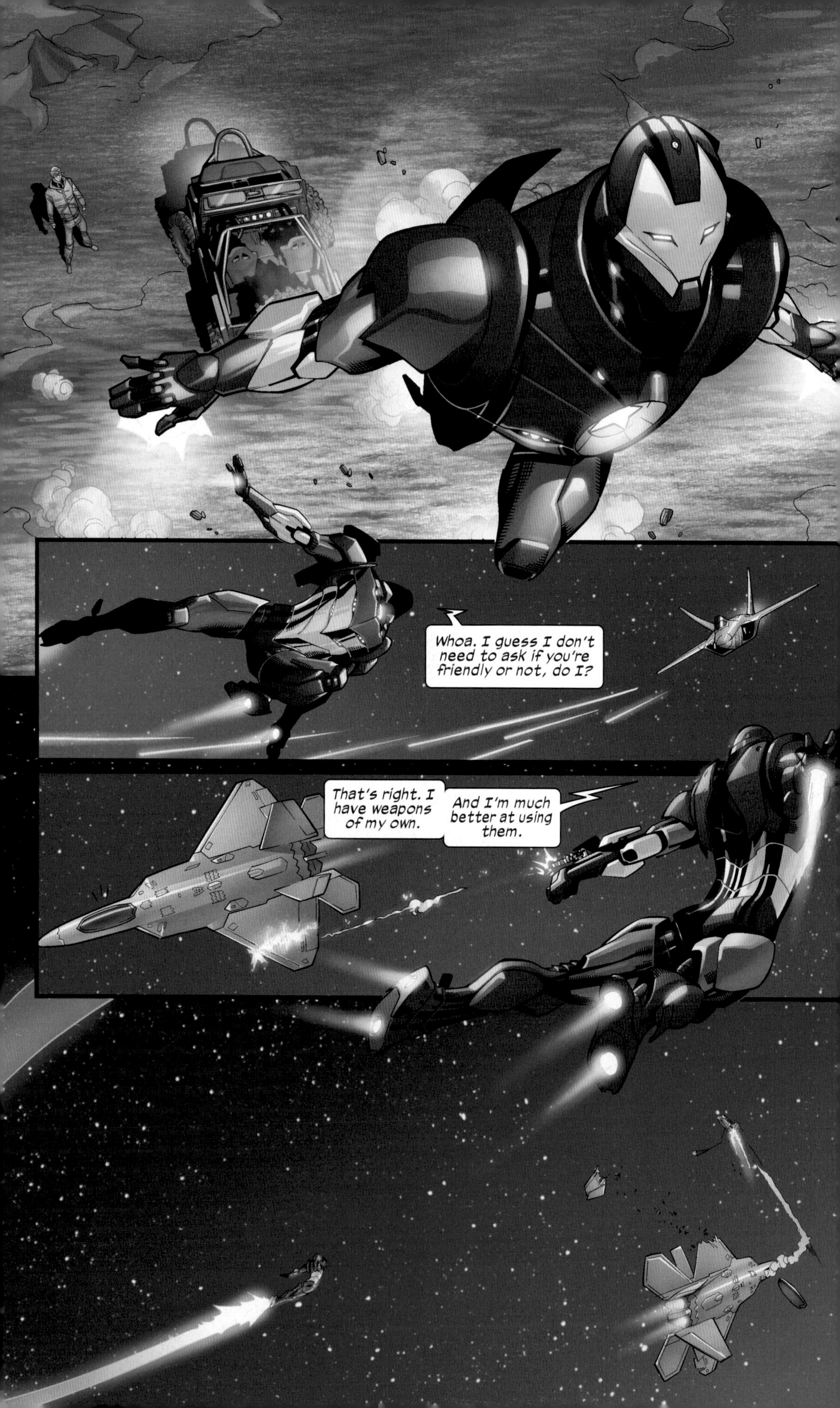
Whoa. I guess I don't need to ask if you're friendly or not, do I?
That's right. I have weapons of my own.
And I'm much better at using them.

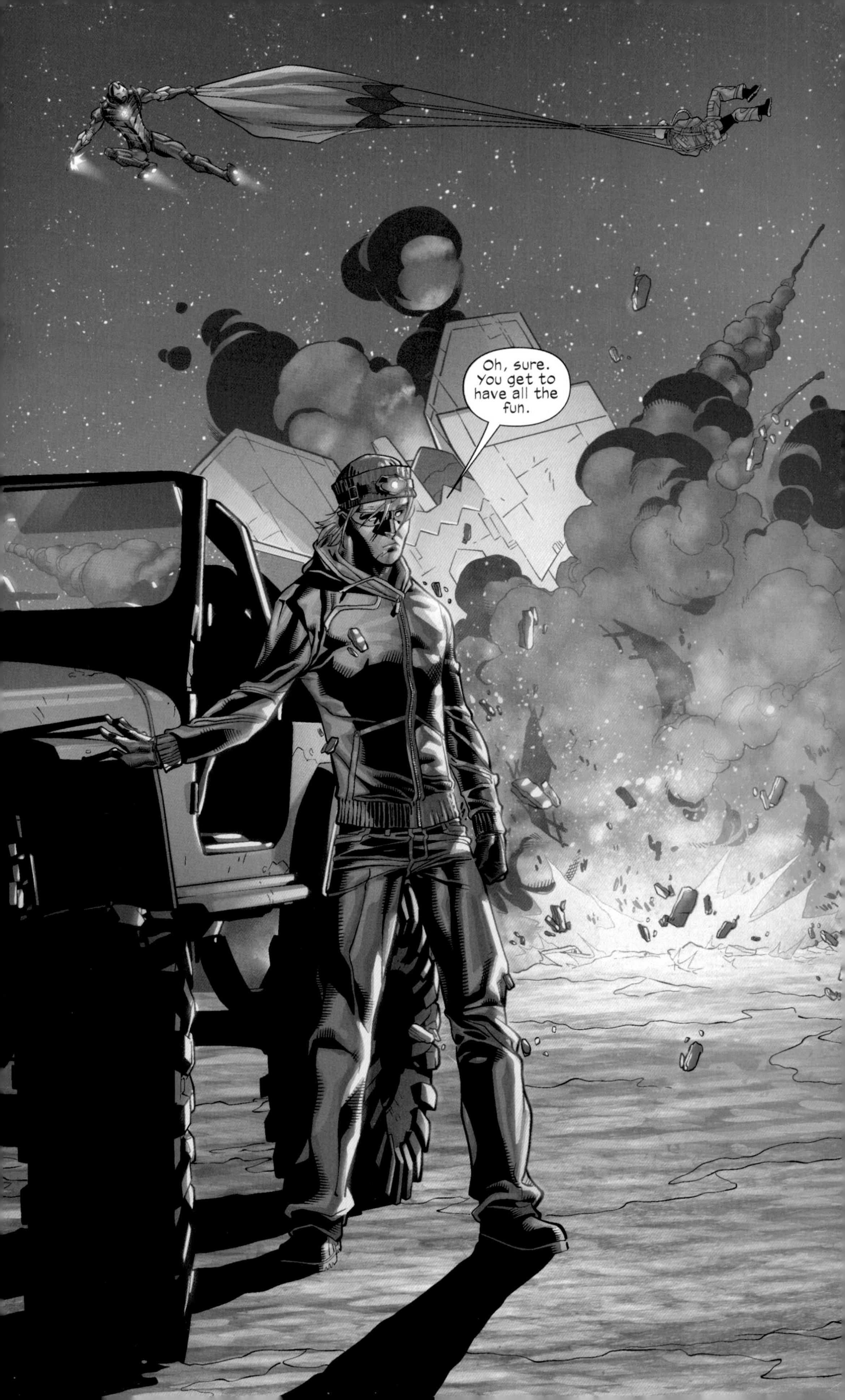
Oh, sure. You get to have all the fun.

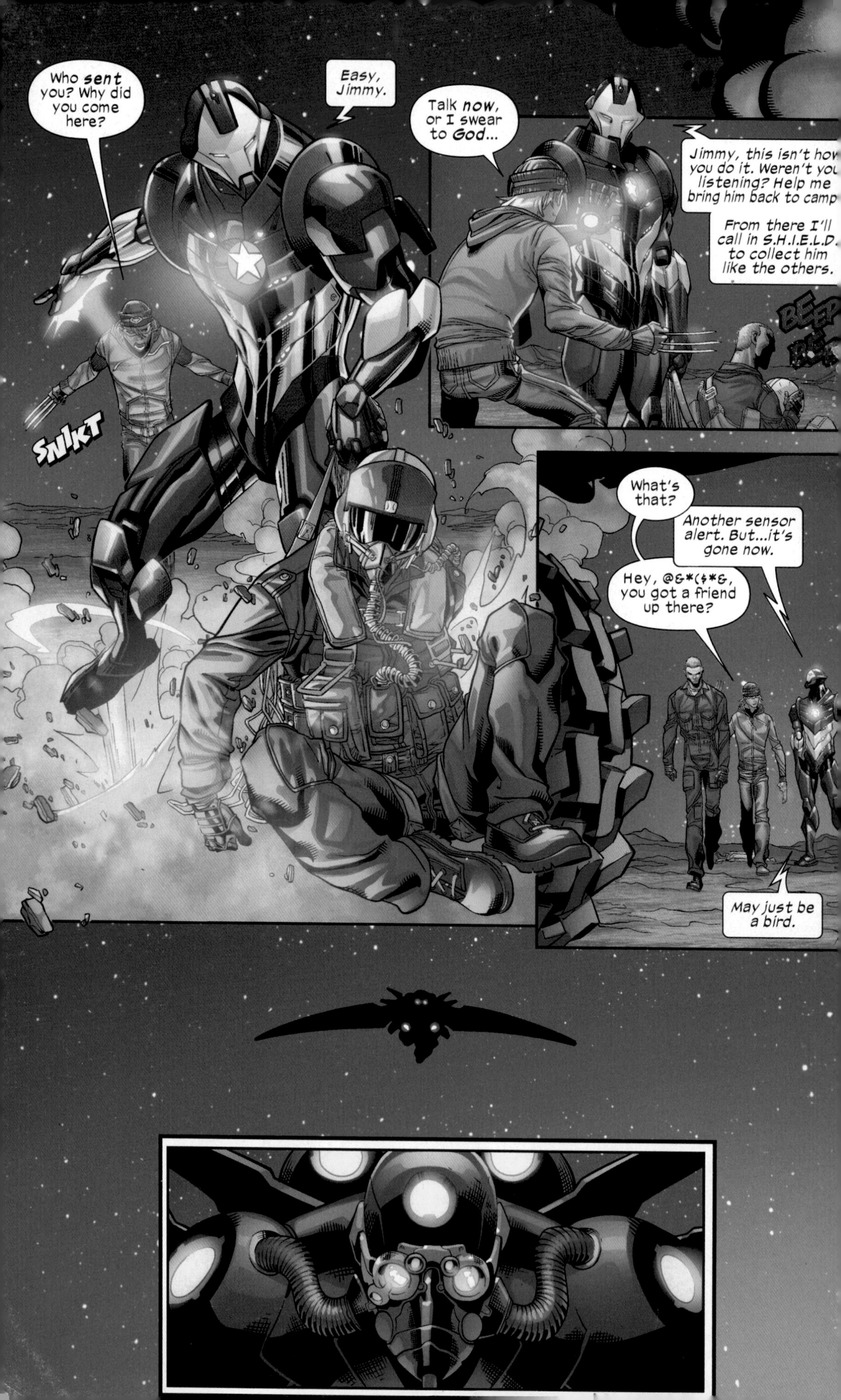
Who sent you? Why did you come here?
Easy, Jimmy.
SNIKT
Talk now, or I swear to God...
Jimmy, this isn't how you do it. Weren't you listening? Help me bring him back to camp.
From there I'll call in S.H.I.E.L.D. to collect him like the others.
What's that?
Another sensor alert. But...it's gone now.
Hey, @&*($*&, you got a friend up there?
May just be a bird.

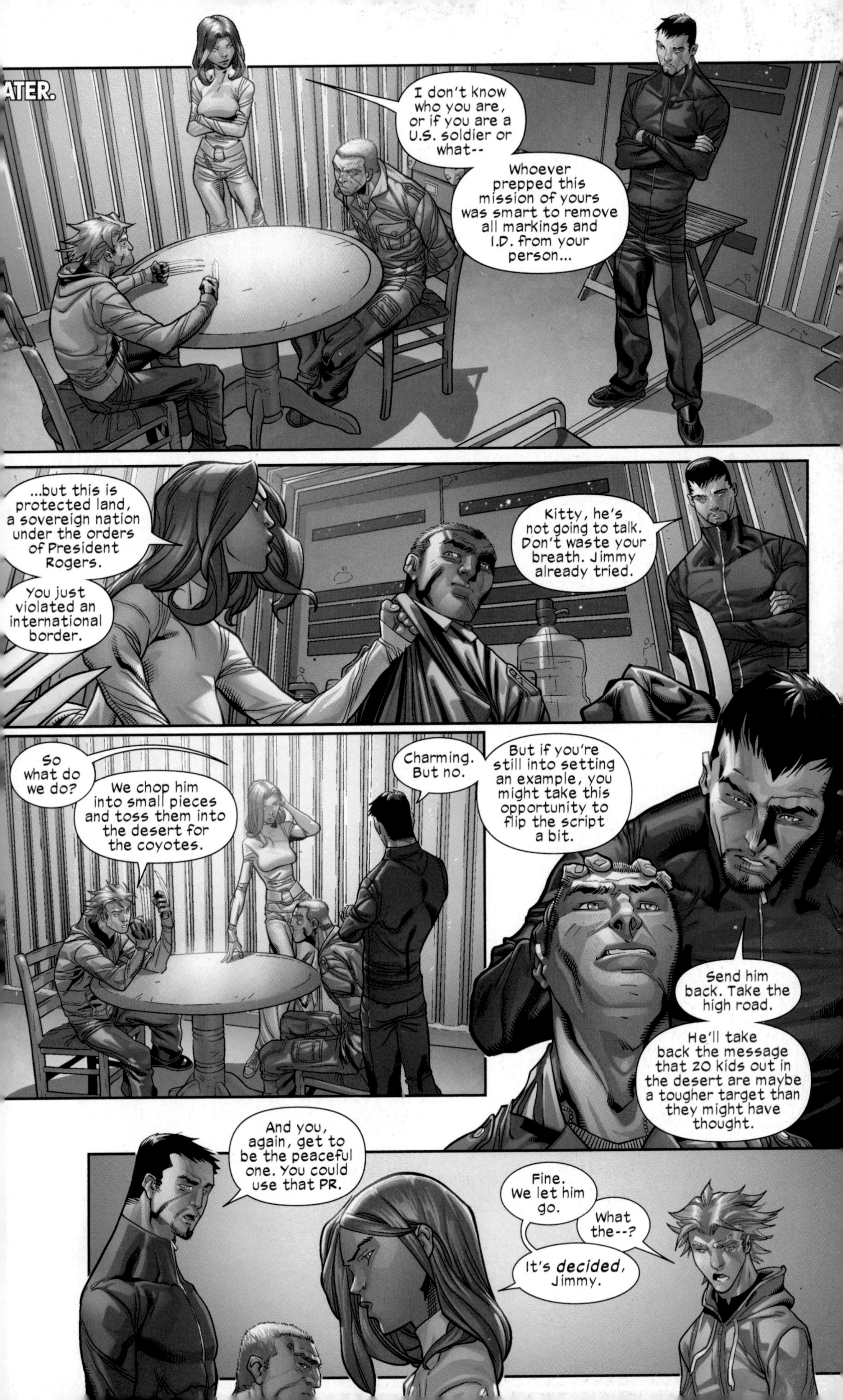
ATER.
I don't know who you are, or if you are a U.S. soldier or what--
Whoever prepped this mission of yours was smart to remove all markings and I.D. from your person...
...but this is protected land, a sovereign nation under the orders of President Rogers.
You just violated an international border.
Kitty, he's not going to talk. Don't waste your breath. Jimmy already tried.
So what do we do?
We chop him into small pieces and toss them into the desert for the coyotes.
Charming. But no.
But if you're still into setting an example, you might take this opportunity to flip the script a bit.
Send him back. Take the high road.
He'll take back the message that 20 kids out in the desert are maybe a tougher target than they might have thought.
And you, again, get to be the peaceful one. You could use that PR.
Fine. We let him go.
What the--?
It's *decided*, Jimmy.

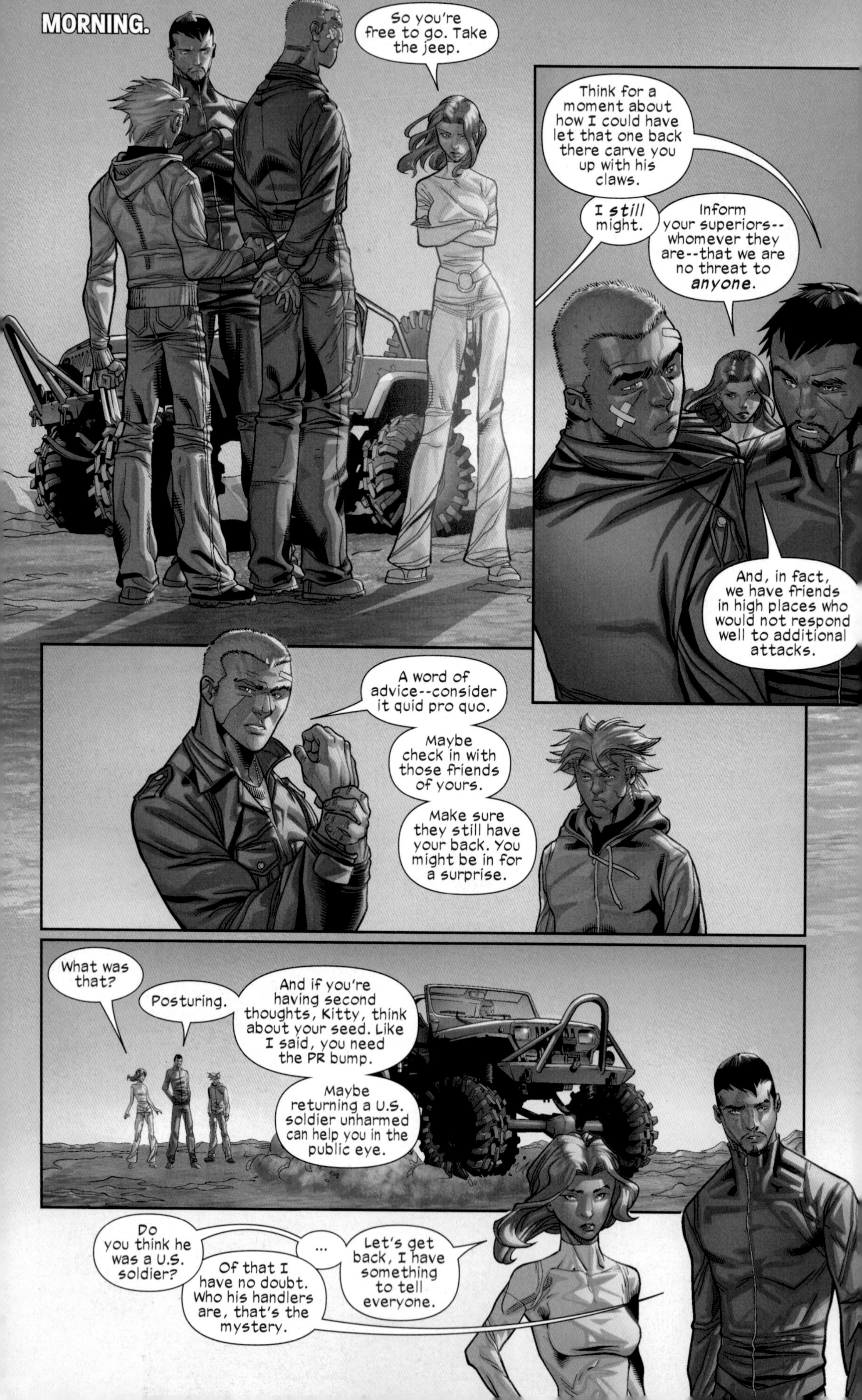
MORNING.
So you're free to go. Take the jeep.
Think for a moment about how I could have let that one back there carve you up with his claws.
I *still* might.
Inform your superiors--whomever they are--that we are no threat to *anyone*.
And, in fact, we have friends in high places who would not respond well to additional attacks.
A word of advice--consider it quid pro quo.
Maybe check in with those friends of yours.
Make sure they still have your back. You might be in for a surprise.
What was that?
Posturing.
And if you're having second thoughts, Kitty, think about your seed. Like I said, you need the PR bump.
Maybe returning a U.S. soldier unharmed can help you in the public eye.
Do you think he was a U.S. soldier?
Of that I have no doubt. Who his handlers are, that's the mystery.
...
Let's get back, I have something to tell everyone.

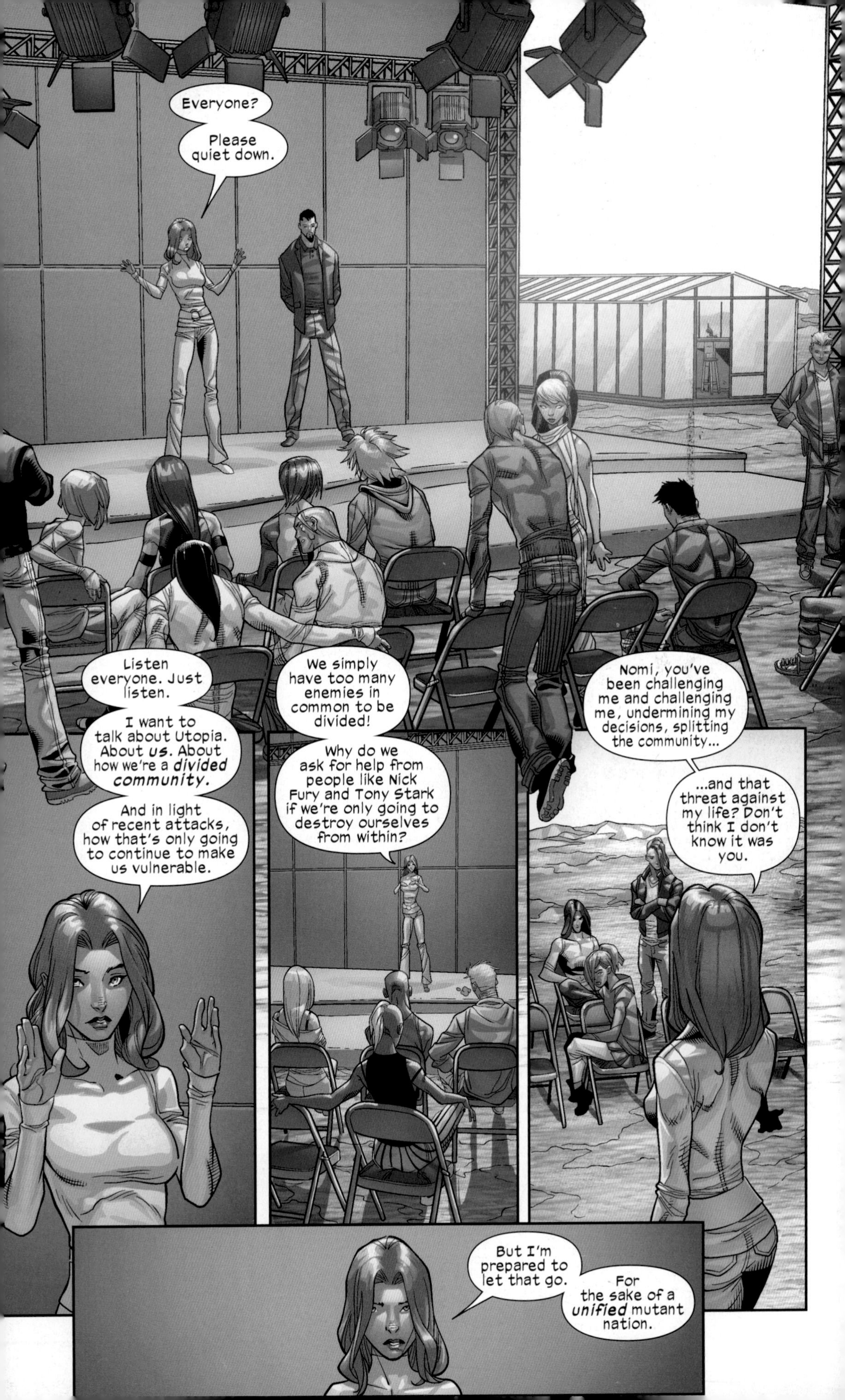

Everyone?
Please quiet down.
Listen everyone. Just listen.
I want to talk about Utopia. About *us*. About how we're a *divided community*.
And in light of recent attacks, how that's only going to continue to make us vulnerable.
We simply have too many enemies in common to be divided!
Why do we ask for help from people like Nick Fury and Tony Stark if we're only going to destroy ourselves from within?
Nomi, you've been challenging me and challenging me, undermining my decisions, splitting the community...
...and that threat against my life? Don't think I don't know it was you.
But I'm prepared to let that go.
For the sake of a *unified* mutant nation.

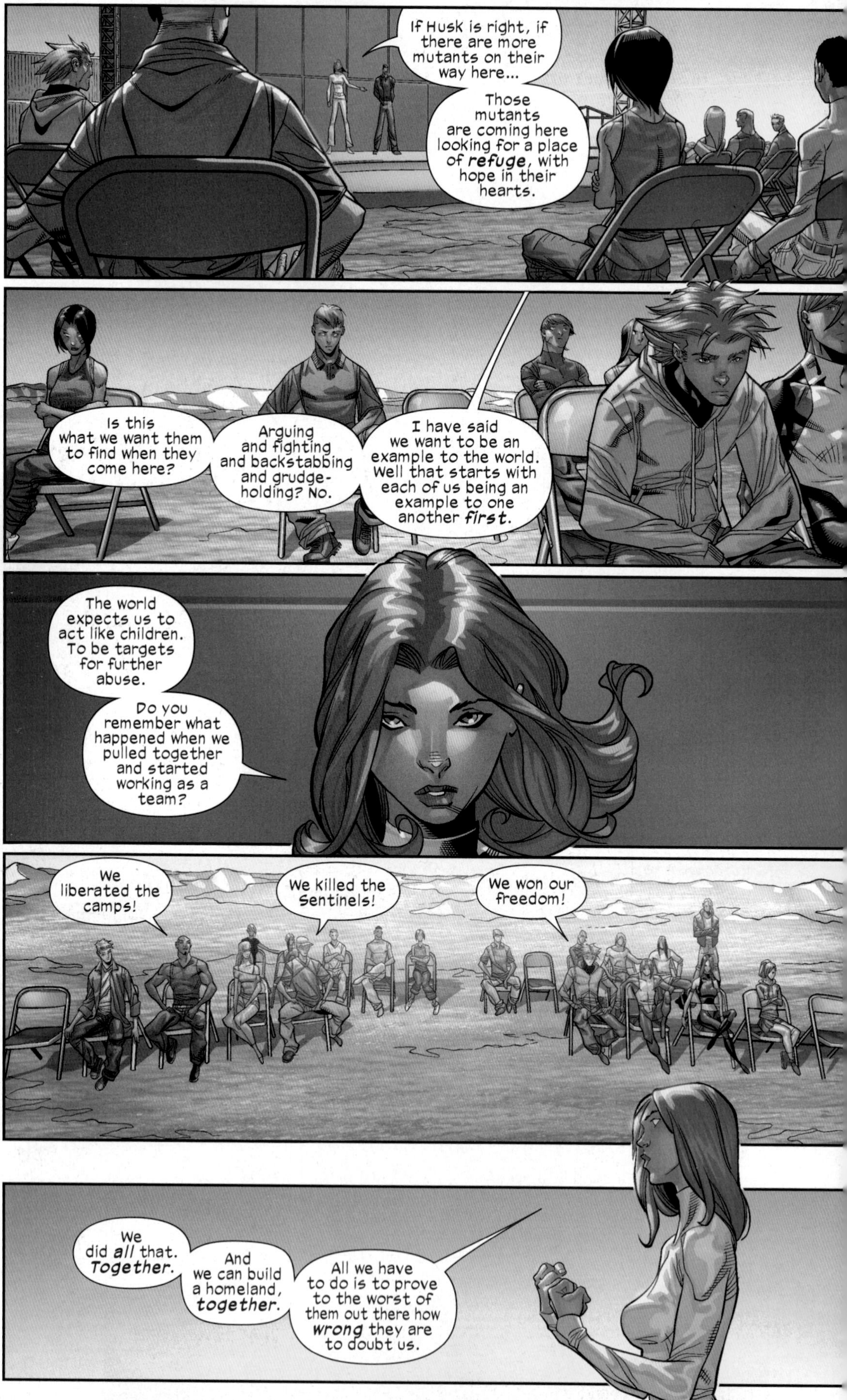

If Husk is right, if there are more mutants on their way here...
Those mutants are coming here looking for a place of *refuge*, with hope in their hearts.
Is this what we want them to find when they come here?
Arguing and fighting and backstabbing and grudge-holding? No.
I have said we want to be an example to the world. Well that starts with each of us being an example to one another *first*.
The world expects us to act like children. To be targets for further abuse.
Do you remember what happened when we pulled together and started working as a team?
We liberated the camps!
We killed the Sentinels!
We won our freedom!
We did *all* that. *Together*.
And we can build a homeland, *together*.
All we have to do is to prove to the worst of them out there how *wrong* they are to doubt us.

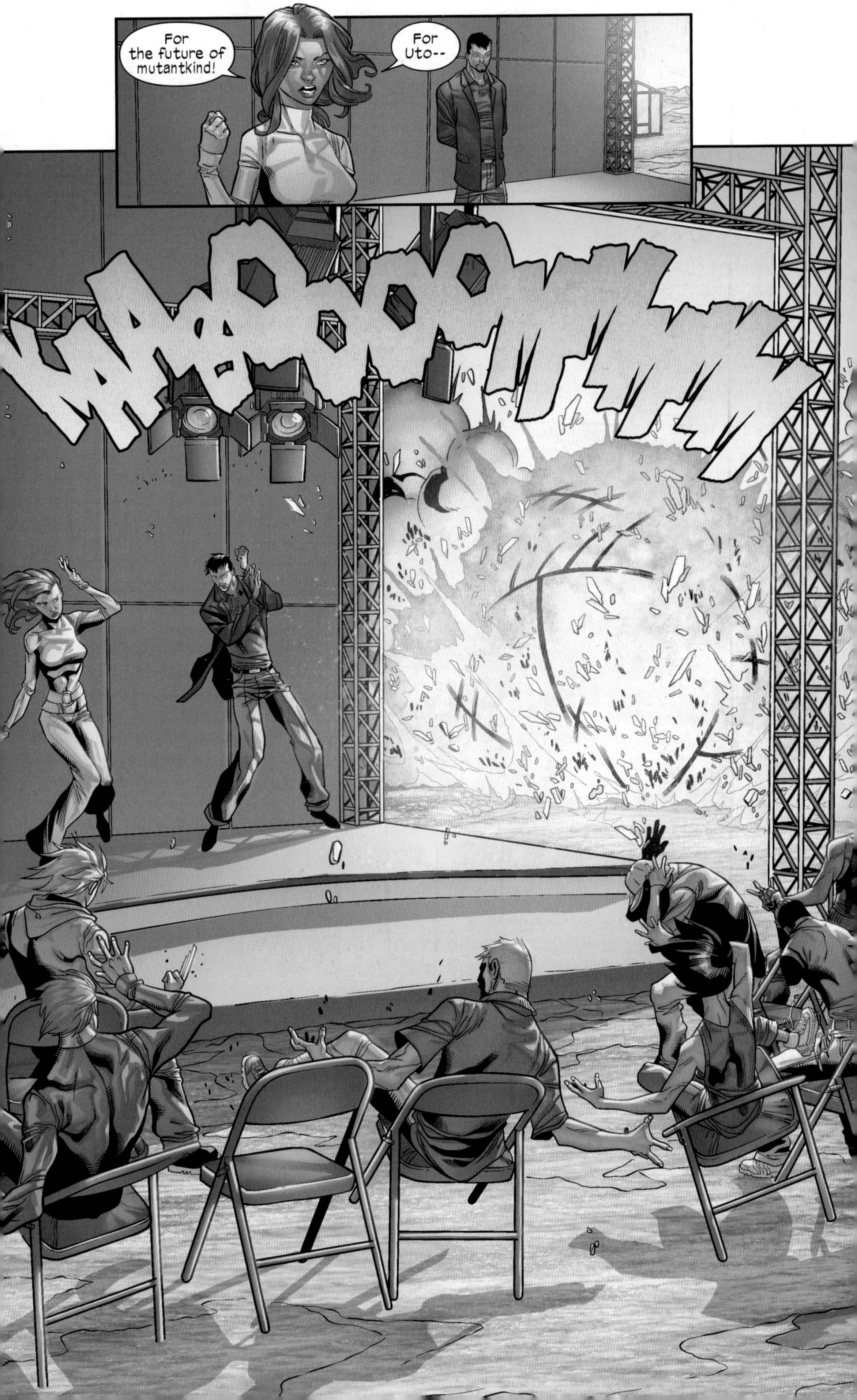
For the future of mutantkind!
For Uto--
KA-BOOOOMMM

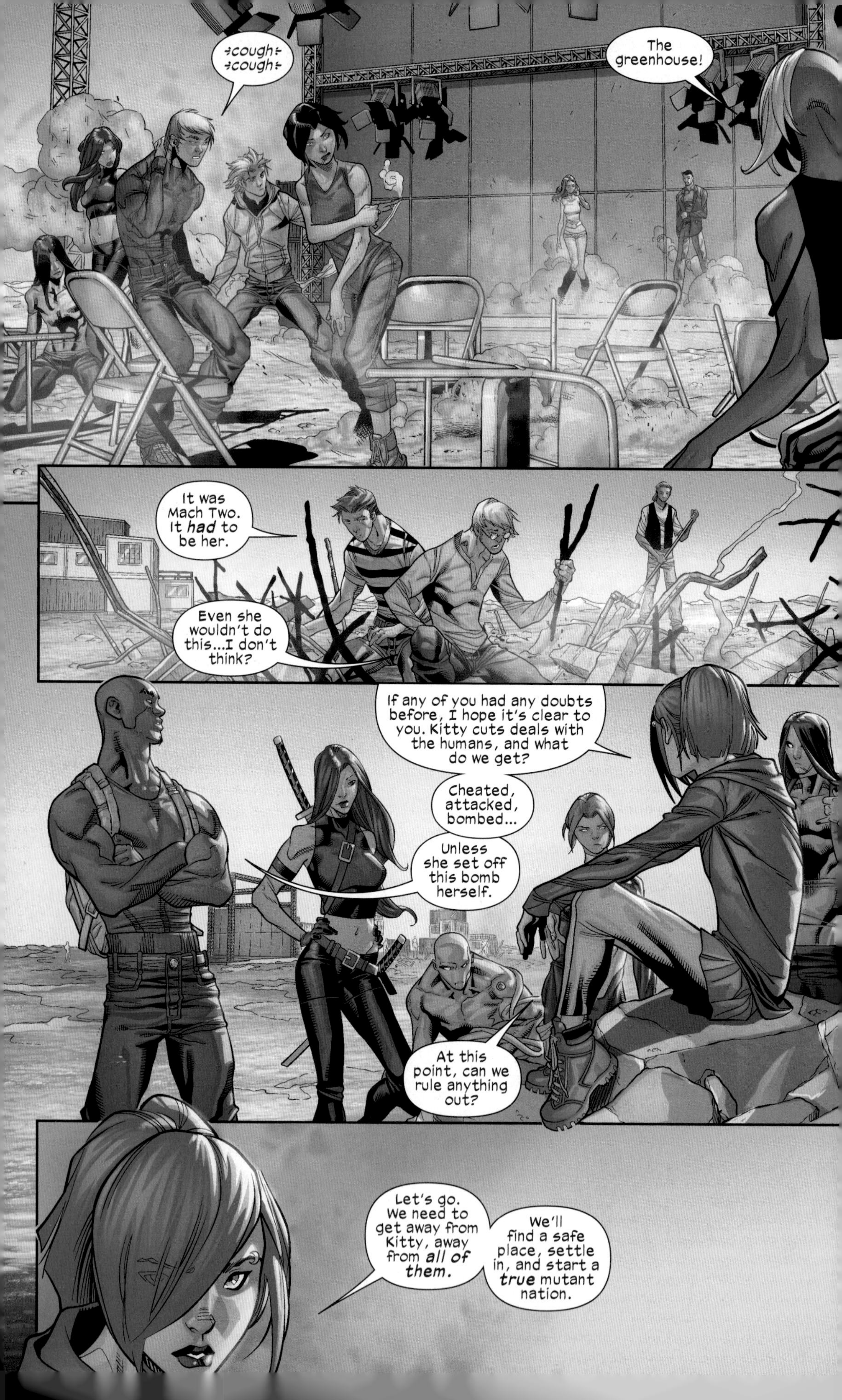

cough
cough
The greenhouse!
It was Mach Two. It *had* to be her.
Even she wouldn't do this...I don't think?
If any of you had any doubts before, I hope it's clear to you. Kitty cuts deals with the humans, and what do we get?
Cheated, attacked, bombed...
Unless she set off this bomb herself.
At this point, can we rule anything out?
Let's go. We need to get away from Kitty, away from *all of them.*
We'll find a safe place, settle in, and start a *true* mutant nation.

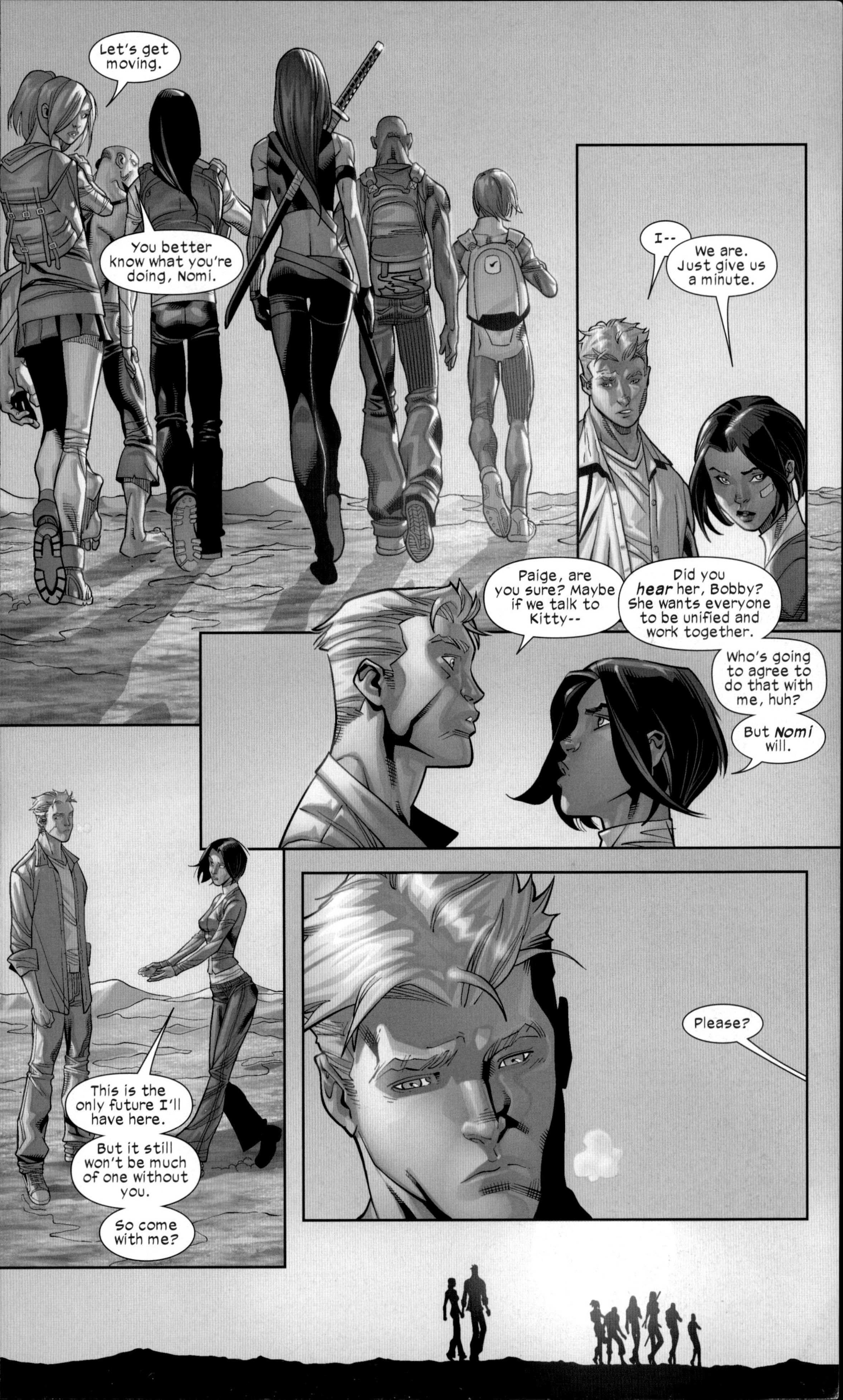
Let's get moving.
You better know what you're doing, Nomi.
I--
We are. Just give us a minute.
Paige, are you sure? Maybe if we talk to Kitty--
Did you *hear* her, Bobby? She wants everyone to be unified and work together.
Who's going to agree to do that with me, huh?
But *Nomi* will.
This is the only future I'll have here.
But it still won't be much of one without you.
So come with me?
Please?

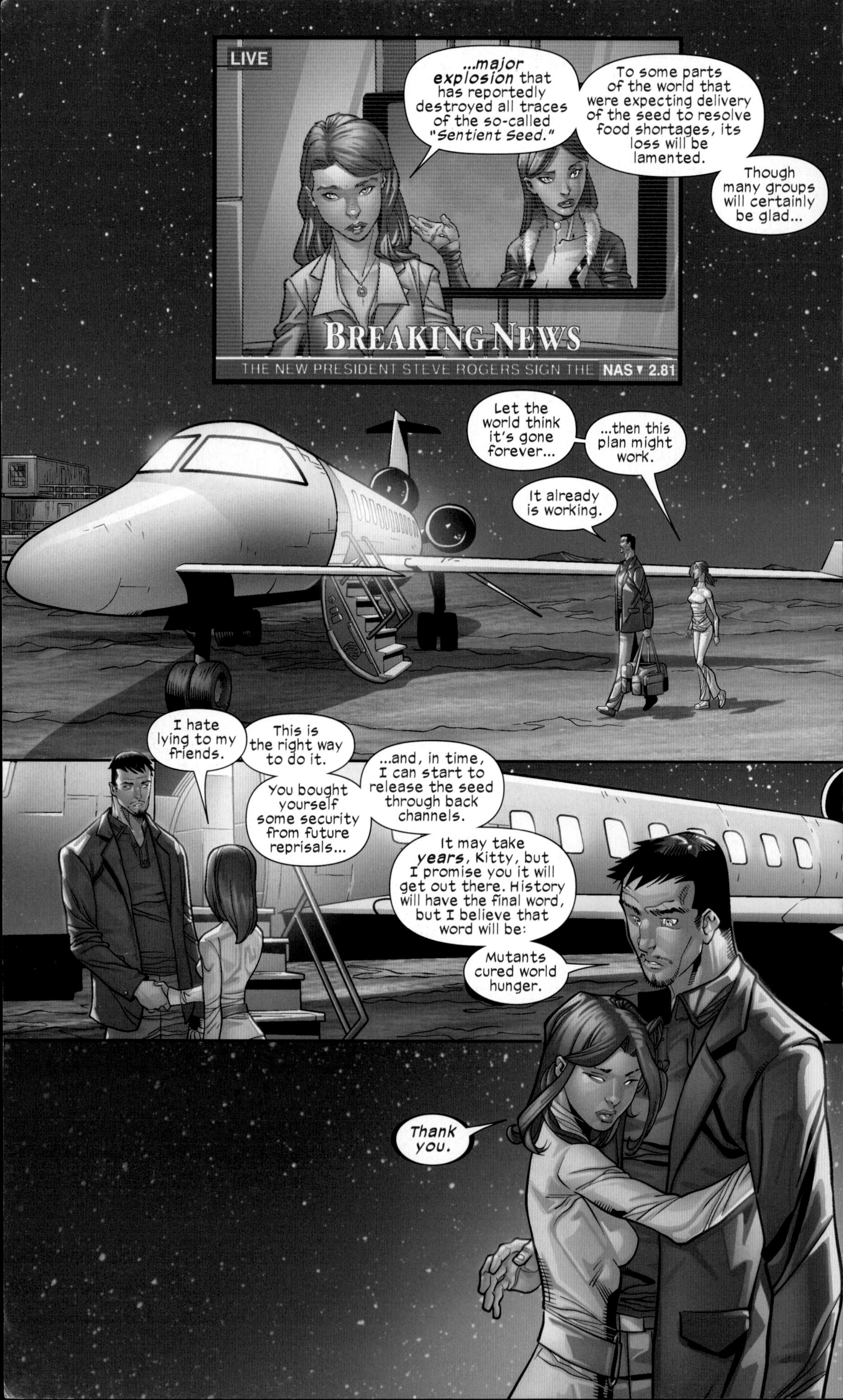
LIVE
...major explosion that has reportedly destroyed all traces of the so-called "Sentient Seed."
To some parts of the world that were expecting delivery of the seed to resolve food shortages, its loss will be lamented.
Though many groups will certainly be glad...
BREAKING NEWS
THE NEW PRESIDENT STEVE ROGERS SIGN THE NAS ▾ 2.81
Let the world think it's gone forever...
...then this plan might work.
It already is working.
I hate lying to my friends.
This is the right way to do it.
You bought yourself some security from future reprisals...
...and, in time, I can start to release the seed through back channels.
It may take years, Kitty, but I promise you it will get out there. History will have the final word, but I believe that word will be:
Mutants cured world hunger.
Thank you.

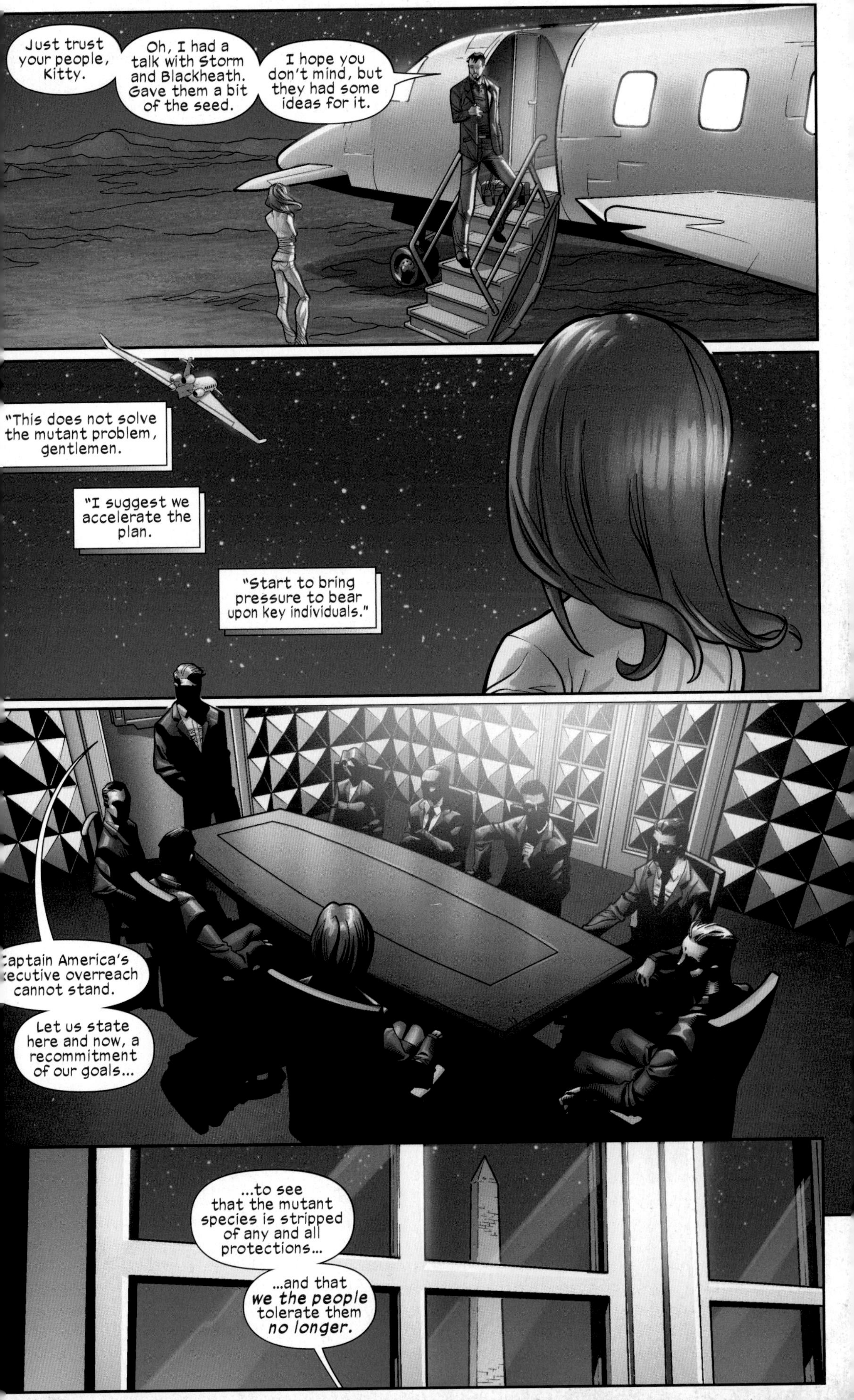

Just trust your people, Kitty.
Oh, I had a talk with Storm and Blackheath. Gave them a bit of the seed.
I hope you don't mind, but they had some ideas for it.
"This does not solve the mutant problem, gentlemen.
"I suggest we accelerate the plan.
"Start to bring pressure to bear upon key individuals."
aptain America's
ecutive overreach
cannot stand.
Let us state here and now, a recommitment of our goals...
...to see that the mutant species is stripped of any and all protections...
...and that *we the people* tolerate them *no longer.*

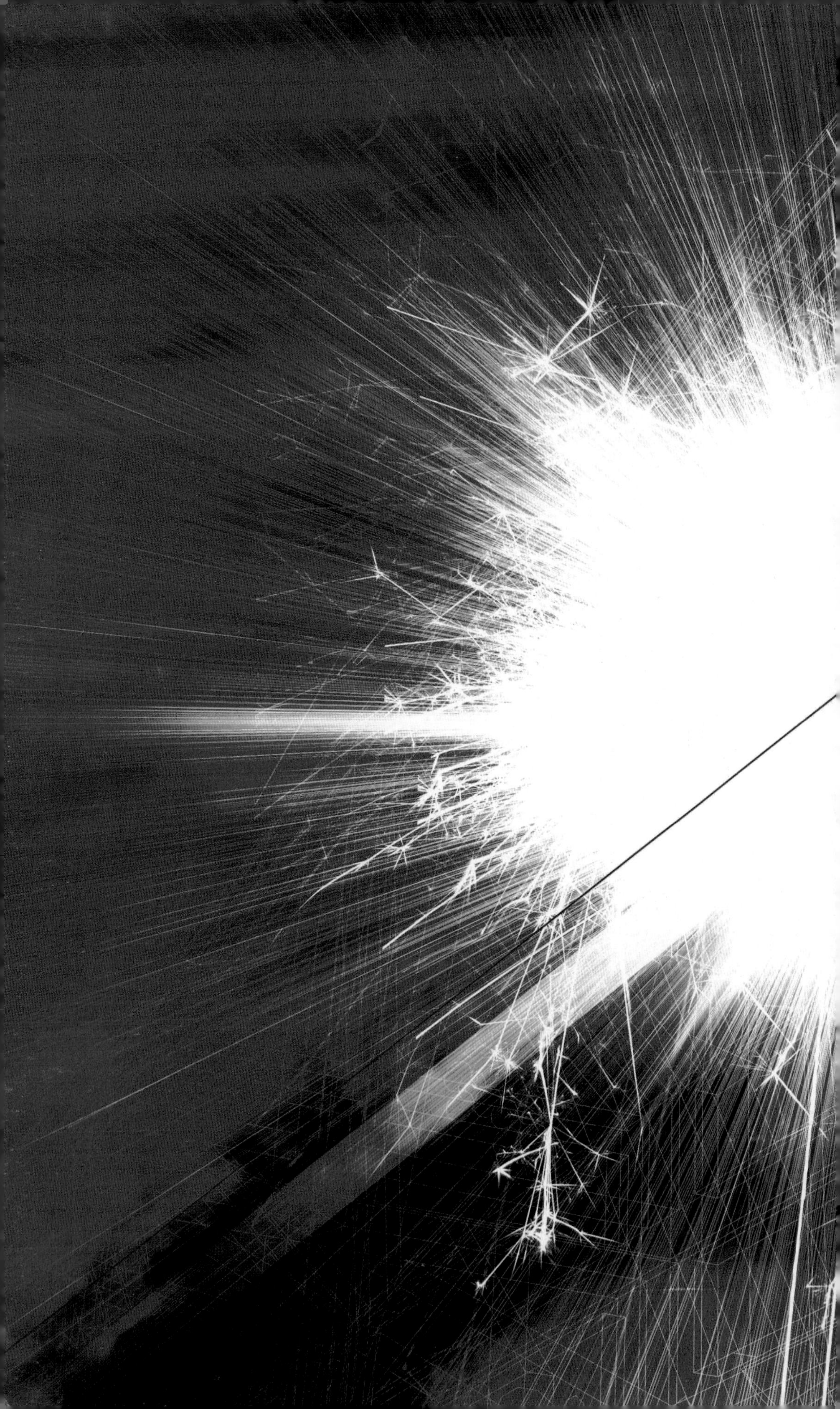

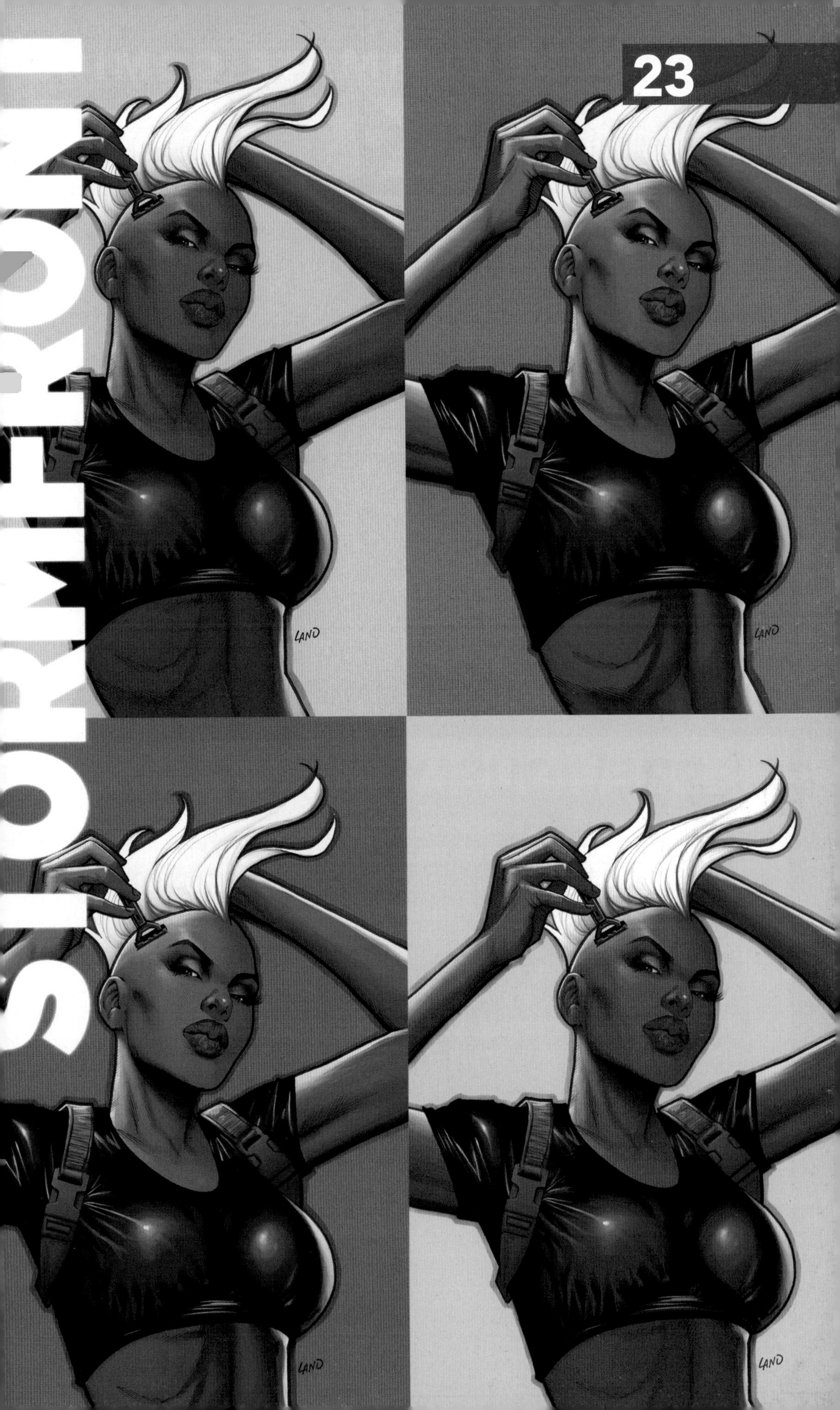
23
LAND
LAND
LAND
LAND

LIVING IN A WORLD
WHERE MUTANTS ARE
HATED AND FEARED MORE
THAN EVER, ONE GROUP
OF YOUNG HEROES HAS
BANDED TOGETHER TO
FIGHT BACK.

ULTIMATE COMICS
X-MEN

PREVIOUSLY:

Under Kitty Pryde's leadership, the war against mutants has ended. The government offered them a treatment to become human. The remaining mutants were relocated to a reservation: Utopia. Among these mutants is Ororo Munroe, known as Storm.

But before Utopia, when the war between the government and the mutants raged on, Storm was a prisoner at Camp Angel, a military-run mutant detention center. Storm, along with Piotr Rasputin, known as Colossus, managed to break free. But there were casualties.

In the struggle, Piotr executed a human officer in cold blood.

This is the story of what happened next.

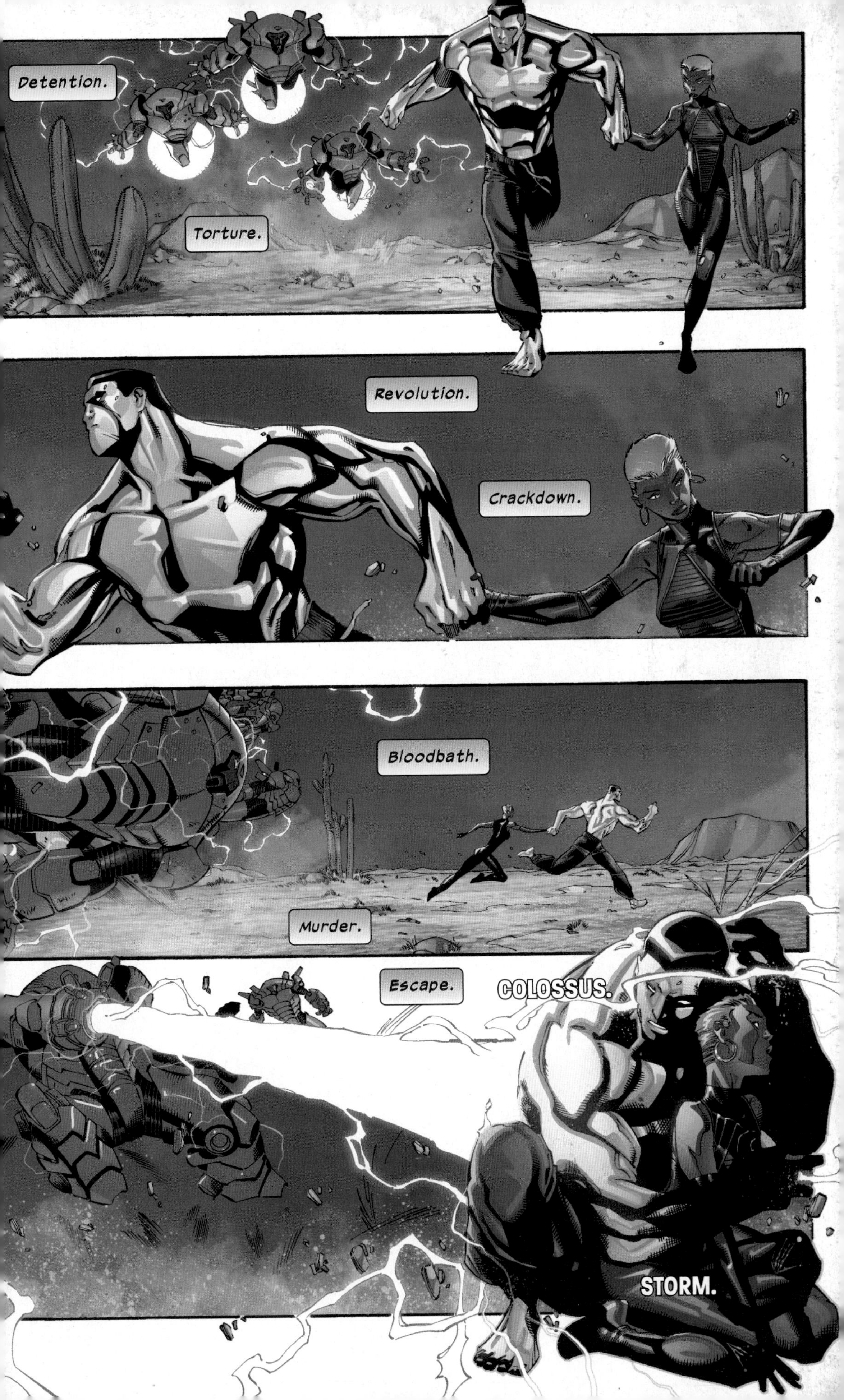
Detention.
Torture.
Revolution.
Crackdown.
Bloodbath.
Murder.
Escape.
COLOSSUS.
STORM.

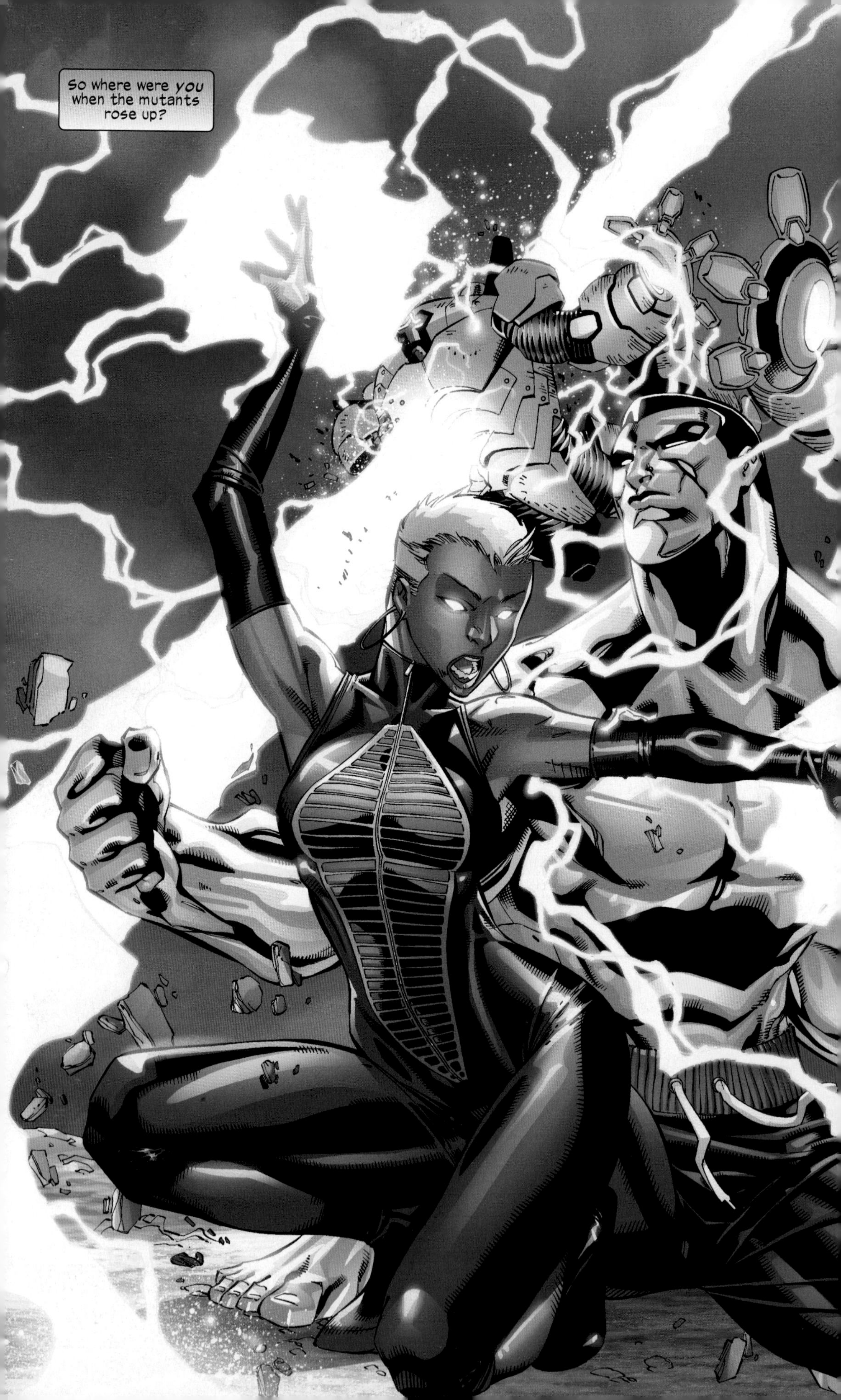
So where were *you* when the mutants rose up?

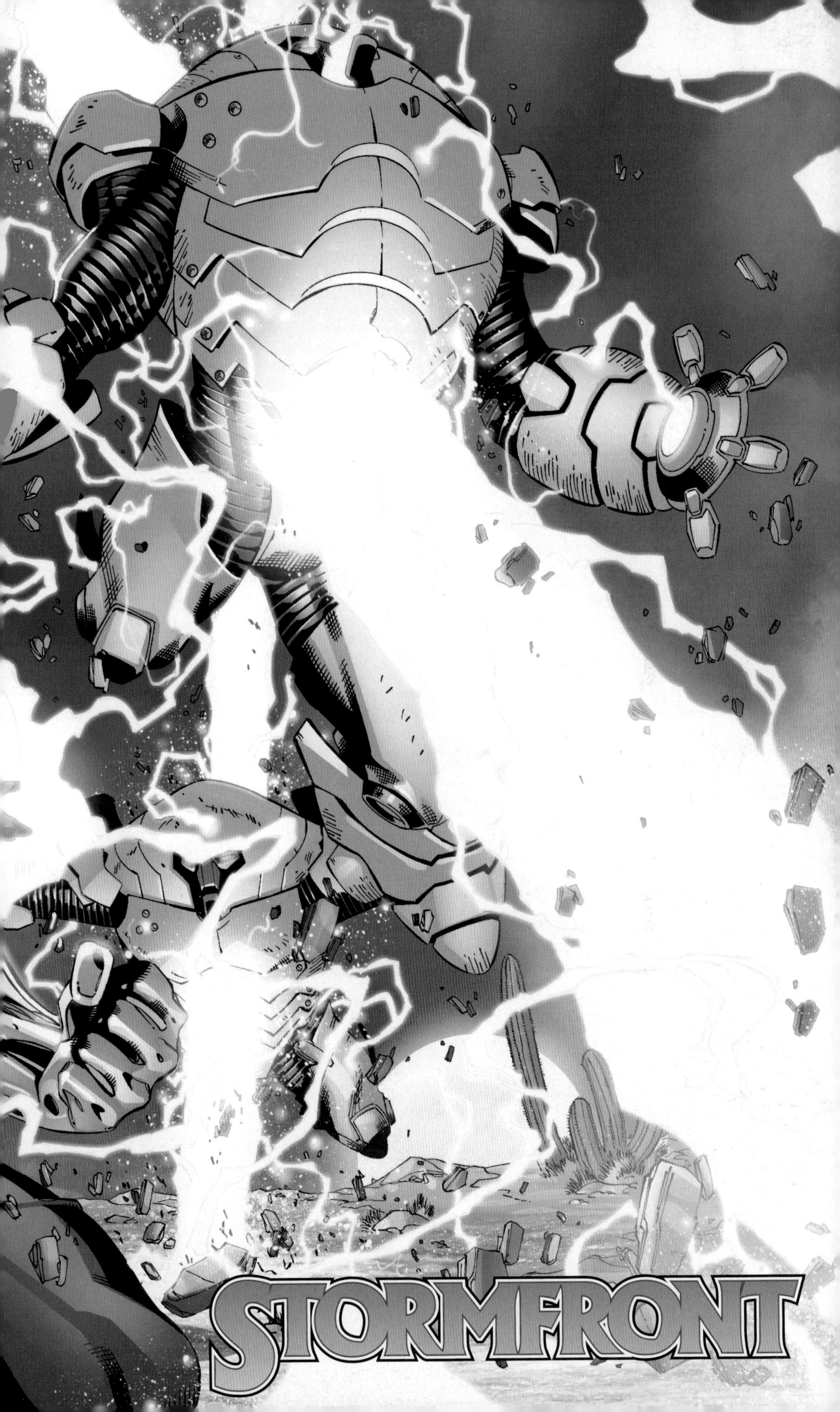
STORMFRONT

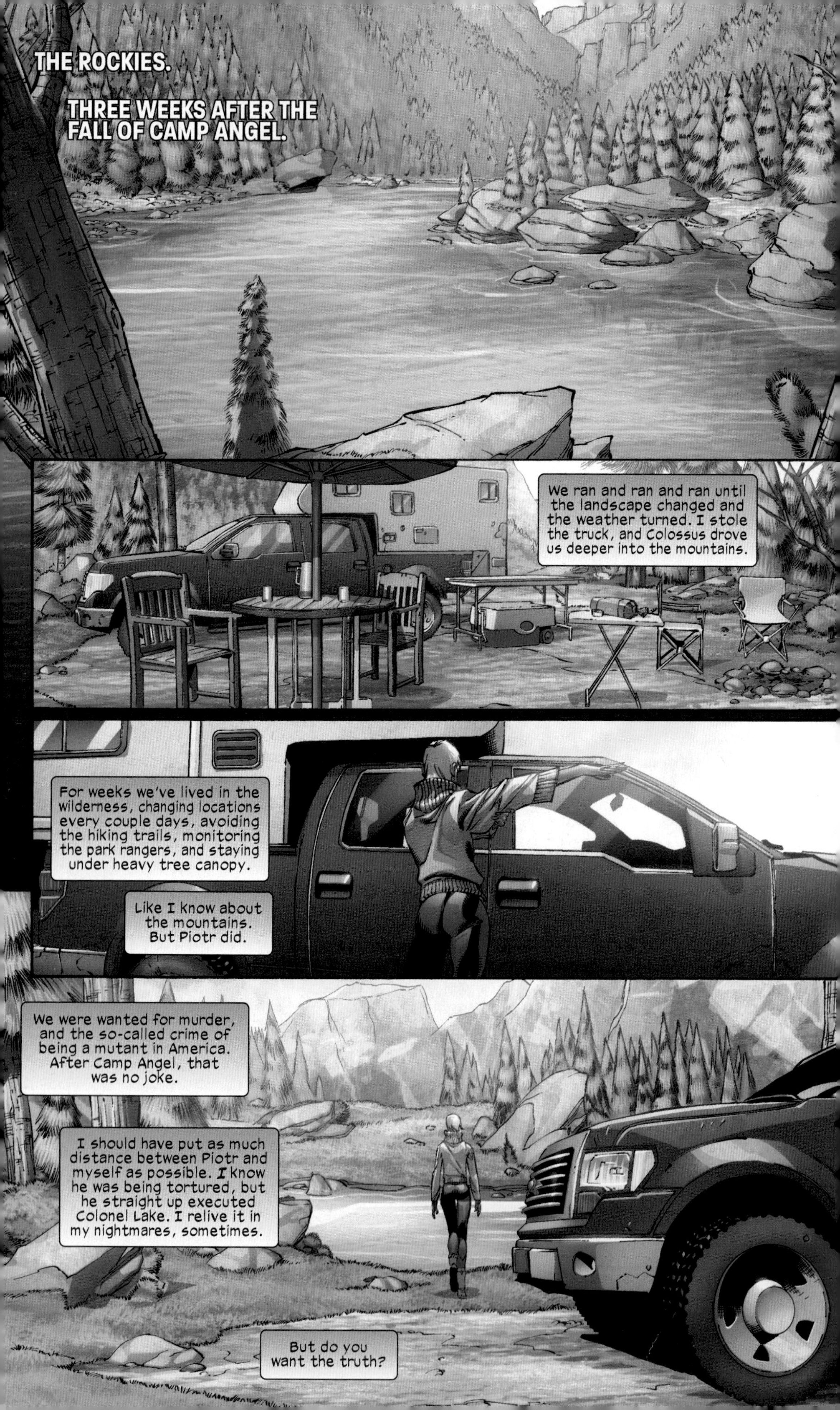
THE ROCKIES.
THREE WEEKS AFTER THE FALL OF CAMP ANGEL.
We ran and ran and ran until the landscape changed and the weather turned. I stole the truck, and Colossus drove us deeper into the mountains.
For weeks we've lived in the wilderness, changing locations every couple days, avoiding the hiking trails, monitoring the park rangers, and staying under heavy tree canopy.
Like I know about the mountains. But Piotr did.
We were wanted for murder, and the so-called crime of being a mutant in America. After Camp Angel, that was no joke.
I should have put as much distance between Piotr and myself as possible. I know he was being tortured, but he straight up executed Colonel Lake. I relive it in my nightmares, sometimes.
But do you want the truth?

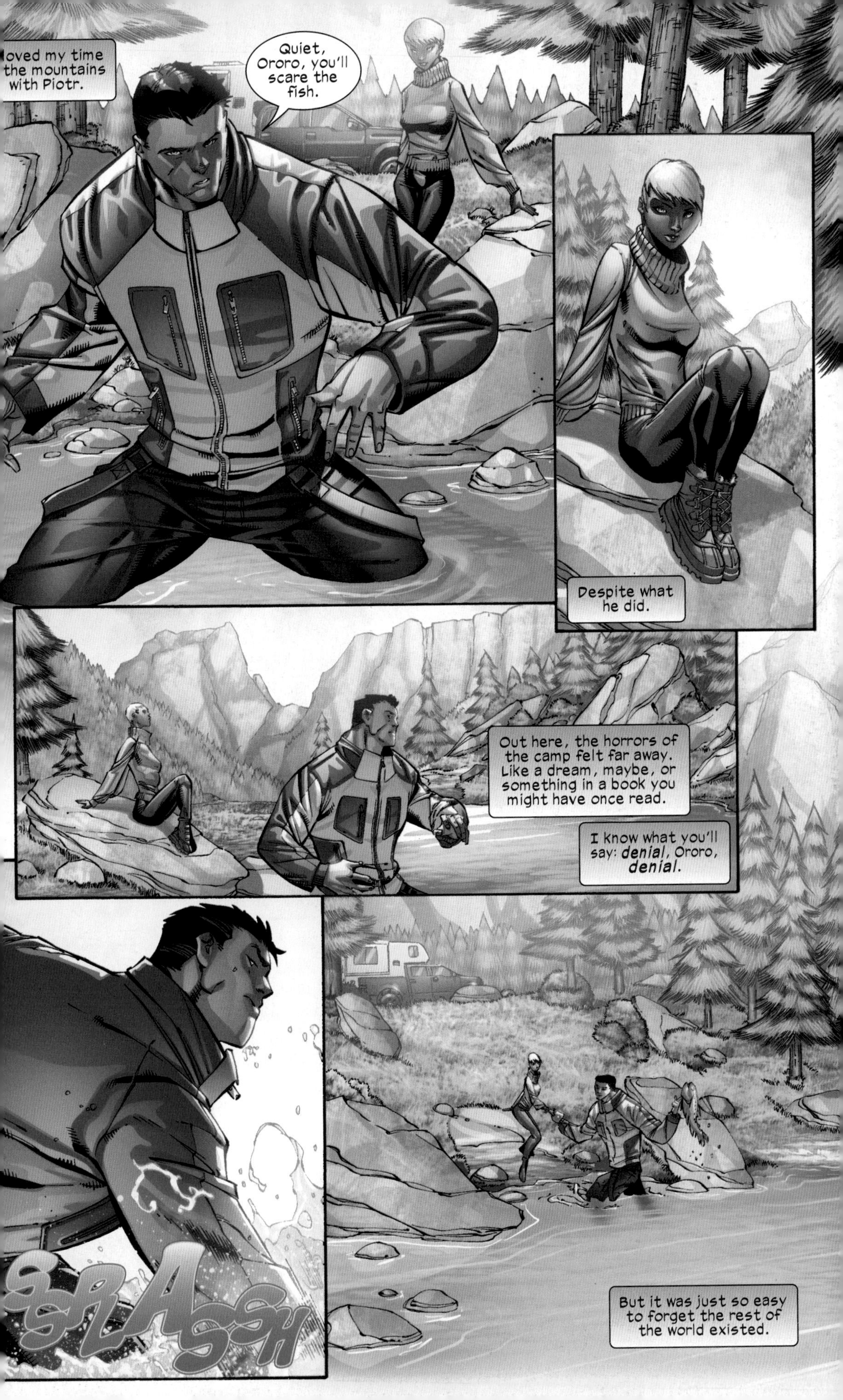

loved my time
the mountains
with Piotr.
Quiet, Ororo, you'll scare the fish.
Despite what he did.
Out here, the horrors of the camp felt far away. Like a dream, maybe, or something in a book you might have once read.
I know what you'll say: *denial*, Ororo, *denial*.
SPLASSH
But it was just so easy to forget the rest of the world existed.

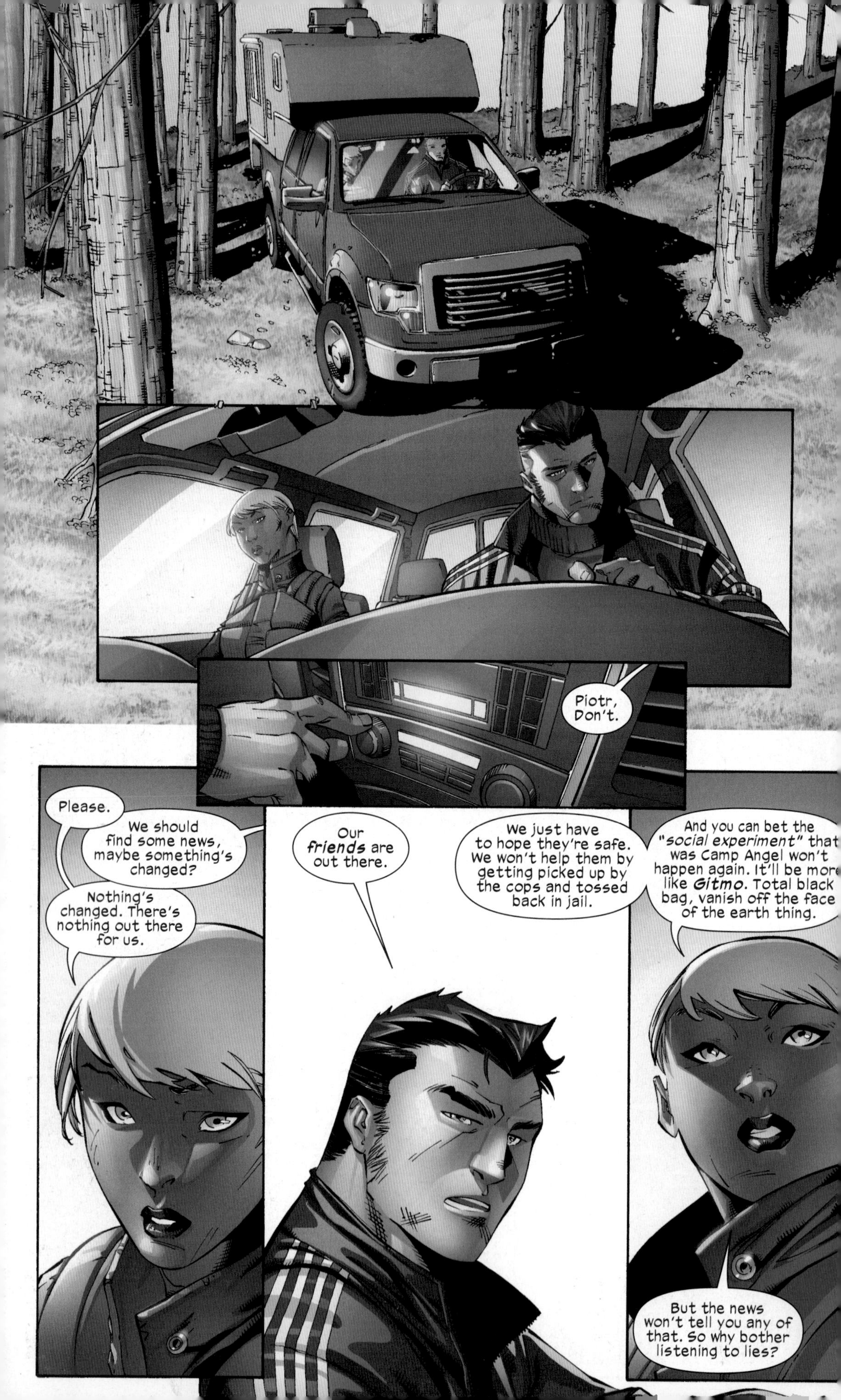

Piotr, Don't.
Please.
We should find some news, maybe something's changed?
Nothing's changed. There's nothing out there for us.
Our *friends* are out there.
We just have to hope they're safe. We won't help them by getting picked up by the cops and tossed back in jail.
And you can bet the "*social experiment*" that was Camp Angel won't happen again. It'll be more like *Gitmo*. Total black bag, vanish off the face of the earth thing.
But the news won't tell you any of that. So why bother listening to lies?

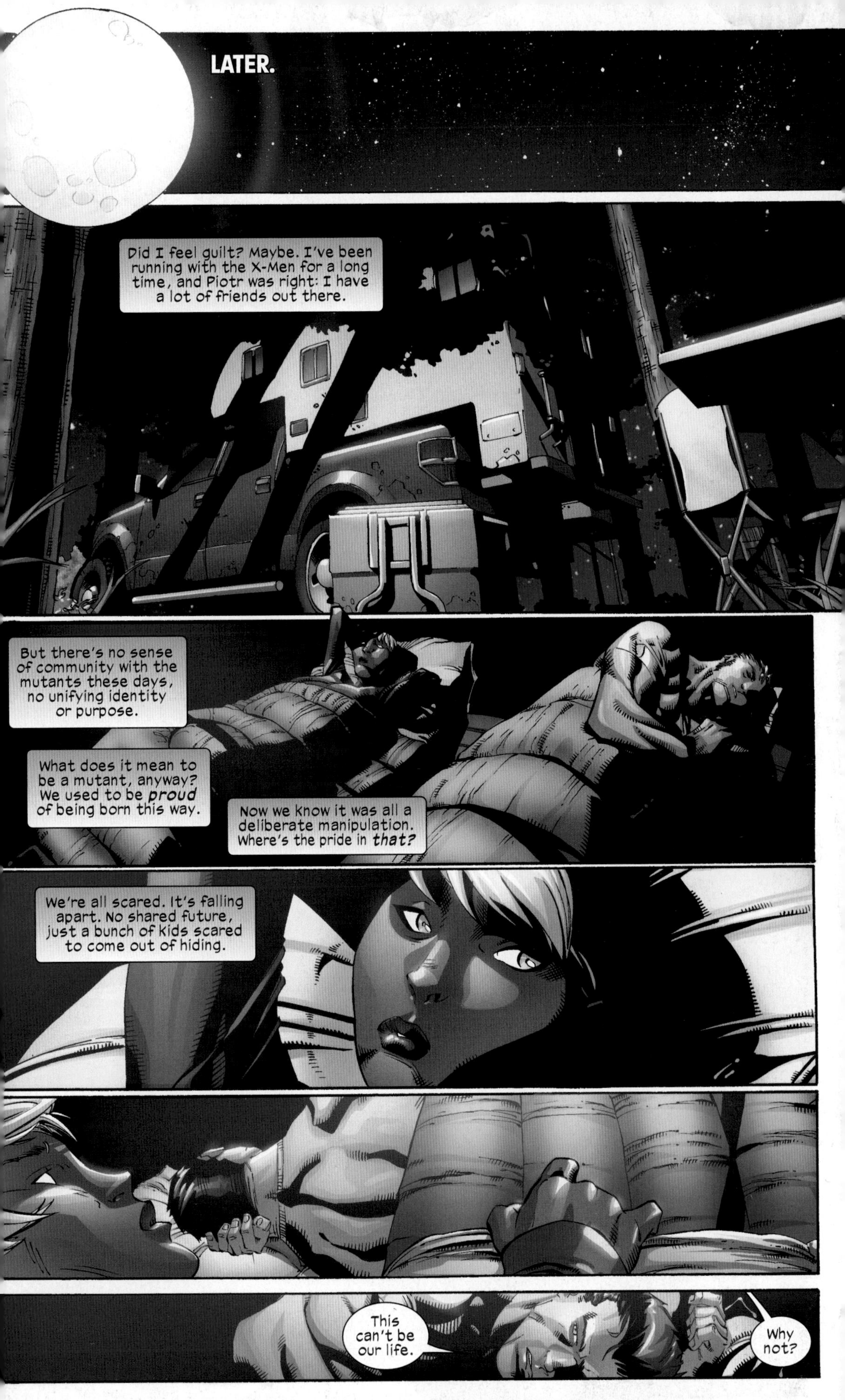
LATER.
Did I feel guilt? Maybe. I've been running with the X-Men for a long time, and Piotr was right: I have a lot of friends out there.
But there's no sense of community with the mutants these days, no unifying identity or purpose.
What does it mean to be a mutant, anyway? We used to be *proud* of being born this way.
Now we know it was all a deliberate manipulation. Where's the pride in *that?*
We're all scared. It's falling apart. No shared future, just a bunch of kids scared to come out of hiding.
This can't be our life.
Why not?

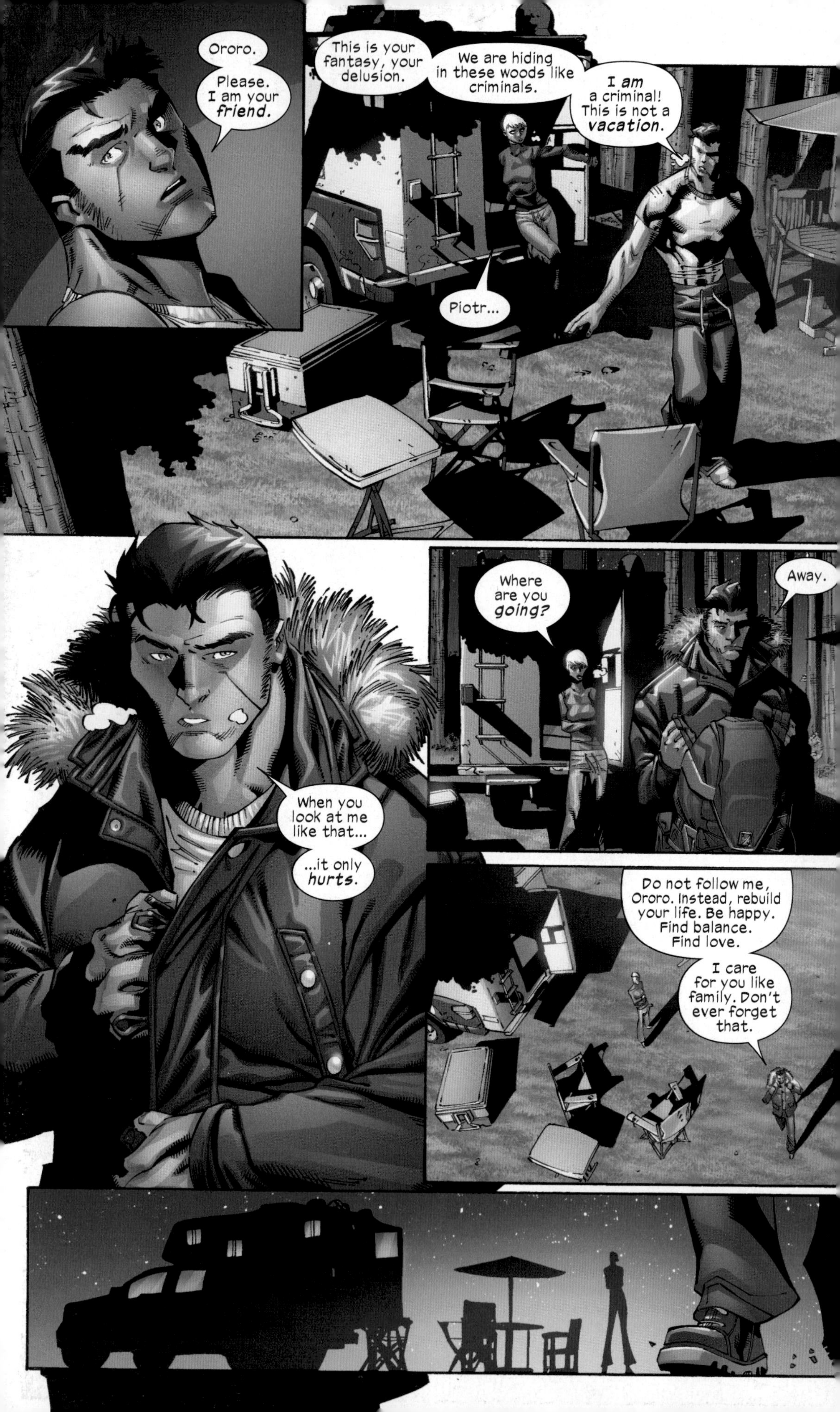
Ororo.
Please. I am your *friend*.
This is your fantasy, your delusion.
We are hiding in these woods like criminals.
I *am* a criminal! This is not a *vacation*.
Piotr...
When you look at me like that...
...it only *hurts*.
Where are you *going?*
Away.
Do not follow me, Ororo. Instead, rebuild your life. Be happy. Find balance. Find love.
I care for you like family. Don't ever forget that.

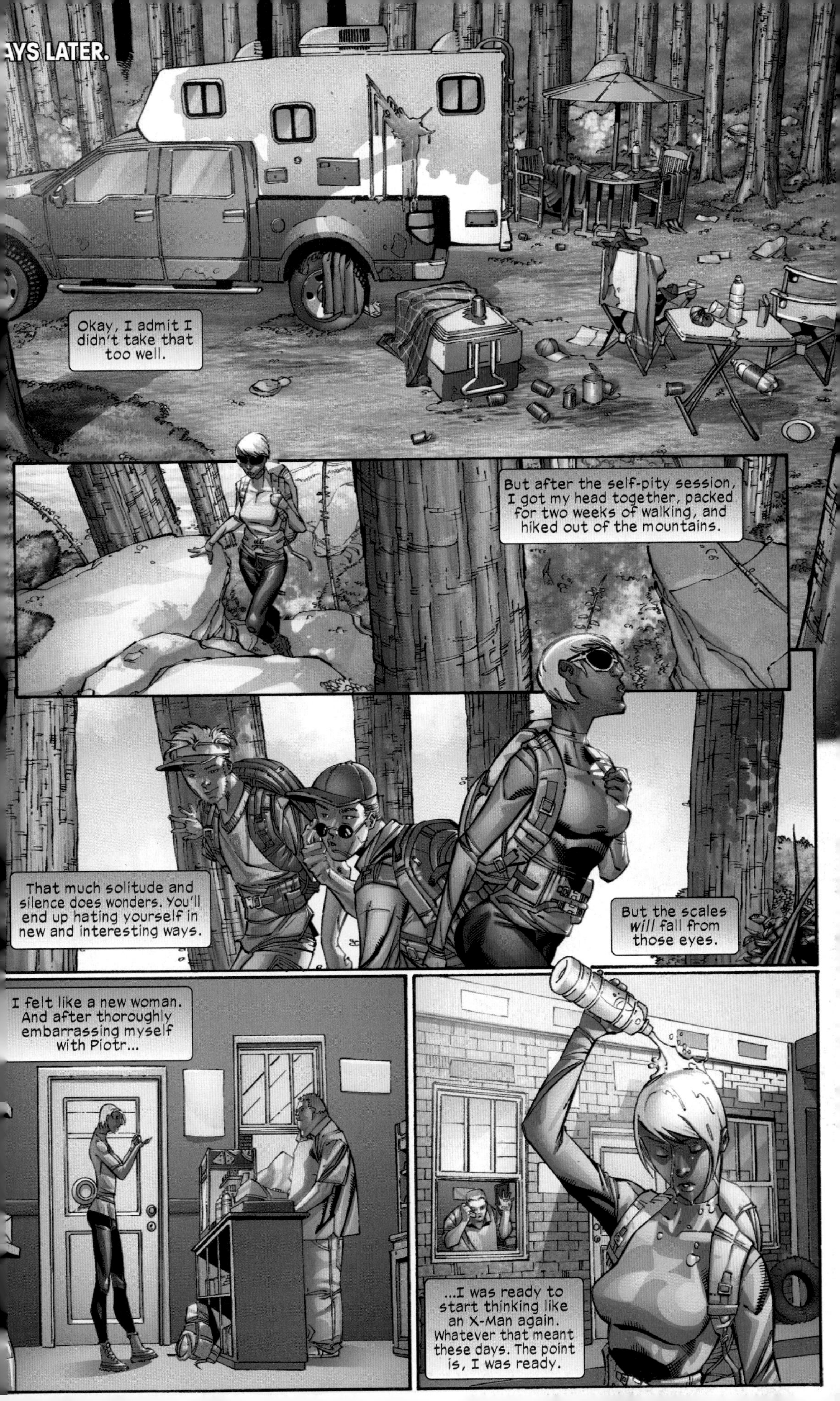

AYS LATER.
Okay, I admit I didn't take that too well.
But after the self-pity session, I got my head together, packed for two weeks of walking, and hiked out of the mountains.
That much solitude and silence does wonders. You'll end up hating yourself in new and interesting ways.
But the scales *will* fall from those eyes.
I felt like a new woman. And after thoroughly embarrassing myself with Piotr...
...I was ready to start thinking like an X-Man again. Whatever that meant these days. The point is, I was ready.

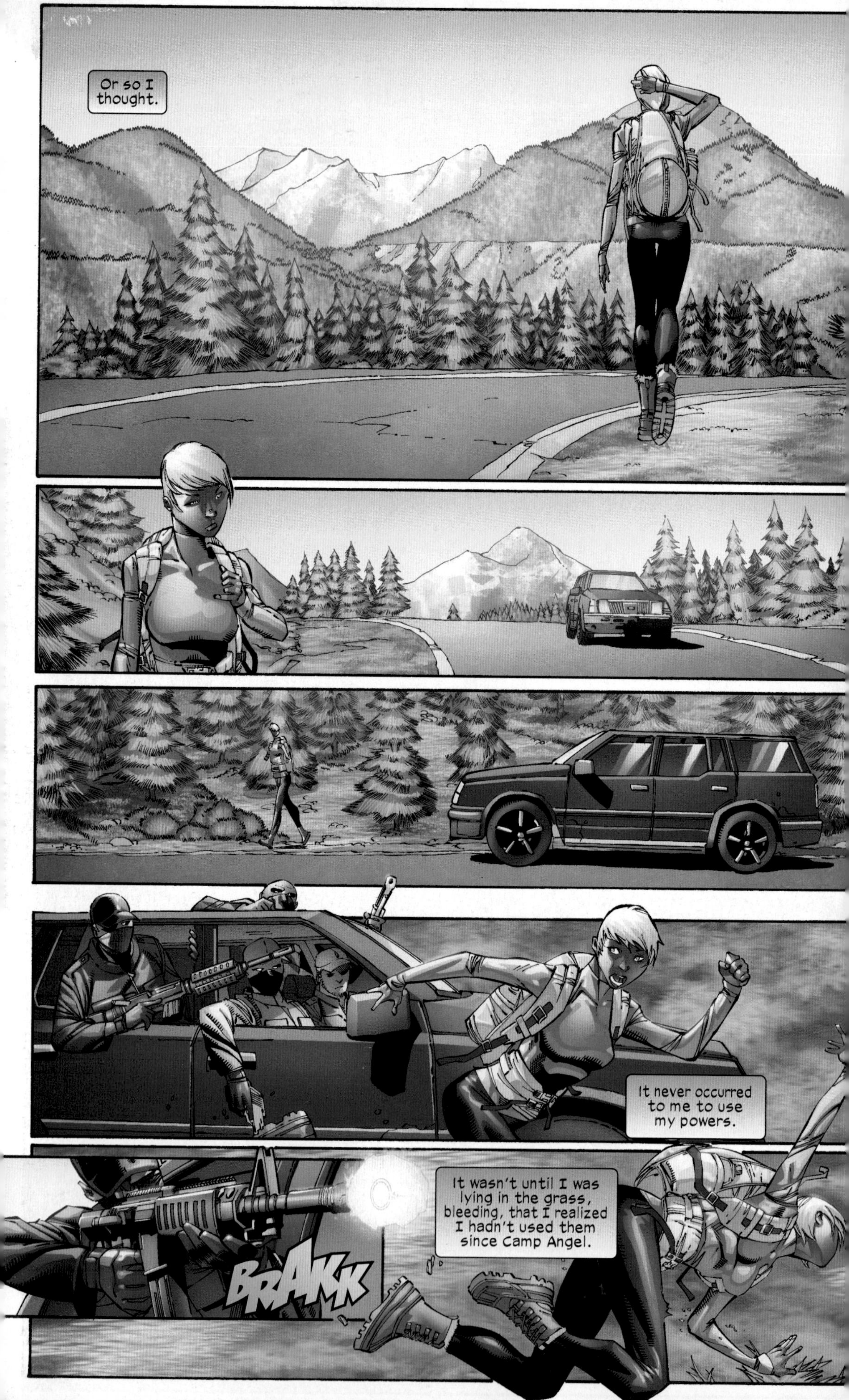
Or so I thought.
It never occurred to me to use my powers.
It wasn't until I was lying in the grass, bleeding, that I realized I hadn't used them since Camp Angel.
BRAKK

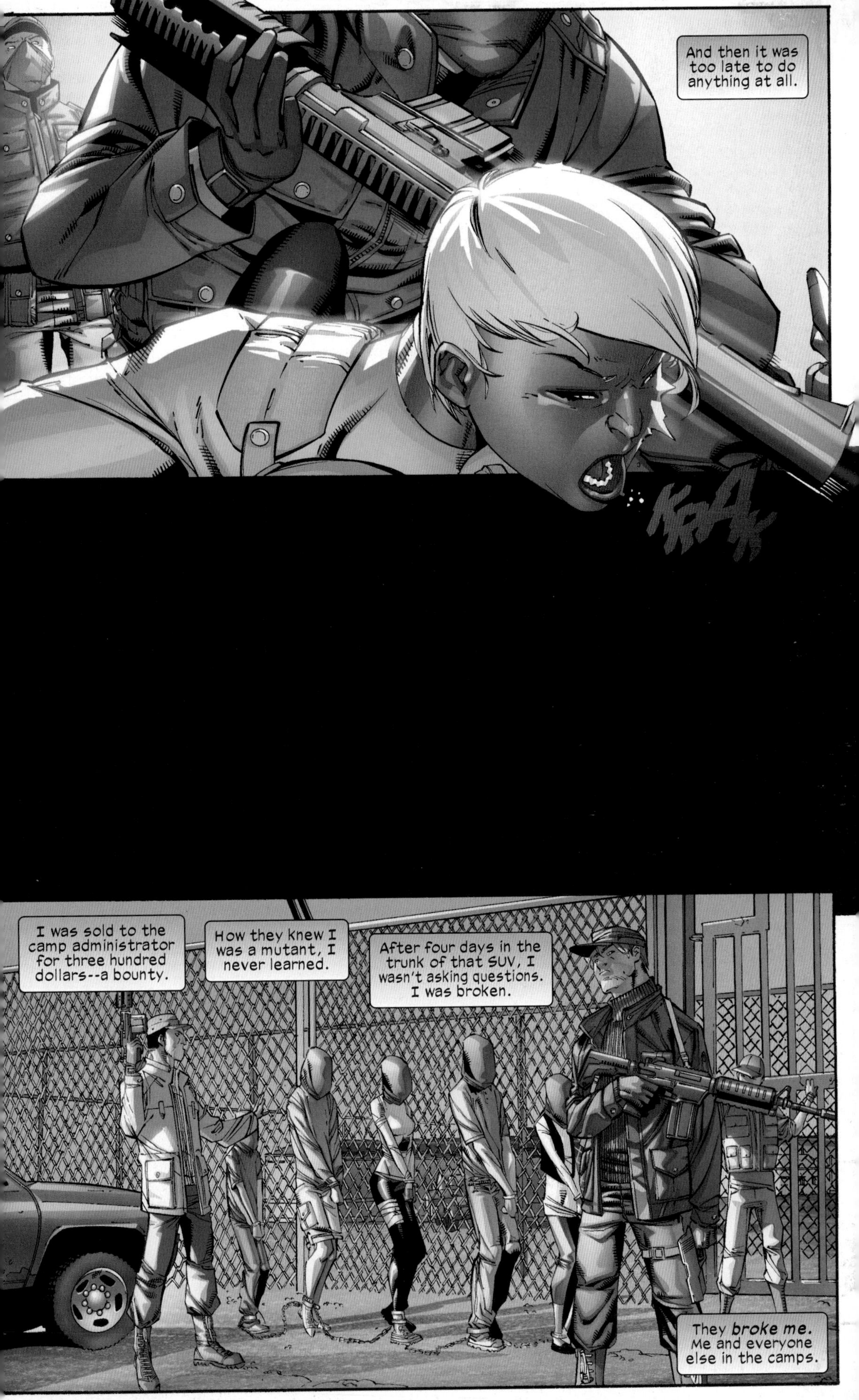
And then it was too late to do anything at all.
KRAK
I was sold to the camp administrator for three hundred dollars--a bounty.
How they knew I was a mutant, I never learned.
After four days in the trunk of that SUV, I wasn't asking questions. I was broken.
They *broke me.* Me and everyone else in the camps.

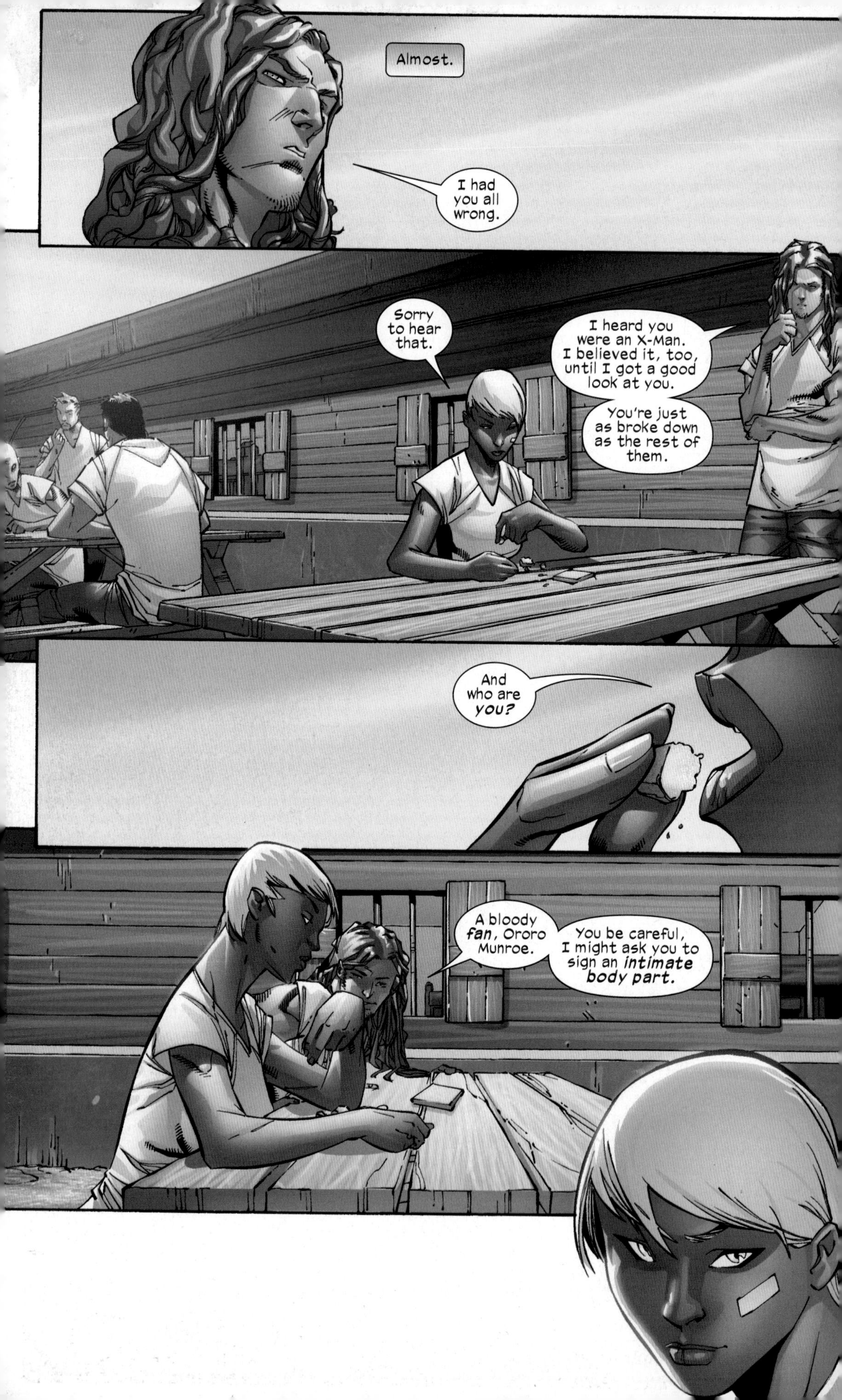
Almost.
I had you all wrong.
Sorry to hear that.
I heard you were an X-Man. I believed it, too, until I got a good look at you.
You're just as broke down as the rest of them.
And who are *you?*
A bloody *fan*, Ororo Munroe.
You be careful, I might ask you to sign an *intimate body part.*

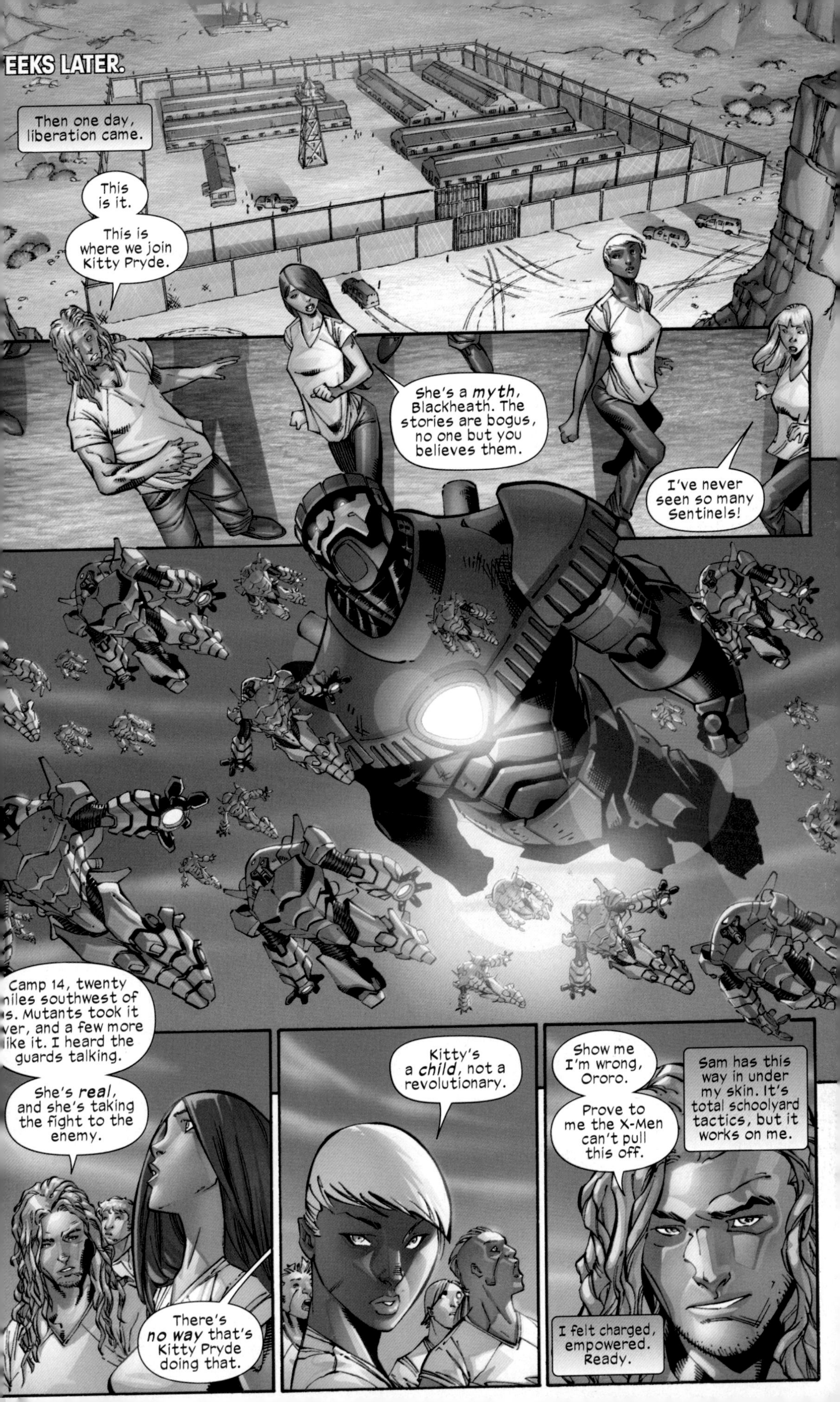
EEKS LATER.
Then one day, liberation came.
This is it.
This is where we join Kitty Pryde.
She's a *myth*, Blackheath. The stories are bogus, no one but you believes them.
I've never seen so many Sentinels!
Camp 14, twenty niles southwest of s. Mutants took it ver, and a few more ike it. I heard the guards talking.
She's *real*, and she's taking the fight to the enemy.
There's *no way* that's Kitty Pryde doing that.
Kitty's a *child*, not a revolutionary.
Show me I'm wrong, Ororo.
Prove to me the X-Men can't pull this off.
Sam has this way in under my skin. It's total schoolyard tactics, but it works on me.
I felt charged, empowered. Ready.

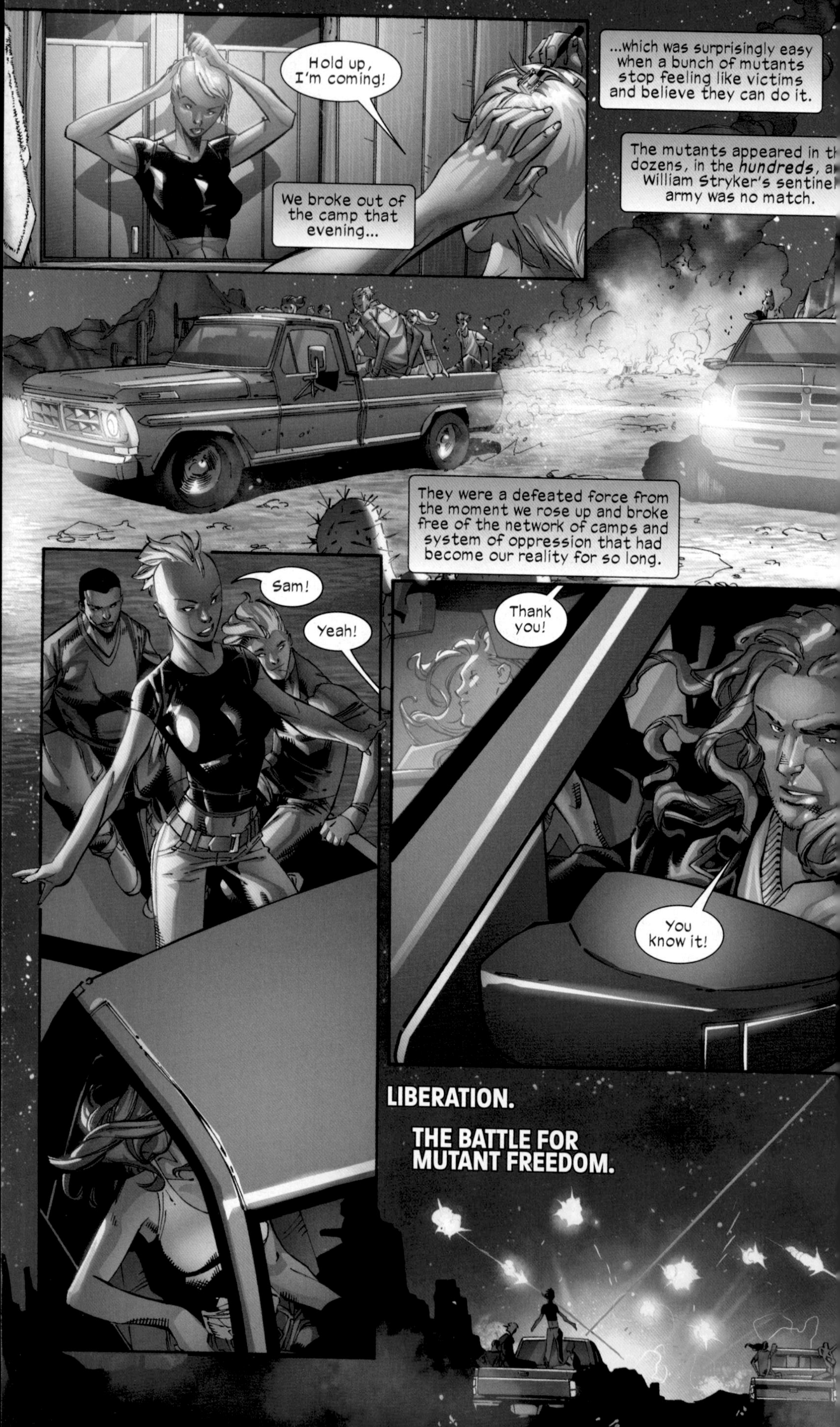

Hold up, I'm coming!
We broke out of the camp that evening...
...which was surprisingly easy when a bunch of mutants stop feeling like victims and believe they can do it.
The mutants appeared in th dozens, in the *hundreds*, a William Stryker's sentine army was no match.
They were a defeated force from the moment we rose up and broke free of the network of camps and system of oppression that had become our reality for so long.
Sam!
Yeah!
Thank you!
You know it!
LIBERATION.
THE BATTLE FOR MUTANT FREEDOM.

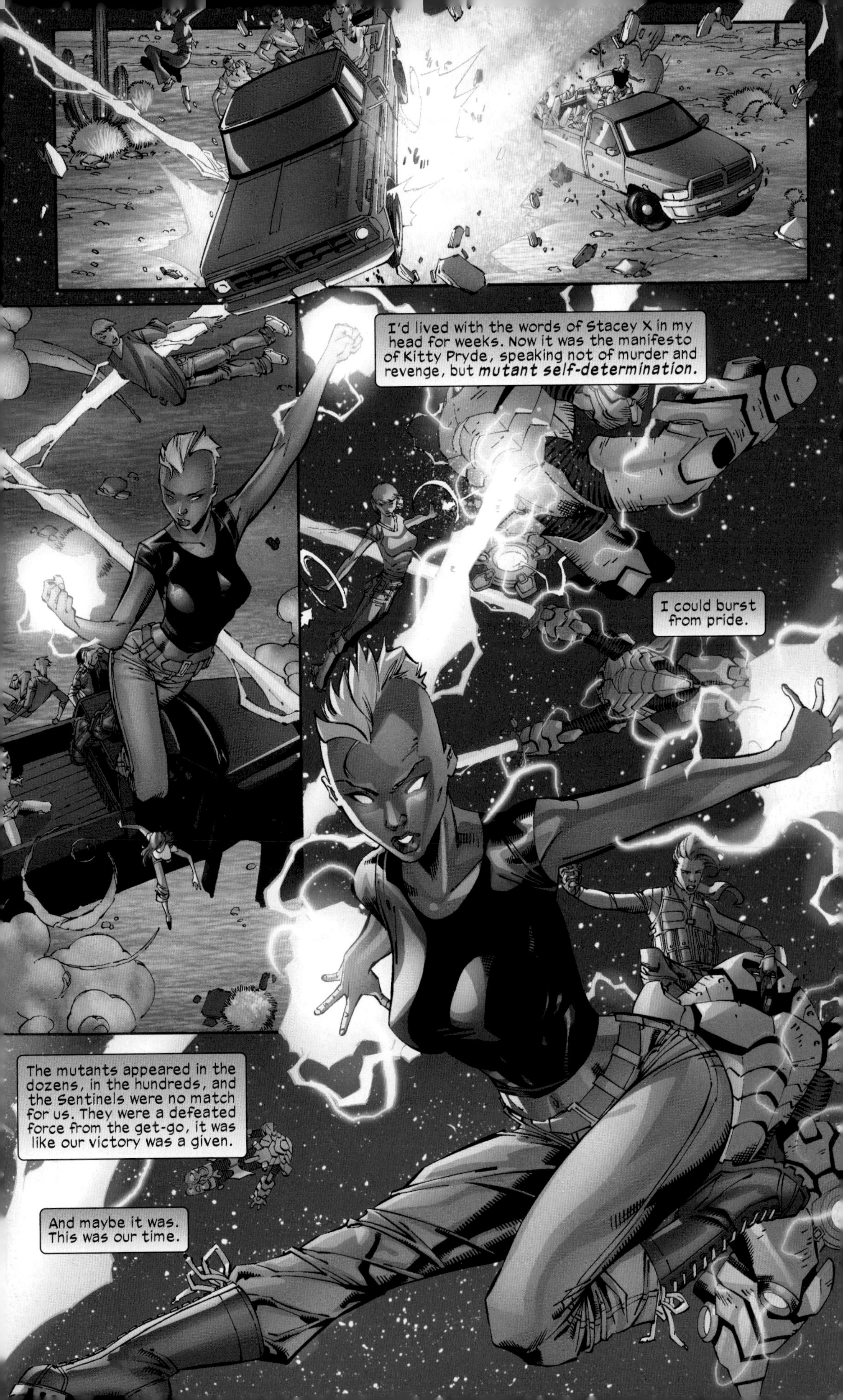
I'd lived with the words of Stacey X in my head for weeks. Now it was the manifesto of Kitty Pryde, speaking not of murder and revenge, but *mutant self-determination.*
I could burst from pride.
The mutants appeared in the dozens, in the hundreds, and the Sentinels were no match for us. They were a defeated force from the get-go, it was like our victory was a given.
And maybe it was. This was our time.

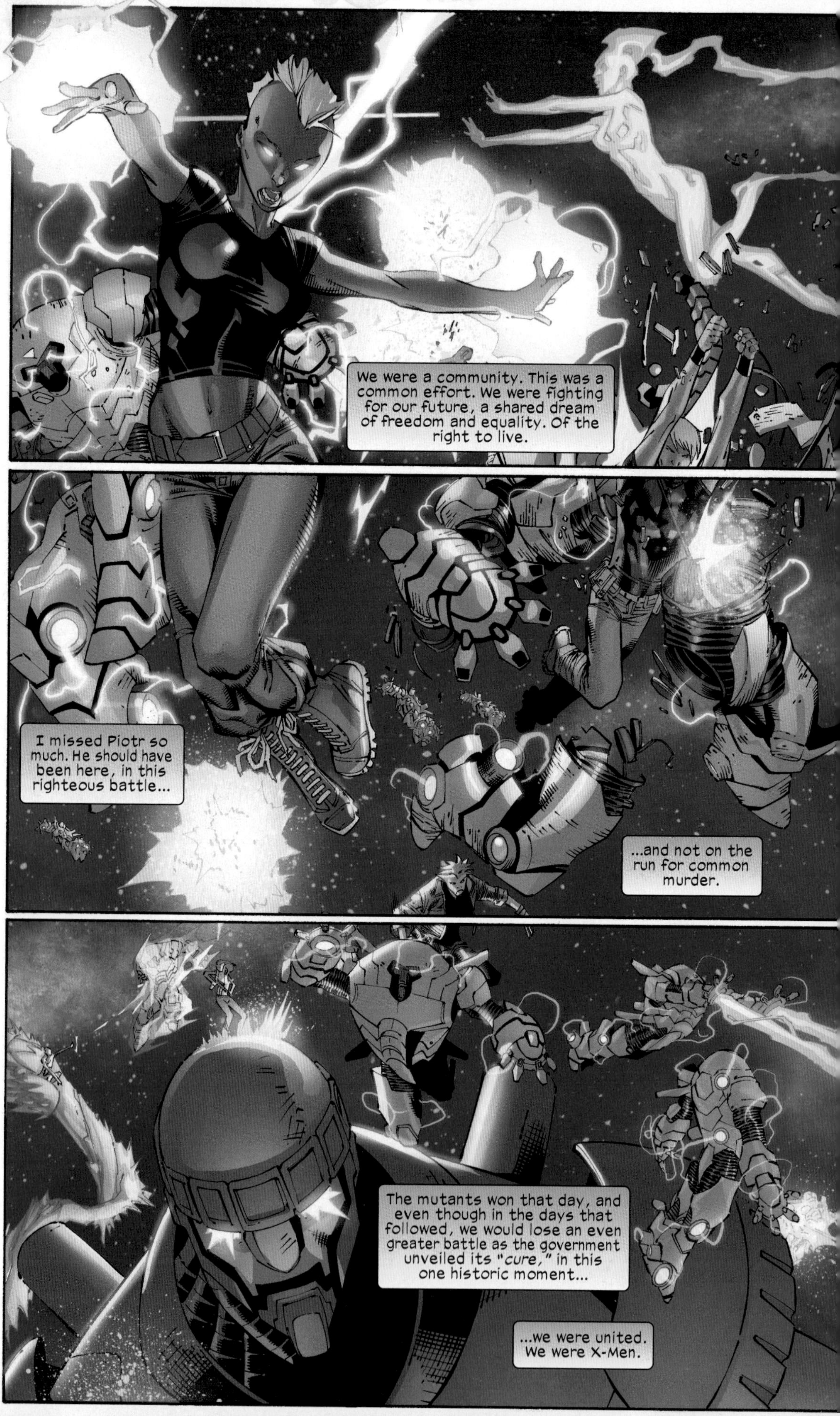

We were a community. This was a common effort. We were fighting for our future, a shared dream of freedom and equality. Of the right to live.
I missed Piotr so much. He should have been here, in this righteous battle...
...and not on the run for common murder.
The mutants won that day, and even though in the days that followed, we would lose an even greater battle as the government unveiled its "cure," in this one historic moment...
...we were united. We were X-Men.

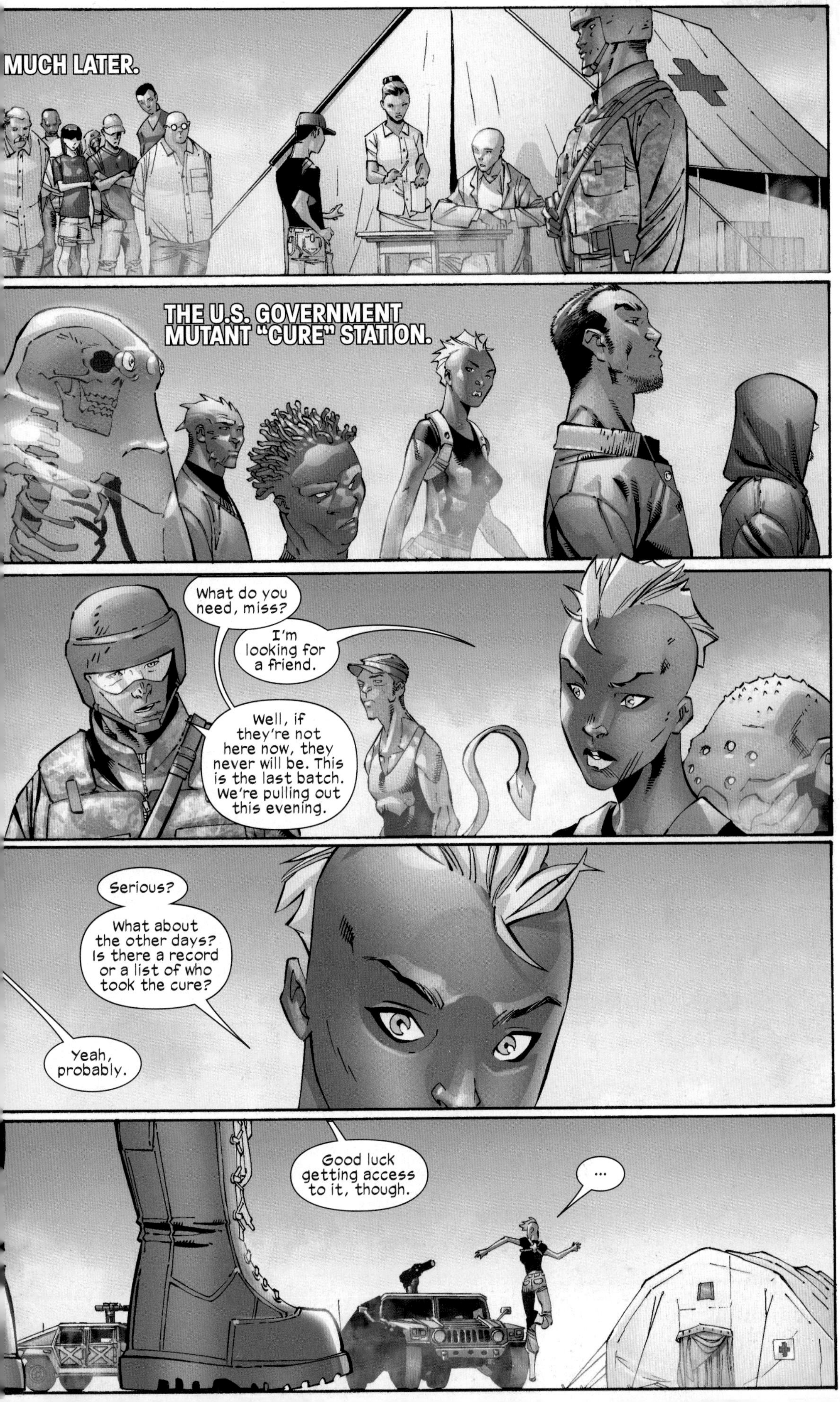
MUCH LATER.
THE U.S. GOVERNMENT MUTANT "CURE" STATION.
What do you need, miss?
I'm looking for a friend.
Well, if they're not here now, they never will be. This is the last batch. We're pulling out this evening.
Serious?
What about the other days? Is there a record or a list of who took the cure?
Yeah, probably.
Good luck getting access to it, though.
...

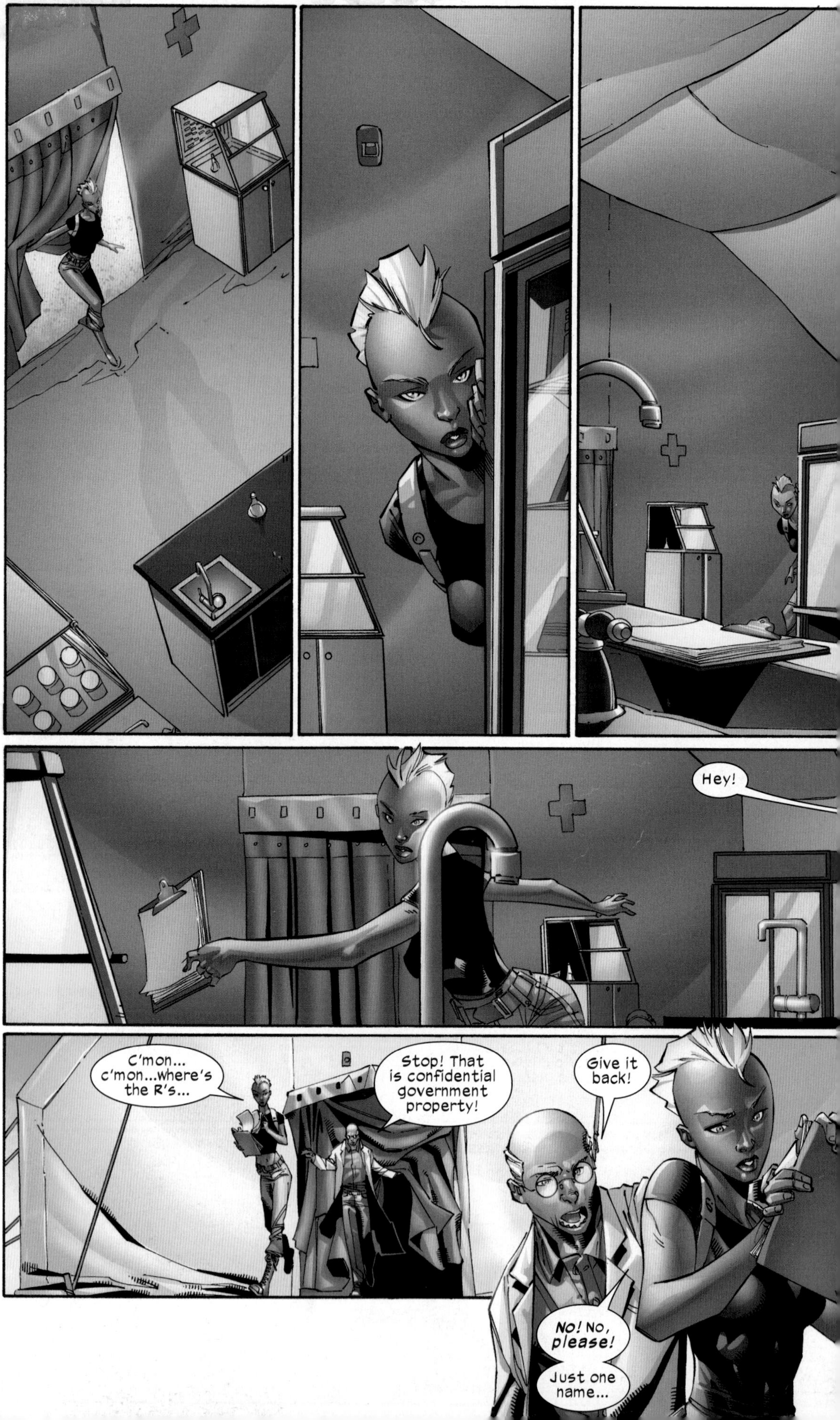
Hey!
C'mon... c'mon...where's the R's...
Stop! That is confidential government property!
Give it back!
NO! No, please!
Just one name...

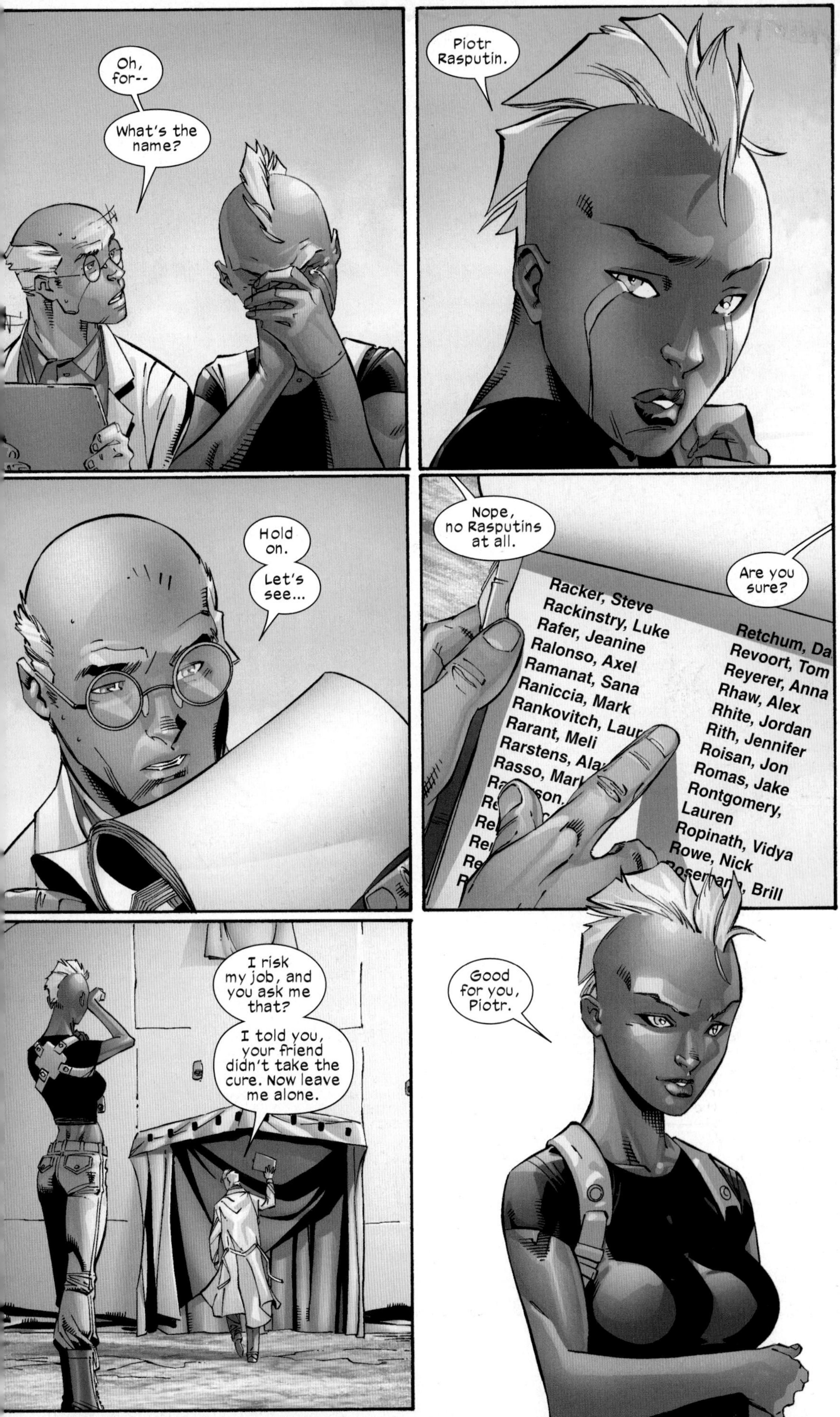
Oh, for--
What's the name?
Piotr Rasputin.
Hold on.
Let's see...
Nope, no Rasputins at all.
Racker, Steve
Rackinstry, Luke
Rafer, Jeanine
Ralonso, Axel
Ramanat, Sana
Raniccia, Mark
Rarant, Meli
Revoort, Tom
Reyerer, Anna
Rhaw, Alex
Rhite, Jordan
Rith, Jennifer
Roisan, Jon
Romas, Jake
Rontgomery, Lauren
Ropinath, Vidya
Rowe, Nick
Are you sure?
I risk my job, and you ask me that?
I told you, your friend didn't take the cure. Now leave me alone.
Good for you, Piotr.

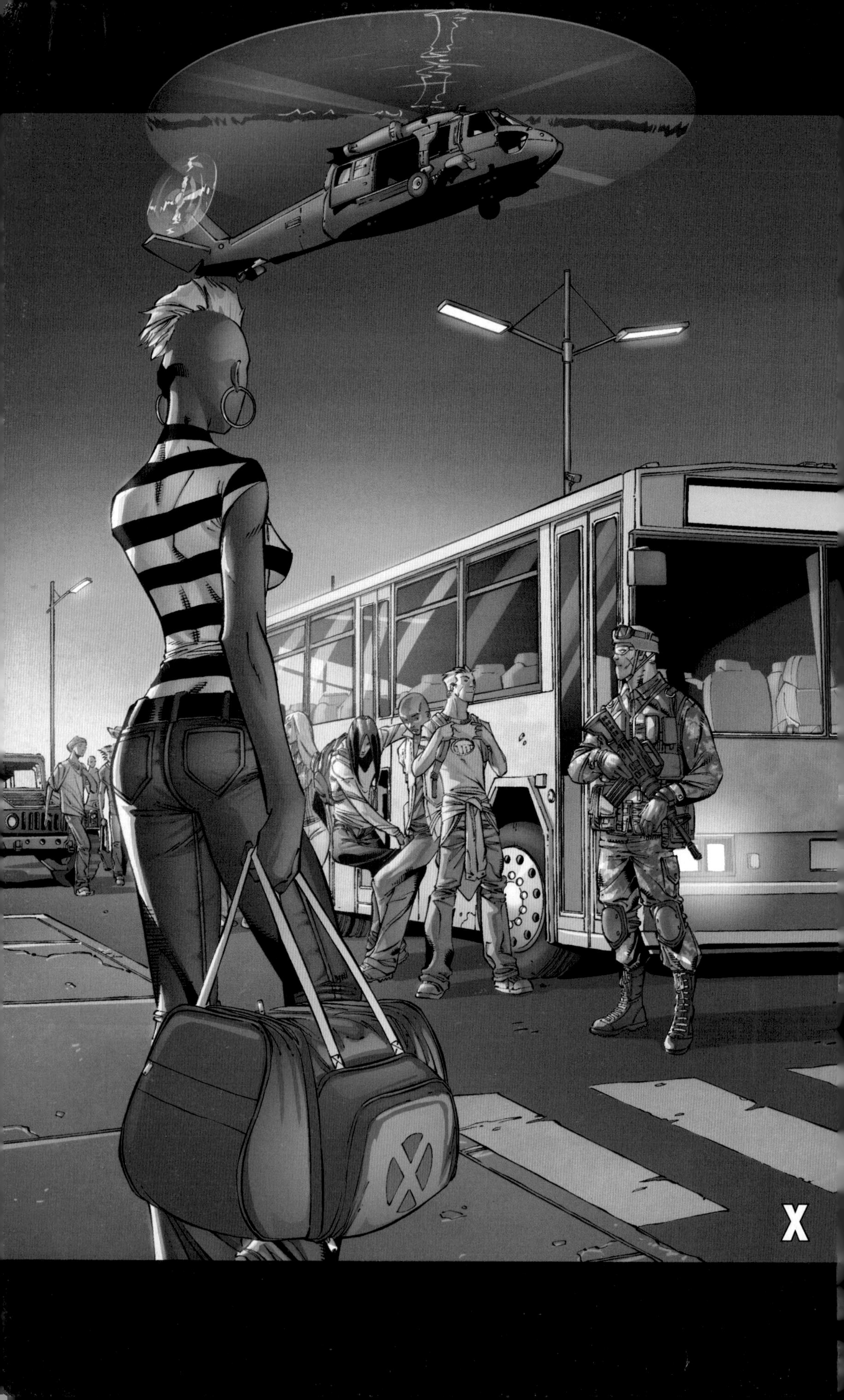

#23, PAGE 1

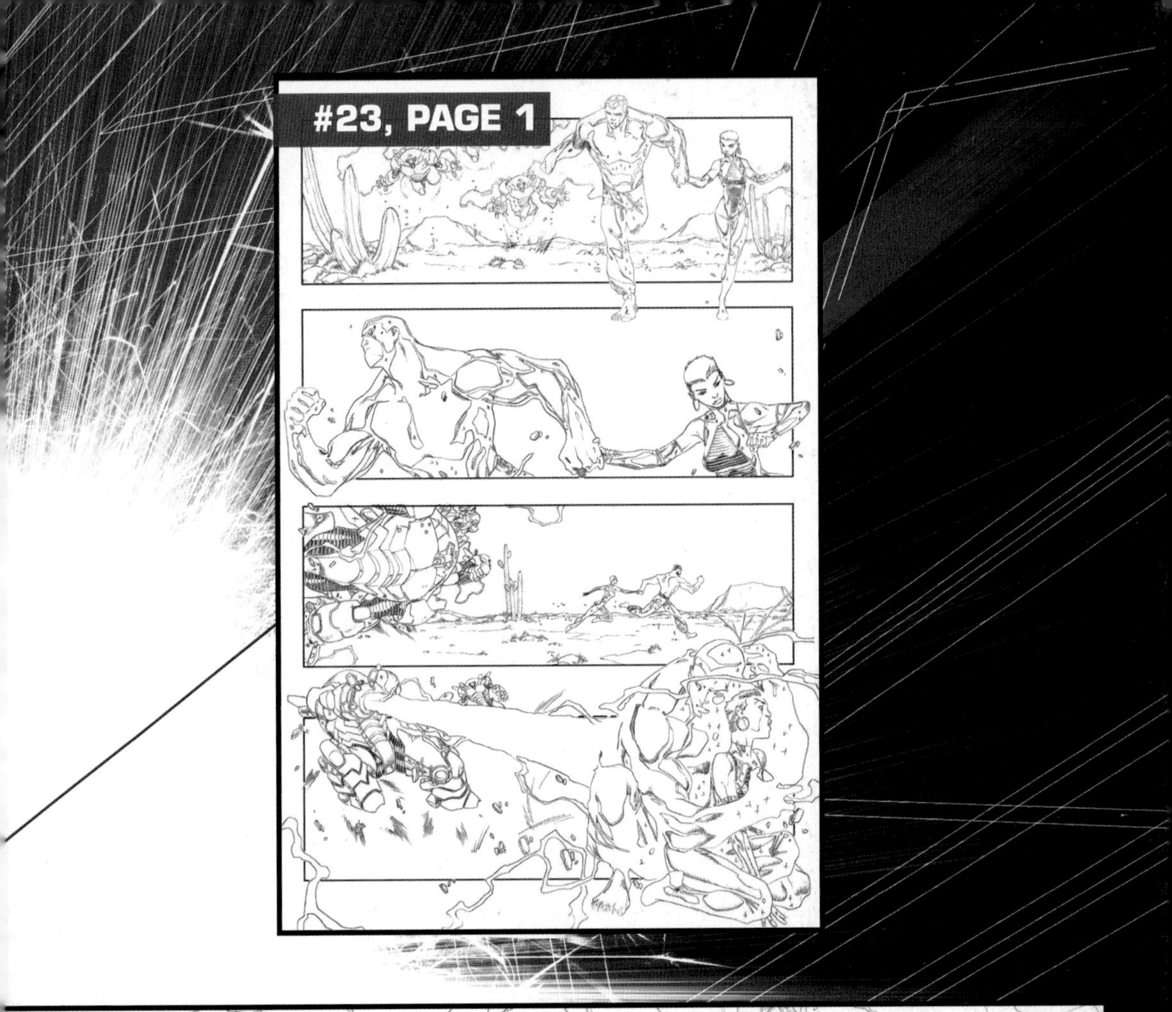

#23, PAGES 2-3

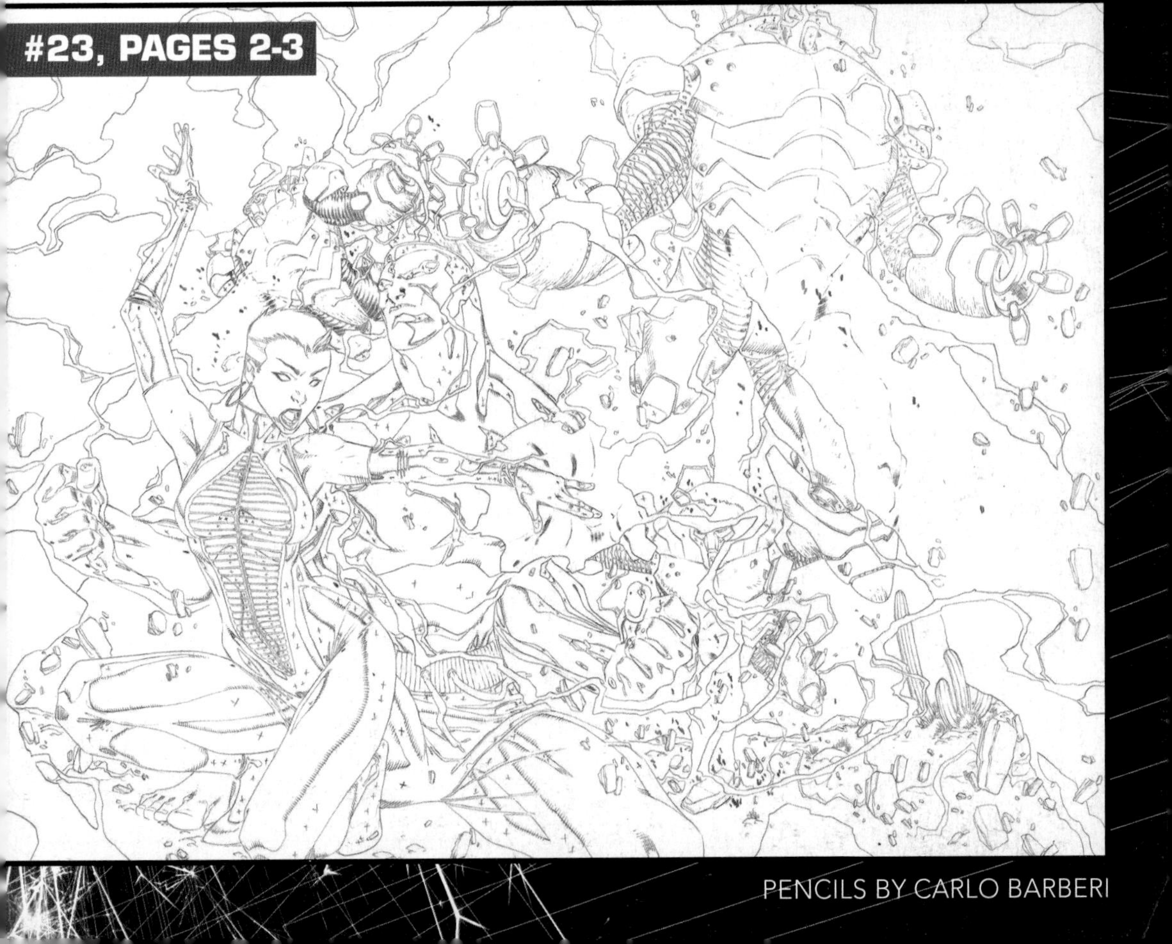

PENCILS BY CARLO BARBERI

#23, PAGE 4

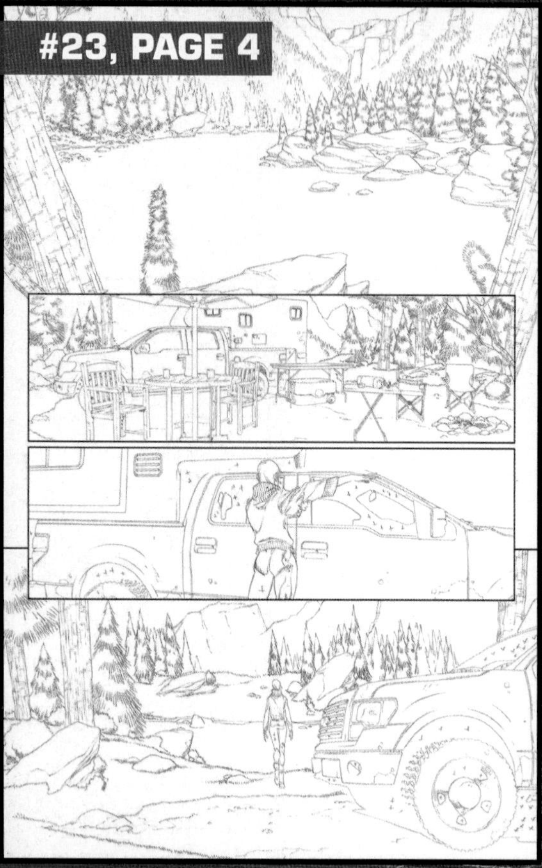

#23, PAGE 5

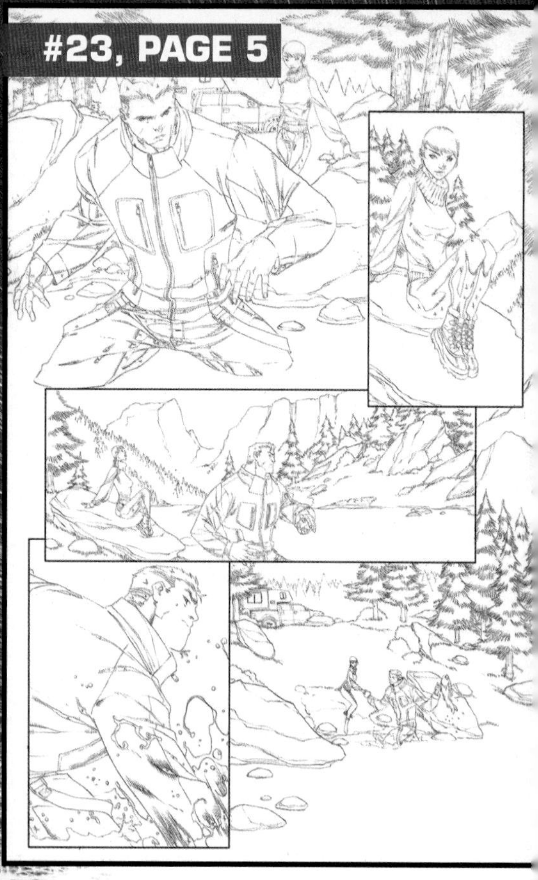

#23, PAGE 6

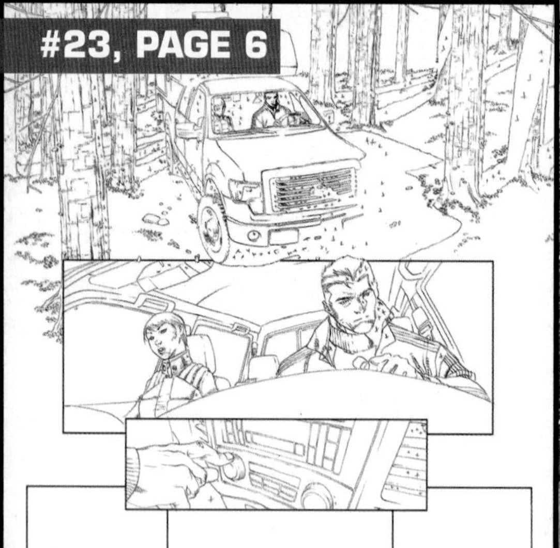

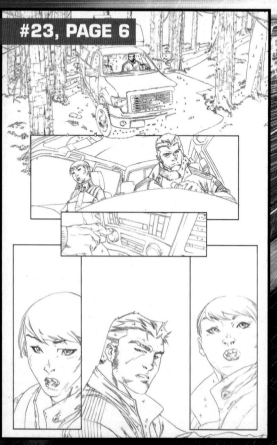

#23, PAGE 7

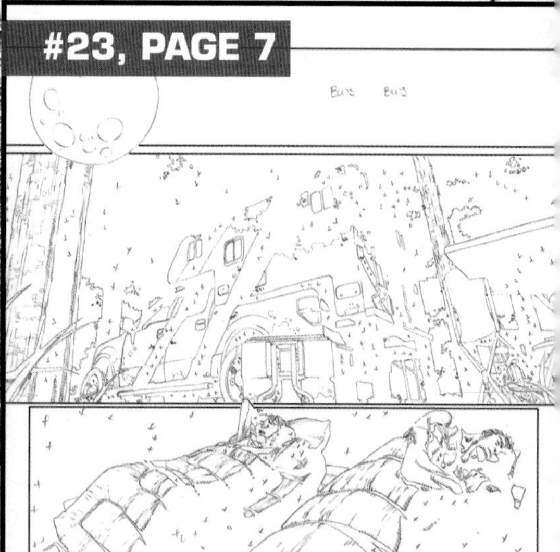

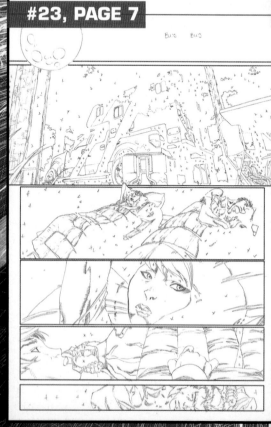

PENCILS BY CARLO BARBERI

#23, PAGE 8

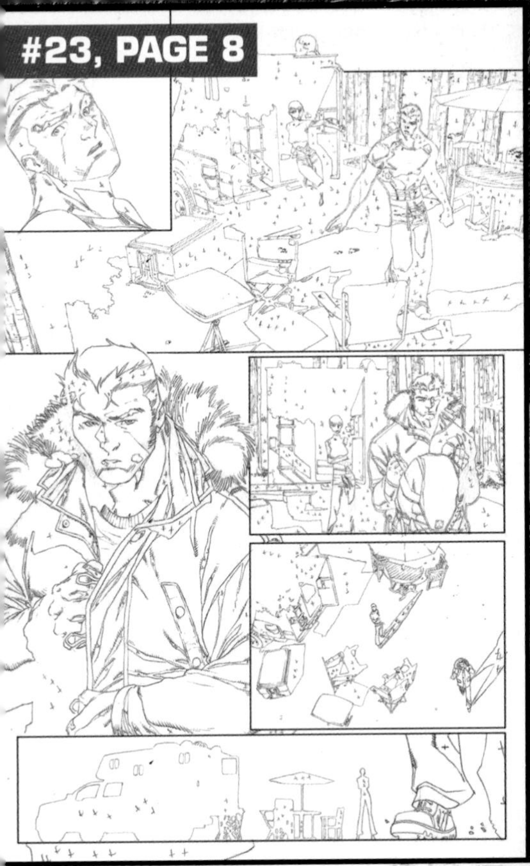

#23, PAGE 9

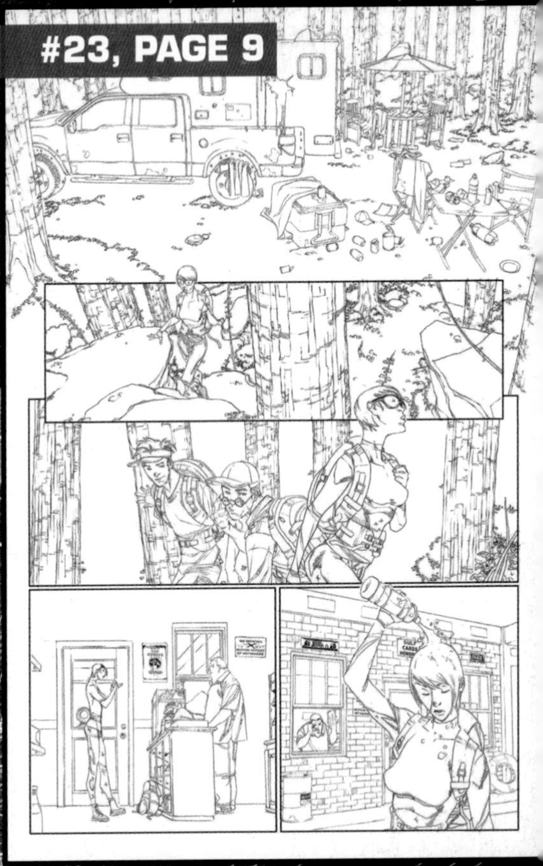

#23, PAGE 10

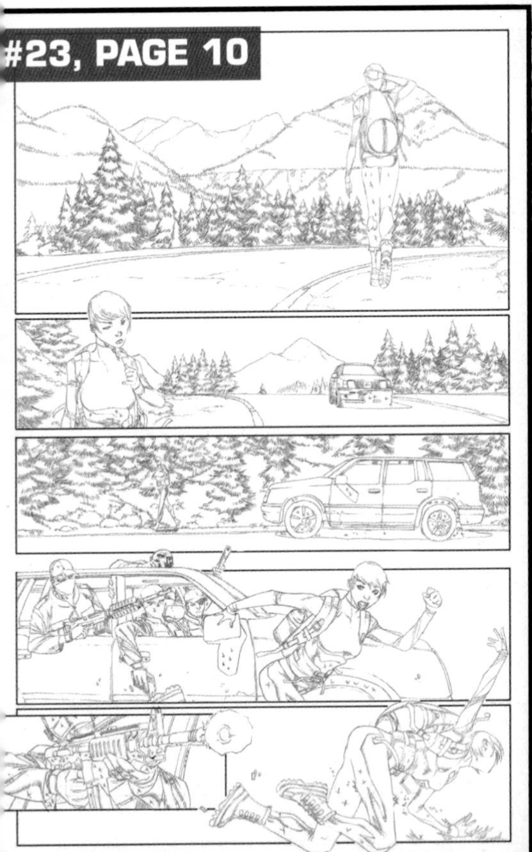

#23, PAGE 11

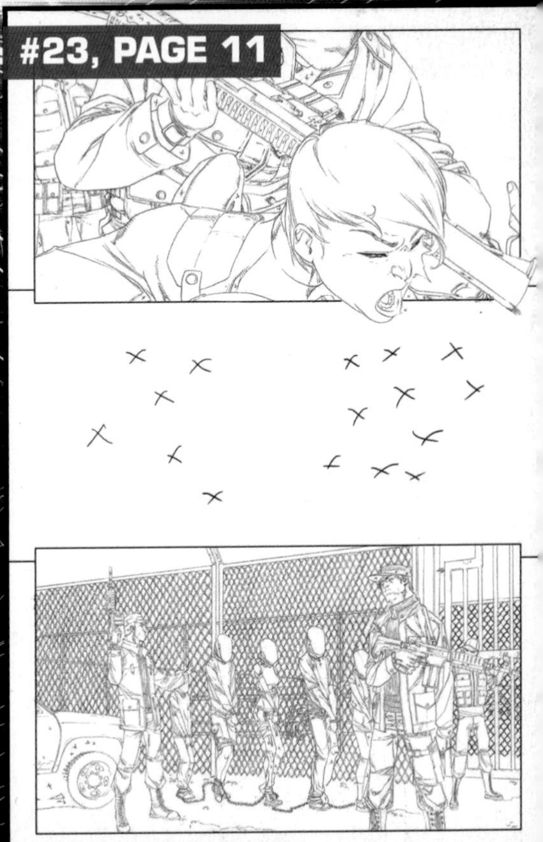

#23, PAGE 15

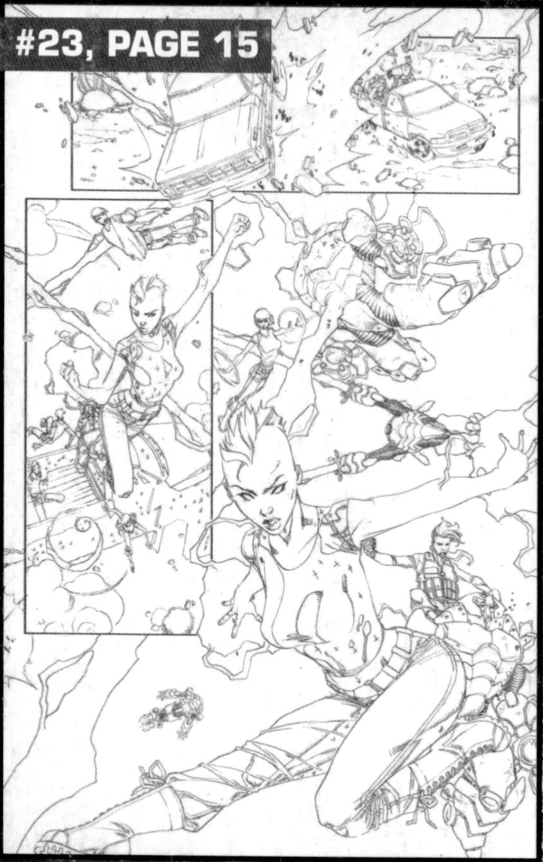

#23, PAGE 16

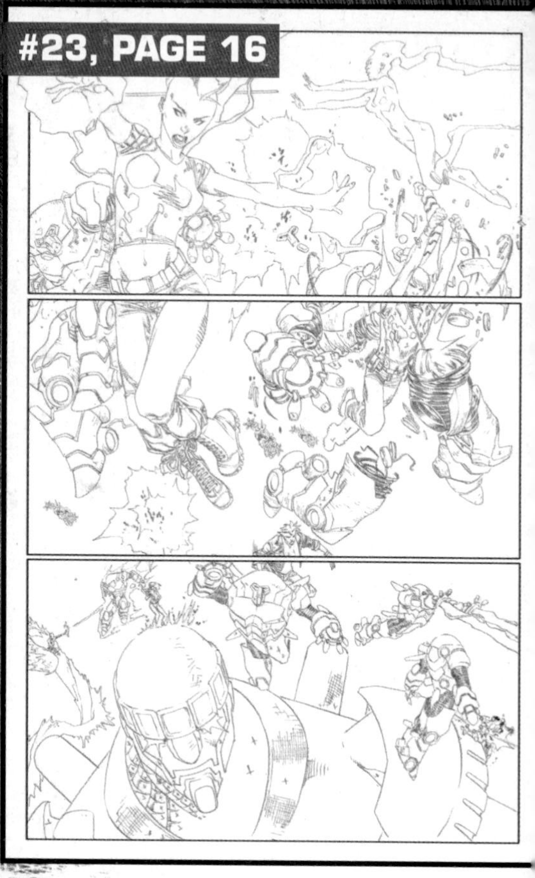

#23, PAGE 17

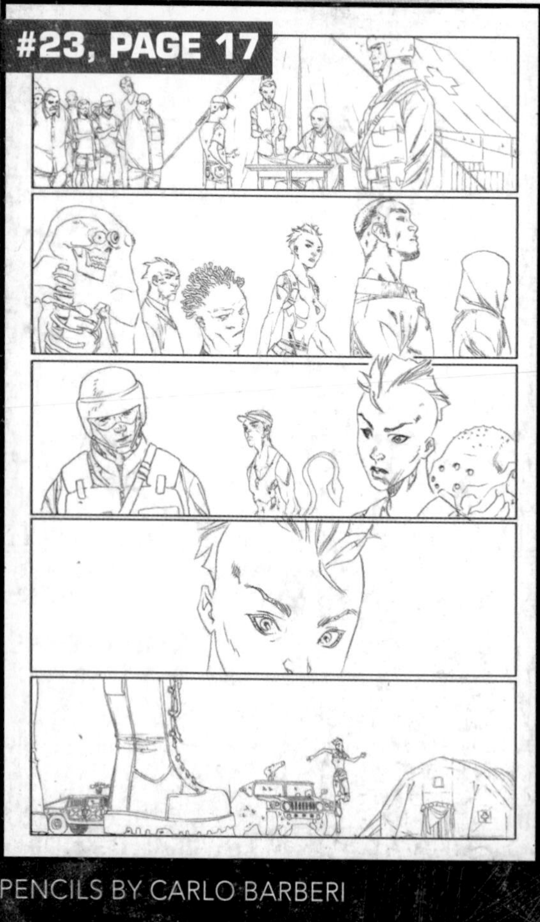

#23, PAGE 18

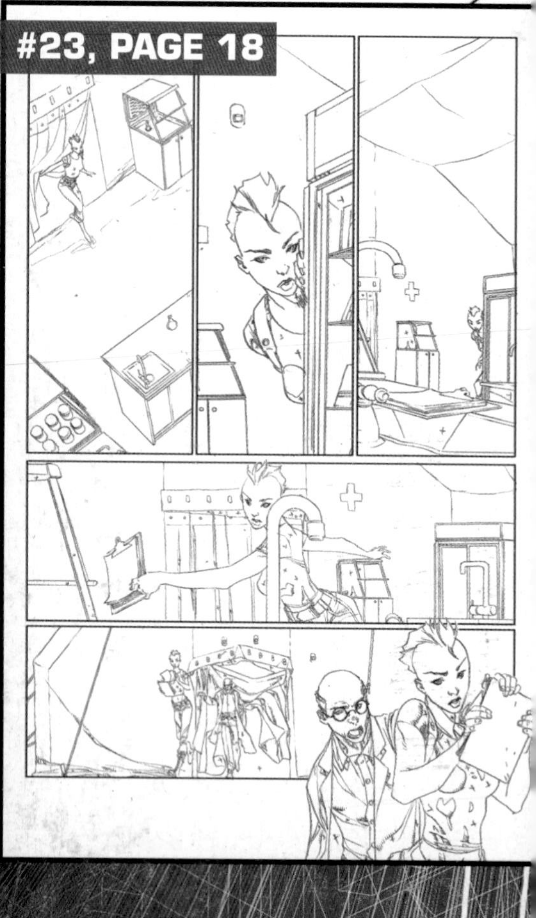

PENCILS BY CARLO BARBERI